Turn It On Again

PETER GABRIEL, PHIL COLLINS & GENESIS

BY DAVE THOMPSON

Backbeat
Books
San Francisco

Published by Backbeat Books
600 Harrison Street, San Francisco, CA 94107
www.backbeatbooks.com
email: books@musicplayer.com

An imprint of CMP Information
Publishers of *Guitar Player, Bass Player, Keyboard,* and *EQ* magazines

CMP
United Business Media

Distributed to the book trade in the US and Canada by
Publishers Group West, 1700 Fourth Street, Berkeley, CA 94710

Distributed to the music trade in the US and Canada by
Hal Leonard Publishing, P.O. Box 13819, Milwaukee, WI 53213

Composition by Michael Cutter
Cover design by Tim Haselman/Michael Cutter
Front cover photo by Michael Ochs Archives.com
Back cover photo of Peter Gabriel, 1973, by ©Armando Gallo/Retna USA/Retna Ltd, USA

Library of Congress Cataloging-in-Publication Data

Thompson, Dave, 1960 Jan. 3–
  Turn it on again : Peter Gabriel, Phil Collins & Genesis / by Dave Thompson.
      p. cm.
  Includes bibliographical references (p. 287) and index.
  ISBN 0-87930-810-9 (alk. paper)
  1. Genesis (Musical group) 2. Gabriel, Peter, 1950– 3. Collins, Phil. 4. Rock musicians—
England—Biography. I. Title.

  ML421.G46T56 2004
  782.42166'092'2—dc22   2004015616
Printed in the United States of America

04 05 06 07 08   5 4 3 2 1

TABLE OF CONTENTS

INTRODUCTION

The roots of this book go back a long way—more than 30 years—to the days when three British boarding school boys (hello, Peter and Andrew) would gather round the music room gramophone to the half dozen or so Genesis albums that were then available: *Trespass, Nursery Cryme, Foxtrot, Live,* and a couple of compilations.

Those were such simple days. The group's first album had yet to be reissued once, let alone the several dozen times it has appeared since then. *Selling England by the Pound* was still off on some distant horizon. Peter Gabriel and Steve Hackett were still members of the group, and Phil Collins was the heavily bearded drummer to whom no one, quite honestly, paid that much attention.

Since that time, of course, everything has changed. The school has gone co-ed, Peter and Andrew have grown up and moved on, and Genesis itself…well, that's what this book is about—the story of a band as it made what was surely the most improbable journey in the history of rock, from obscure cult to international superstars and from progressive-rock doyen to pop-chart darlings. It's the wellspring from which no less than six remarkable and, again, unique solo careers have sprung. And those half a dozen albums have swollen to occupy several very long shelves of recordings.

It would, of course, be an open-minded listener indeed who could claim to have loved every record that every member of the band has been involved with, who could swing from "Supper's Ready" to "Sussudio" without a pause for breath, who could rate "Big Time" as highly as "Biko," and who thinks *Invisible Touch* is as rousing as *A Trick of the Tail*.

From the outset, then, let it be known that the 13 year old who believed *Foxtrot* was the greatest record ever made has remained in control of this book—attempting to tell the story of Genesis without him would have sucked the joy out of the entire project and would have rendered it little more than a giant discography. Some albums will receive pages of praise, others a mere sniff of acknowledgment, and some, as the story splinters into so many solo careers, do not appear at all, not because I disdain them (well, not always) but because to do justice to every record released within the Genesis family tree would require not one book, but ten. The discographies at the end of this book make that clear.

What this book does attempt to do is follow the major thread, the story of Genesis itself, as the group's activities were molded not only by its own successes and failures but by the world that was turning around it.

No band exists in a vacuum. No matter how hard the individual musicians may try to isolate themselves, the rest of the world still rotates around them, and it would be a solitary outfit indeed that could carry on its own sweet path without ever noting anything that spun off in its direction. Genesis, though it has been called a lot of things over the years, has never been condemned as isolationist. Rather, it often appears its eyes are even wider open than most bands, granting it an awareness that allows Genesis to experiment with new ideas and principles that the rest of the pack may not notice for months to come.

Through the early years, that world was small and insular, a comfortable roost within one of the most visionary record company rosters of the age. Later, as the band's success expanded, so the members' horizons broadened with it, to catapult first Peter Gabriel and Steve Hackett off on solo careers of their own, then Tony Banks and Mike Rutherford, and, finally, Phil Collins—a man to whom, now, everybody paid attention and who repaid that attentiveness with a string of era-defining hit singles and albums.

But, though many observers would claim that Collins's success did more to shape Genesis throughout the last 15 years of its life span than any other point of reference, the truth is far more complicated and fascinating than that, and that—all of that—is what this book is about. It is not an insider's tale of sex, drugs, debauchery, marital breakups, and personal breakdowns—that, if it needs to be told, is for the band members' themselves to impart. Neither is it a fly-on-the-wall account of the ins and outs of Genesis's business practices, for that, again, is the musicians' own business.

Rather, it is the story of a band as it forms, develops, succeeds, and survives in a world that is filled with other bands; it is a document of the ideas, interactions, and inspirations that, for close to 40 years now, have shaped and sharpened, shattered, and shadowed the musicians whose names will forever be associated with the one group they all have in common.

Genesis's first LP was called *From Genesis to Revelation*, and now that its own final chapter has been written, following the group's final disbandment in 1998, it remains a brilliantly conceived title. Over the course of its career, the group's activities, impact, and, most of all, music have indeed been described as biblical in scope and dimension. This is the story of how that all came to pass.

CHAPTER ONE

A GENTLEMAN AND SOME SCHOLARS

The British public school system has turned out some remarkable chaps over the centuries. No matter that *public* in this context more accurately translates as excruciatingly private…exclusive, even. It is said that the Battle of Waterloo, the tumultuous conflict that ended little Corporal Napoleon's dreams of world domination, was won on the playing fields of England, by stout laddies schooled in the virtues of a virtuous life. But Waterloo was just one moment of warring among many.

From Parade Ground to Parliament, the men who forged the British Empire were themselves forged at the great schools of England. The sporting types who ran, jumped, kicked, and hit their way into the records books of the amateur age learned their skills on the playing fields of Eton, Harrow, and Charterhouse. And, when British soccer organized the sport's first-ever national competition, the FA Cup, in 1872, the public schools dominated the tournament, and the game's first heroes lined up not for multimillion-dollar corporations but for the Old Etonians, Old Harrovians, and Old Carthusians.

Captains of industry, captains of men, royalty and writers, barristers and bishops…F.O. Grenfell, one of the first soldiers to win the Victoria Cross for gallantry during World War I, attended Eton; so did George Orwell, author of *1984* and *Animal Farm*. Novelist John Galsworthy was educated at Harrow; Prince Charles attended Gordonstoun. Charterhouse gave the world Baden Powell, the founder of the modern scouting movement, and the composer Ralph Vaughan Williams.

The public school system had sent its progeny venturing down every walk of life you could name. Except one. It had never created a "pop star." So, when a former Charterhouse pupil, 17-year-old Kenneth "Jonathan" King stepped out in 1965 to score a worldwide hit with the wistful "Everyone's Gone to the Moon," his academic background raised as many watching eyebrows as any of his many other talents. Now the race was on to follow in his footsteps.

Although its present-day campus is comparatively modern, Charterhouse will celebrate the 400th anniversary of its foundation in 2011, 400 years since one Thomas Sutton decided to build a school for needy scholars and pensioners on the site of what had once been one of the most beautiful abbeys in central London, close by what is now Smithfield meat market.

Charterhouse takes its name from the French town of Chartreux and the austere religious order that was established there by St. Bruno. The first English house of the order—the first Charterhouse—was founded by King Henry II at Witham in Somersetshire in 1181, and, over the next four centuries, until Henry VIII set about dissolving the Papist monasteries, the order flourished throughout England. The London Charterhouse was stripped of its finery and demolished, but the site retained its name, and Thomas Sutton saw no reason to change it.

> Barbaric cruelty and bullying was still part of the natural order.

Charterhouse remained in London for the next two-and-a-half centuries, until the grime and noise of the ever-growing, ever-industrializing city became too overwhelming. Finally, the headmaster of the day, the Reverend Dr. Haig Brown, announced that the entire campus was to be bodily transported south of the city to a new 200-acre site north of the River Wey in what was then the sleepy village of Godalming in Surrey and where it has lain, prospering, ever since.

Entry to Charterhouse is controlled through the Common Entrance Exam, which tests aspiring students in mathematics, English, science, history, geography, religious studies, and modern languages. Boys enter at age 13, to begin their studies in what the British educational system refers to as the fourth form; they remain for three years, through the sixth form, at which point they are destined for university. The school year itself is divided into three quarters: the Oration Quarter, running from September to Christmas; the aptly named Long Quarter, spanning January to Easter; and the Cricket Quarter, bowling through to the summer break.

The five boys who would, before they departed the school, form themselves into a group called Genesis, began arriving at Charterhouse in September 1963, with the appearance of Peter Brian Gabriel and Anthony George Banks, two 13 year olds born six weeks apart, on Feb. 13 and March 27, 1950, respectively.

Their backgrounds could scarcely have been more different—Banks was the son of a school teacher who actually specialized in getting children through the Common Entrance Exam that was the door to a public school education; Gabriel's father was an electrical engineer and inventor, instrumental in the development of radar flight simulators and, though nobody paid any attention at the time, the first-ever TV system that employed fiber optics…cable television, in other words. "Thirty years ago," Gabriel explained in 1994, "he was trying to sell the idea of cable TV and home shopping, but no one was interested. And that's what I grew up with, really. Although I didn't have his technical and creative skills, I still had some of the excitement of that vision."

The pair became fast friends very early in their school career, as they both found themselves forced to acclimatize to the surreal world into which they were suddenly plunged. The public school life documented in Thomas Hughes's classic novel *Tom Browne's Schooldays* (itself set at Rugby School) was more than a century old by the time Gabriel and Banks arrived at Charterhouse, but few of the boys who attended the establishment in Browne's days would have been overly shocked by what they found there in the 1960s.

Fagging, the system by which the youngest boys did the every bidding of their elders, continued in full swing, and the ultraformal discipline that modern educators would come to describe as barbaric cruelty and bullying was still part of the natural order.

Contact between the school and the outside world—mixing with kids from the village, for example—was discouraged, so, in fact, was any form of identification with the common herd beyond the Charterhouse walls. One did not attend public school simply to be educated. One was taught to be a leader, and the first step toward that was to instill a sense of superiority in every child who passed through those halls.

But the outside world was slowly creeping in through the pernicious influence of television, of the media, of rock 'n' roll, that bastard musical form that, for eight years now, had torn up everything that society had once deemed was the destiny of the younger generation—torn it up and replaced it with dreams. By fall 1963, the Beatles were almost a full year into their British hit-making career; as Gabriel and Banks received their first taste of life at Charterhouse, so the Fab Four's "She Loves You" was commencing its own inexorable rise to spend the first of six weeks atop the U.K. chart.

Behind the Beatles, too, a wild ferment was kick-starting every juvenile fantasy imaginable, as the buoyant "beat boom" sounds of the Rolling Stones, the Searchers, Billy J. Kramer, and the Mojos each conspired to change the face of British pop music forever. Even within the cloistered seclusion of Charterhouse, its walls dripping with tradition and history and discipline, it was impossible to avoid the music and impossible to escape its influence. And that was before Jonathan King came along.

With its own music center named in memory of Ralph Vaughan Williams, Charterhouse certainly promised some kind of grounding to any aspirant musician among its annual intake of new students, although pop music itself would never become a part of the curriculum. Indeed, any would-be teen idols entering those halls of learning were better off keeping their mouths bolted shut when it came to apprising the masters of their personal ambitions, unless they wanted to be buried beneath a storm of withering scorn or worse. Only in the Billiard Room could they truly relax with the racket, cranking up the volume on a battered Dansette record player and dancing wildly for the 90 minutes a day that the machine was allowed to operate.

Nevertheless, the braver lads persisted, and by 1965, the dormitories and common rooms of Charterhouse were alive with the sound of so many practicing pop groups, each one hacking out its personal rudimentary versions of the hits of the day. And, again, its impact was all pervading. Tony Banks, for example, arrived at the school intent on studying classical music. But then he fell in with Gabriel, and, slowly, his outlook broadened. The first song he ever worked out on a piano was Tommy Roe's "Sheila," but one of the first he tried to actually put music to was "Sammy the Slug," Gabriel's own first attempt at songwriting.

Paramount among these amateur noisemakers was an outfit formed by one Anthony Edwin Phillips, soon after he arrived at Charterhouse in April 1965, aged 14. The son of a southwest London merchant banker, Phillips was already an experienced guitarist by the standards of the day. Attending St. Edmunds Preparatory School in nearby Hindhead, he and another guitar-playing student, Rivers Job, led their own combo, the Spiders. The group broke up, of course, when the members moved onto different schools, but when Job and Phillips were reunited at Charterhouse, the spirit of the Spiders was instantly rekindled.

They were joined by vocalist Richard MacPhail, who originally auditioned as drummer but took the microphone when his bandmates discovered he knew the words to most of the Rolling Stones' catalog, and, soon afterward, by drummer Rob Tyrrell. Christening themselves Anon (pointedly without the "definitive article" although editors the world over have insisted on adding one), the group's first rehearsals took place in an empty classroom, before they graduated to the Green Room, a storage area located beneath the stage in the school's main hall.

With their repertoire seldom straying far from MacPhail's knowledge of the Stones' catalog, Anon recruited their final member that summer. The grandly named Michael John Cleote Crawford Rutherford was born on Oct. 2, 1950, and entered Charterhouse shortly before his 14th birthday, in September 1964.

Like Phillips, he had played in a pop group, the Chesters, while at prep school. Later, however, he admitted that his time with the group may have been better spent learning how to *tune* his guitar, as opposed to attempting to play it. However, he also had little concern for the effects his style may have on any tender ears in attendance, and by the time Anon caught up with him, Rutherford was already regarded among the most rebellious kids in the school. According to legend, he was indulging in a bout of underage drinking at a local pub when the initial approach was made.

Contrary to every regulation, Rutherford kept a motorbike at the same hostelry, and he and a friend, Richard Pickett, were no strangers to taking unauthorized journeys beyond the school grounds, even venturing as far afield as London, if there was a gig they wanted to see. He was, the school authorities soon determined, "an undesirable element," and several of his associates received stern lectures on the perils of mixing with the likes of him.

With such a cachet already attached to him, Rutherford's unveiling as Anon's new rhythm guitarist raised the group's stature from just a bunch of tiresome fifth formers banging away at their instruments to something that the older, cooler cats may want to pay attention to, and, on Dec. 16, 1965, Anon made its public debut at the school Christmas concert.

Sandwiched between the customary fare of comedy skits, satirical sketches, musical and dramatic pieces, and a short film, Anon was scheduled to play three songs—"Oh Baby (We've Got a Good Thing Going)," Chuck Berry's "Talkin' 'Bout You," and "Mercy Mercy," all three painstakingly learned from the Rolling Stones' most recent album, *Out of Our Heads*.

It was not a carefree performance. Rutherford's guitar lead failed before Anon even launched into its opening number, and by the time the set was over, it was apparent that some people wished that it had stayed in a state of inoperativeness— school headmaster Mr. van Oss was seen standing with his fingers plugged into his ears throughout the performance.

Emboldened by the reaction of their peers, however, Anon plugged on, becoming such regulars at parties and the like that, early the following term, vocalist MacPhail's parents recommended he leave the group so as to concentrate better on his studies. He acceded to their demands, and Mike Rutherford stepped briefly up to the microphone. However, his career, too, was curtailed after a long-forgotten transgression saw his housemaster, Mr. Chare, bar him from playing any further part in the group. Although the school had learned to tolerate its denizens' rock 'n' rolling, it never accepted it, and the uneasy truce that developed was itself dominated by any master's ability to bar a student from playing music, for as long as he saw fit. According to Rutherford, Mr. Chare essentially prohibited him from playing his instrument throughout his entire Charterhouse career.

> Rutherford was, the school authorities soon determined, "an undesirable element."

One can readily understand the school's attitude. Rock 'n' roll was, after all, the sound of teen rebellion, unbridled insolence, and unfettered exuberance. Not yet a commodity to be tamed and marketed like so much fast food by the burgomasters of the music "industry," it was long hair and loud noise, disrespect, and dirty dancing. It was everything, in fact, that Charterhouse and the other public schools stood shoulder to shoulder against, with the masters' resistance to its encroachment therefore no more surprising than the stands they may have taken against promiscuity, theft, drugs, or any other social ill.

It was their willingness to actually let the music even exist that shocks, although once Jonathan King had proven what was possible in the world of pop—he followed his hit single with his own national television series, the weekly *Good Evening*—any attempts to truly stand against the tide would have been futile.

Shorn of Rutherford, Anon turned again to Richard MacPhail, who not only engineered his own return but who also introduced a new rhythm guitarist, Mick Colman—who, in turn, delivered an entire new dimension to the group's ambition when he teamed with Phillips to begin writing original material. Little of it was memorable, even by schoolboy standards—Colman later described one number, "She's Got Those Lopin' Shoulders," as the worst song he ever wrote.

Slowly, however, the band began to piece together a repertoire of which they were proud, and in April 1966, Anon booked themselves two days of recording time at a tiny home studio set up by another Carthusian, Brian Roberts, on Wellesley Road in Chiswick, southwest London. Roberts's father was a doctor, and the studio occupied a small room above the garages next door to his surgery. It was scarcely state of the art; it was scarcely even soundproof. But Anon made the most of it nevertheless, laying down versions of three of their own songs—"Patricia," "Don't Want You Back," and "Pennsylvania Flickhouse," plus the inevitable Stones cover, the baroque gentility of "Lady Jane"—itself an indication of the ambition coursing through Anon's veins.

Weeks later, with the end of the school year approaching, Anon signed up for another Charterhouse concert. Richard MacPhail was instrumental in organizing the event and quickly rounded up two other groups to fill the bill.

His period of punishment over, Mike Rutherford had now formed a new outfit, the Climax, and readily agreed to open the concert. Next up, however, was an act that apparently existed in little more than name and intention alone—Peter Gabriel and Anthony Banks's the Garden Wall.

Though they were older than the members of both Anon and the Climax, Gabriel and Banks had nevertheless proven slow in getting their personal musical ambitions off the ground. Gabriel fancied himself as a drummer at the time and had bashed around with a couple of groups, a dance combo called M'Lords and, alongside the ubiquitous Rivers Job, a soul group, the Spoken Word. He also filled in with a jazz act, the League of Gentleman.

Yet even as he drummed, he dreamed of other roles. "Sammy the Slug" had tapped a new ambition in the boy—still writing songs, he was keen to sing them as well. But there was no room in rock 'n' roll for a singing drummer and nobody to take one seriously should such a hybrid ever emerge. The Garden Wall was Gabriel's attempt to break out from behind his kit and find out if he could carry a show. Adding trumpeter Johnny Trapman to the lineup, he then surrendered his drums to Chris Stewart.

Like Gabriel and Banks, Stewart had spent much of his Charterhouse career lurking on the fringes of the school's musical ferment, seemingly ambitious but never going so far as to pull an actual band together. He took to drums after finding his attempts to learn guitar met with parlous failure, recalling how he "blithely stumbled through 'House of the Rising Sun' with no idea why corridors were clearing and study doors slamming."

Drums, on the hand, seemed to fall naturally to his command—or, at least, Charterhouse's branch of the Army Corps, a compulsory activity for every boy in the school, thought so. Stewart joined the Corps' band and drums musical wing and "was issued with a little book of drum music, a pair of hickory sticks, and a snare drum." And the instrument became "a strange sort of obsession. You carried your sticks everywhere, and, at mealtimes, you'd do it with knives and forks, rattling out marches on the refectory tables."

Even as this bold new venture became reality, however, the Garden Wall found itself drastically shorthanded and was forced to borrow both Anthony Phillips and the inevitable Rivers Job from Anon before they were able to take the stage. It was a ragtag assemblage that prepared for this momentous show, then; it would only be in later months that history could look back at the event and pinpoint it as the first occasion upon which the five founding members of Genesis played together on stage—albeit spread across three different bands.

Gabriel struck few people as a born performer. Rather, if asked to select a career for him to follow, most of his friends would have pointed him in the direction of fashion. Rooting around in his grandfather's attic one day, Gabriel discovered a remarkable-looking old hat, and, having found a manufacturer willing to run off a number of copies (the London, Piccadilly-based, Dunn and Co.), he took to touring the boutiques of swinging mid-'60s London to sell them. The venture was a marked success. Singer Marianne Faithfull, then in the first flush of her pop success, became one of his customers, and when Gabriel saw her on television's *Juke Box Jury*, resplendent beneath one of *his* hats, he admitted he nearly wet himself.

Emboldened, Gabriel moved into other arenas. For two shillings a go, he would dye his schoolmates' clothes whatever fancy colors they liked. This exercise, however, was less successful. A stranger to the world of colorfast dyes and fabrics, Gabriel's creations transformed every white shirt and cricket jersey into a sea of psychedelia.

Anthony Phillips insisted, "My first recollections of Pete were that he was the last conceivable person on earth to be a rock star. He was quite pudgy...he was like a barrel. And very quiet. He was always a bit slow delivering his speech and thoughts." But he thought nothing of climbing onto tables in the dining room to sing..."he was well into James Brown"...and, though he made people wait for his words, "he had a very individual way of expressing things, and it [was always] worth the wait."

> "At mealtimes, you'd do it with knives and forks, rattling out marches on the refectory tables."

The Garden Wall's debut was not, unfortunately, one of those occasions. Gabriel's singing was nervous and his bandmates were clearly under-rehearsed; in fact, they had not rehearsed at all. Though they intended to open the show with a 12-bar blues number, they neglected to figure out how to end it. So they didn't, simply playing on and on until finally, Richard MacPhail climbed on stage, quieted the musicians, and suggested they launch into their next song, a group original—at which point, one of the masters ran to the stage, demanding an immediate end to the nightmarish proceedings.

֎ ֎ ֎

Anon returned to the recording studio during the summer, 1966, following another change of personnel. The group had already booked themselves into Tony Pike Sound studios on Drybergh Road, Putney, when Mick Colman announced he was unable to make the date. Mike Rutherford slid easily back into his place, and Anon cut two songs, new and improved versions of "Pennsylvania Flickhouse" and "Don't Want You Back." The song "Pennsylvania Flickhouse" alone was then singled out to be pressed onto a one-sided acetate disc…Anon's first record. A grand total of six copies were pressed, one for each member of the band and one for Brian Roberts, with whom they had recorded the original version of the song.

Through the Oration Quarter, Anon rehearsed and partied on, but by the time of the next end-of-term concert in December 1966, it was clear that the band had exhausted itself. Following that final show, Rutherford and Phillips alone continued to take their musical endeavors at all seriously, writing songs together and venturing up to Brian Roberts's studio to record them.

It was as they prepared for one of these trips that the pair decided one particular song required keyboards. Tony Banks, widely regarded as the finest player in the school despite the lack of action that still dogged the Garden Wall, was their inevitable choice; inevitable, too, was Banks's insistence that he bring Gabriel along to the session to augment (and, quickly, replace) Rutherford's unwilling vocals and also to exact payment for the session—the recording of one of the Garden Wall's own songs, "She Is Beautiful." The addition of drummer Chris Stewart soon after completed a quintet that none of the members had ever even intended to form.

Tony Banks is adamant when he insists, "We had no intention of being a live band. I had no desire to be on stage." Rather, the quintet considered itself a songwriting co-operative whose musical abilities were required only for demoing the songs that other artists, they were convinced, would rush to record. As Anthony Phillips later put it, "We had this idealistic image…."

But, according to Chris Stewart, they quickly fell into the swing of things. "We played at school functions and at parties in the holidays and, somehow or other, got a reputation as the best group in the school." Their repertoire was comprised, in the main, of soul and R&B, "which was what Gabriel loved most," Stewart remembered. "'When a Man Loves a Woman,' 'Knock on Wood,' 'Dancing in the Street'— Otis Redding, Percy Sledge, Wilson Pickett."

"He was tremendously influenced by Otis Redding," Anthony Phillips agreed. "In a way, we used to joke about his 'soul' voice. But that's what he used to do." Attempts at coming up with original material, Stewart continued, saw them pilfer "occasional melodies [from] the hymn book."

As 1967 unfolded, and with Mike Rutherford now concentrating on bass guitar, the still unnamed group continued demoing its own material with Brian Roberts. The ensuing cassette tapes seldom went any further than their immediate circle of friends. As the end of the Cricket Quarter approached, however, an excited murmur began circulating Charterhouse that the forthcoming Old Boys Day would bring a special treat for every pop fan in the school. Jonathan King was coming back.

King later admitted that his sole motivation for returning to the school was "to show off. I'd written and sung a monster hit record and become a POP STAR! Ghastly for poor old Charterhouse! The pupils, of course, adored it…I ousted Baden Powell as their most famous Old Boy. So, to irritate the masters and delight the students, I returned in triumph."

Hastily, the band with no name set about assembling a tape of their best efforts to hand over to the Great Man in the hope that he might be able to point such aspiring songwriters in the right direction. Drawing from the stockpile of Brian Roberts "productions," they selected the softly lilting "Patricia," with its earnestly strummed acoustic melody and a percussion line that sounds like somebody rapping a table, the brightly sing-along "Try a Little Sadness," and the eerily portentous "She Is Beautiful." The paranoid epic "That's Me," "Don't Wash Your Back," and, finally, "Listen on Five" completed the cassette.

The players were too nervous to make the delivery themselves and press-ganged a friend, John Alexander, to make the presentation for them. Playing the tape back, however, the initially skeptical King found himself at least intrigued—"I liked the sound of the songs, especially the vocals of the lead singer, Peter Gabriel."

Within weeks of receiving the tape, King contacted Gabriel to suggest they meet to discuss their future face to face. That was where "I…agreed to produce some tracks with them in the school holidays and christened them Genesis to celebrate the start of my serious career as a producer." Then he dispatched the five schoolboys back to the studio, partially to discover what "real" recording equipment may make of them but, more important, to get something down on tape that King could play to other ears.

Gabriel was acting as Genesis's spokesman at the time, but he gave little credit to his efforts. "I did most of the selling of the band, which was very unsuccessful," he shrugged. "Jonathan King…was the only person in the business who would touch us. Actually, I think it was…the fact that he'd been to the same school that appealed to him."

In fact, King was not the only entrepreneur to receive a copy of the tape. With Gabriel still thrilled by his hat's appearance on *Juke Box Jury*, the singer also dispatched one to disc jockey David Jacobs, the Saturday evening TV's show's host. One of Jacobs's associates later claimed the accompanying note actually mentioned the hat; "they thought we'd listen because we'd remember the hat. But we didn't."

Jacobs elaborated, "For a start, the sound balance was atrocious." As so many other young acts have discovered as they set out on their journey, it didn't matter how good the songs may or may not be if it wasn't actually possible to listen to them without your every nerve end screaming for mercy.

Jonathan King professed himself similarly utterly underwhelmed by the tape's sound quality but persevered. Indeed, he later pointed out that it was indicative of the strength of the songs on this first tape that two of them, "Patricia" and "She Is Beautiful," would soon find themselves being reworked for inclusion on the group's debut album, as "In Hiding" and "The Serpent," respectively, while a third, "That's Me," would make it onto their first B-side.

King was no stranger to "launching" new talent; late in 1965, he seized upon the completely unknown Hedgehoppers Anonymous and wrote and produced a Top Five hit for them, the multipurpose assault on the supersensationalist media of the day, "It's Good News Week." Now he was working as an assistant to Sir Kenneth Clark, head of Decca Records, a position that already gave any artists he "discovered" a head start in the

> "Gabriel was the last conceivable person on earth to be a rock star."

A&R stakes. Now all King had to do was persuade others at the label that Genesis was worth taking a chance on, and the band did not let him down. For one hour, the quintet found itself ensconced within the so-historic Regent Sound studios in

London, wherein so many rock legends cut their own recording teeth. There, and in that impossibly brief span of time, Genesis cut four songs, revisions of "Try a Little Sadness" and "She Is Beautiful," plus "The Image Is Blown" and "Where the Sour Turns to Sweet."

Decca was impressed. The past few months had seen the British music scene flower in a manner that few people could ever have expected, a psychedelic blossoming that took its lead from the West Coast of America but its soul from the Beatles' recent experiments with both sound and songwriting. *Sgt. Pepper's Lonely Hearts Club Band* was a matter of mere weeks old at the time, and the world was still coming to grips with the bold steps forward that it represented, but already the scramble was on to broach the same far-out frontiers that the Fabs had attained.

By mid-1967, Decca had already taken the first strides toward attuning itself with this new spirit of adventure, inaugurating the Deram label as an outlet for many of its more enterprising acts. A new keyboards-and-classics inspired version of the veteran Moody Blues and an oddball young singer-songwriter named David Bowie ranked among the new label's first recruits. Other new signings, divided between Deram and Decca itself, would include such picturesquely named combos as Tintern Abbey, the Accent, the Syn, the Attack, the Fairytale, Felius Andromeda, Human Instinct, and the 23rd Turn-off—outfits bound, if only for a few hazy months, to become arch-staples of the British psychedelic rock scene. Though the music therein was less prone to whimsy and more thoughtful and musicianly, still Genesis's first professional demo tape seemingly destined them to fit seamlessly in alongside all these others.

In early August 1967, Genesis signed their first record contract, at the same time as King himself moved to sign them to the Jonjo Music publishing company he had launched with his partner, Joe Roncoroni. The full weight of that organization would thus be placed behind them, both as songwriters and as recording artists in their own right.

Whereas the Decca contract spanned just one year, Peter Gabriel later claimed that King's publishing deal was for ten, binding the quintet to Jonjo until 1977. It was a fairly standard offer by industry standards of the time, and the five teens happily signed it. But King reckoned without the musicians' parents, none of whom took this pop music lark even half as seriously as their offspring. So far as they were concerned, music was simply a sideline to the five's now fast-approaching move into the real world, where their Carthusian education would surely carve them safe careers in law, accountancy, and the like. "They were pretty horrified when they learned what we'd done," a rueful Gabriel admitted.

"But fortunately we were all minors, so the contract was void. So then we entered into a legal contract, supported by [our] parents' signatures, for one year." By way of an advance on future publishing royalties, each of the musicians received the princely sum of £10 apiece.

King had already determined how Genesis's recording career would begin, and toward the end of the month, he accompanied them to Advision Studios to produce what was intended to be their debut Decca single, a full-blooded reprise of "Where the Sour Turns to Sweet."

The session was a disaster, as nerves and inexperience—on the part of musicians and producer alike—combined to create a recording that all concerned readily admitted was unreleasable. The tape was shelved and, sensing that King was deeply disappointed by the performance, Genesis devoted itself to getting back onto his good side.

Throughout the fall, Genesis was furiously writing and demoing new material, songs that ranged in intent from the awkward "Hair on the Arms and Legs," whose portentous mood and ethereal harmonies had little in common with that peculiar title, to "Barnaby's Adventure," "Lost In a Drawer," and "Hidden in a World of Dawn." Anthony Phillips contributed a number of piano pieces, including "Creation," "Fivers," and "Passepied," several of which would be revisited during his own future solo career, within the multipart *Private Parts and Pieces* series of instrumental albums. "I remember Tony Banks not being terribly impressed by my cross-hand technique, and he was probably quite right," Phillips laughed. "They liked some of the pieces, but 'Creation' was probably a bit beyond the pale."

> "We had no intention of being a live band. I had no desire to be on stage."

The most significant of these early recordings was "The Mystery of the Flannan Isle Lighthouse," one of the earliest ever manifestations of the mighty epics that would soon become one of Genesis's best-loved calling cards—albeit in little more than two-and-a-half minutes.

The track was based upon one of the most enduring of all maritime mysteries, the events that occurred on the Flannan Isle lighthouse on Dec. 15, 1900. Standing off the Atlantic coast of the Scottish Isle of Lewis, the lighthouse had been in operation for little more than a year when a passing steamer reported that the light itself was not operating, despite the entire area being encased in a thick fog bank that would persist for much of December—the lighthouse itself remained invisible from land until Dec. 29.

A relief boat, the *Hesperus*, was sent to investigate, but storms kept her at sea for ten days before she was finally able to land at the lighthouse on Dec. 26. There, the crew was astonished to find no trace at all of the three men who crewed the structure. The clock on the inner wall had stopped, there was no fire in the grate, and all the beds were empty. A meal was prepared but lay uneaten. The final log entry was at 9 a.m. on Dec. 15.

Wilson Wilfred Gibson's poem, "Flannan Isle," was the first to immortalize the mystery, in 1912; since that time, the tale has inspired an opera, Peter Maxwell Davies's *The Lighthouse* and even an episode of television's *Dr. Who*—Gibson's poem is quoted in part during the story *The Horror of Fang Rock*. Into the early '90s, Hector Zazou's *Songs from the Cold Seas* album features its own musical recounting of the disappearances, "Lighthouse."

Genesis's contribution to this canon, while suffering from a handful of factual inaccuracies (the island lies 15 miles from land, not 47), certainly captures much of the mystery and magic that still affords the lighthouse's desolate setting and, again, stands as something of a blueprint for what the group would go on to create. King, however, was less than impressed. For all the intrigue and prophetic vision of "The Mystery of the Flannan Isle Lighthouse," it was discarded by King, who then pronounced himself similarly unimpressed by anything he heard on this latest tape.

Having dropped the tape off at King's Jonjo Music offices in London's SoHo Square, the band waited weeks before, on Nov. 29, fellow Jonjo director Joe Roncoroni wrote to Gabriel regretting, "we were not very impressed—the previous batch you did are, in our opinion, much better." There was no need for despair, however; Roncoroni was keen to meet with Gabriel for "a chat" as soon as the singer could get back up to London.

King later admitted that he was very uncertain how Genesis should be marketed. For a time, it appeared that there were problems coming from every direction—no sooner had he christened the band Genesis, for example, than Decca pointed out that there was already a group of that name operating in the United States and suggested that he look further afield. King at least agreed to consider the handful of new ideas that were passed along, but having dismissed Gabriel's Angels and the Champagne Meadow, he returned to his original decision, only for the nomenclature confusion to continue as another band, the Gods, released an LP titled *Genesis*.

Further difficulties arose in the studio. King would be the first man to admit that his forte lay in pop music, even as Genesis's talents leaned in more serious directions entirely. His decision to try and find a middle ground between the two instincts was, with the hindsight of experience, always doomed to failure—at the time, however, it seemed possible simply because no one else had yet proved it was *imp*ossible.

The so-called progressive rock boom that would make stars of Barclay James Harvest, the Edgar Broughton Band, and so forth, was still away in the future. Only Procol Harum, with the chart-topping "Whiter Shade of Pale" earlier in the year, and the Moody Blues, with the hit single "Nights in White Satin," had offered any indication whatsoever that there was commercial mileage to be gained from "going progressive," and even the Moodies' effort had yet to achieve the classic status that attends it today.

Something *was* stirring within the Moody Blues' disavowal of rock's American roots; however, in their decision to look to their own country's traditions for inspiration and endeavor—something that would ultimately resolve itself into a largely British and wholly European musical force. But, entering the U.K. chart at the very end of December 1967, "Nights in White Satin" climbed no higher than No. 19 and did so at precisely the same time as Genesis and King were still trying to nail their personal immediate ambitions into place.

The group was shooting in the dark. Other developments in the same fermenting field were still to unfold—Deep Purple had yet to commence its inexorable shift away from its early devotion to the Vanilla Fudge; the Nice was still best regarded as the backing musicians for soul singer P.P. Arnold. Other bands destined to become irrevocably associated with the progressive genre—Yes, King Crimson and Emerson Lake and Palmer—were yet to be unveiled; and others still, such as the one-album-old Pink Floyd, were as much in the dark as Genesis and Jonathan King. If anybody needed look outside of themselves in search of the direction in which they hoped to travel, they had a long wait ahead of them.

16

CHAPTER TWO

FROM REVELATION TO GENESIS

Having abandoned "When the Sour Turns to Sweet," Genesis took another stab at cutting its first single at Regent Sound in December 1967. Two months later, on Feb. 2, Decca released the ensuing "The Silent Sun."

Contrary to the band's visions for the song but effortlessly in keeping with Jonathan King's sharp eye for the commercial wellspring, "The Silent Sun" emerged a tight, string-driven ballad, stately and sufficiently harmonic to earn comparisons with the then-similarly styled Bee Gees. Flip the blue-and-silver labeled seven-inch, however, and its B-side, "That's Me," did little to maintain the deception, as Gabriel's vocal, smooth on the other side, adopted a manic crackle that was perfectly in keeping with the song's thoughtful portrayal of dark paranoia.

Unfortunately, few people listened to either side. Plunged into a marketplace dominated by the likes of "Everlasting Love," "The Ballad of Bonnie and Clyde," Englebert Humperdinck, and the Monkees, "The Silent Sun" snatched a handful of vaguely impressed reviews and then sank from sight—just as the *New Musical Express* review predicted it would: "I'm still not sure what the enigmatic lyric is about, but I gather it refers to a girl! Anyway it's certainly a thought-provoking song that holds the attention throughout. Competently handled by Genesis, with a beautiful flowing arrangement of violins and cellos. A disc of many facets and great depth, but it might be a bit too complex for the average fan."

King was even more enthusiastic (of course!), informing readers of his weekly newspaper column that the first King production "in almost a year—[is by] a group of young, fresh, 15/16/17 year olds called Genesis. Simple sounds; plaintive, high, wheeling strings; lyrics of intensity and purity. It needs a lot of airplay, but I'm sure you'll grow to love it. Remember when you were innocent? That's what it's all about—'The Silent Sun that never shines.' Take it, and then, to your hearts if you feel like I do about it."

Undeterred by the single's failure, the following month found Genesis back in the studio, taking over Central Sound Studios on Denmark Street, in the heart of London's Tin Pan Alley, to record the songs "Hey," "I'm Here," "There Was a Movement," and the intriguingly titled "2.30 Park Time (AM PM)." But, even as they worked, an audacious scheme was hatching in the musicians' minds, one that would see so much of what they had already recorded cast aside, never to see the light of day again. (A mere fraction of Genesis's 1967–68 output has seen even bootleg release.)

Instead, they intended turning their attentions toward a full-fledged concept album, a field of musical ambition that only the Beatles' *Sgt. Pepper* and the Pretty Things' *SF Sorrow* had, so far, truly grasped. Pete Townshend was talking about it, and the leviathan *Tommy* was not far away. But still Genesis was venturing into uncharted territory, with an ambition that was amplified only by their announcement of what its chosen concept would be. Punning on their own name, they were going to take on the Bible, from Genesis to Revelation. "It was a semiconcept," Gabriel corrected later. "We had this fairly loose theme and greased in a few things that shouldn't have been there…."

Looking to capitalize on the smattering of goodwill engendered by "The Silent Sun," and to mask the band's silence as they worked toward the LP, a second Genesis single was issued on May 10 although with little hope, surely, of improving upon its predecessor's showing. Stately and impassioned though it once again was, "A Winter's Tale" was scarcely the most eye-catching title to release, just as Spring began to kick into its stride.

Once again, the *New Musical Express* was enthusiastic enough about this "absorbing disc," with its "pulsating crescendo" and "impressive…gripping" lyric. "The melody could have done with a little more substance," the review continued, but still it was a "chart possible." Sad indeed that neither Decca nor the *NME* reviewer chose to flip the record over before release. "One-Eyed Hound" was another of the group's excursions into supernatural territory, but it rocked with a fuzzy abandon, a squalling thunderstorm triggered by a guitar refrain that was pure Jimi Hendrix. It may never have become a hit, but it would have raised eyebrows that its politely understated A-side could never have affected.

Genesis was still rehearsing the material destined for the LP when drummer Chris Stewart departed, shortly after the release of "A Winter's Tale." Unlike his bandmates, he had never taken a career in the music industry too seriously; neither were his parents even halfway as accommodating as his collegues when it came to balancing his academic and future life against having fun in a pop group. Armed with a £300 pay-off from Jonathan King, "to clear up the question of any future rights in the recordings," Stewart later mused wryly, the drummer headed away to a life in farming, and only the occasional dip back into his musical dreams—one short-lived gig found him playing drums with a circus act. Later still, Stewart would establish himself as

> "I'm still not sure what the enigmatic lyric is about, but I gather it refers to a girl!"

a travel writer of some renown, first for the *Rough Guide* series of venturesome handbooks and then in his own right—his autobiographies *Driving Over Lemons* and *A Parrot in the Pepper Tree* rate among the most delightful (and, as an aside, successful) travel books of the 21st century so far.

Stewart was replaced in the lineup by John Silver, a friend of Gabriel's whose abilities as a drummer were handsomely augmented by a family house near Oxford, to which his new bandmates were regularly welcomed to rehearse during the school holidays. Other friends, too, came through for the group. One David Thomas hailed from a veritable country house in South Warmborough, Hampshire, and the group became constant guests there, as well, reveling in the bucolic atmosphere as they worked toward writing and mapping out the now-looming Bible album.

Sessions at Regent Sound saw Genesis make its first serious stab at laying down the skeleton of the album—ten songs were demoed, but the sheer enormity of the project before them saw any sense of cohesive concept still far out of reach. "Where the Sour Turns to Sweet," "Am I Very Wrong," "In the Beginning," and "In the Wilderness" would all eventually make their way into the framework. But "One Day," "The Magic of Time," "There Is a Movement," "Humanity," "Everything Is Love," and "You Got to Be Perfect" were destined for nothing more than the curio shelf. "There were one or two musical ideas which I think would have been quite interesting," Gabriel later complained, "but we weren't allowed to do them because they were thought not to be commercial. There was [one] track, 'A Place to Call My Own,' [which was] the first of the bigger numbers we do with lots of mood changes…an eight-minute thing…of which 30 seconds got on the record."

> A squalling thunderstorm triggered by a guitar refrain that was pure Jimi Hendrix.

Nevertheless, Banks insisted, "Jonathan was really quite kind, and he liked our songs and didn't try to influence us. I don't think we'd really sorted out a direction at that time, though, and we were still rather amateurish in the studio."

Slowly through the summer of 1968, *From Genesis to Revelation* took shape, with the band locked inside Regent Sound Studios with producer King and ace arranger Arthur Greenslade overseeing the lush and lavish strings with which the music would be draped.

The recordings concluded in September, and the band members prepared to launch the next stage of their academic careers. Tony Banks was off to Sussex University to read physics, mathematics, and philosophy. Mike Rutherford was entering Farnborough Technical College; Gabriel and Phillips were to remain at Charterhouse to work toward their A-level exams.

From Genesis to Revelation was set for release the following March. A single, the long-delayed "Where the Sour Turns to Sweet," would follow in June. But the group was, as their studies continued, necessarily able to do little to promote either, and when the sales figures were finally drawn in, *From Genesis to Revelation* was revealed to have shifted a mere shade more than 1,000 copies in the United Kingdom—690 in stereo, 350 in mono. A few more ears may have been pricked up over the next year or so, as the slightly Pink Floyd-ish ("Astronomy Domine") "In the Beginning" was culled for inclusion on the budget-priced progressive sampler album, *Wowie Zowie! The World of Progressive Music*, nestled alongside such attractions as William R. Strickland's spooky "Computer Love," American rockers Touch's "Down at Circes' Place" and the now-ubiquitous Moody Blues. But it would be another five or six years before Genesis fans were again granted an opportunity to hear *From Genesis to Revelation* in its entirety, by which time the band had moved so far beyond its parameters that any kind of comparison, or even fair evaluation, was all but impossible.

Reissued on both sides of the Atlantic in 1974 (when it promptly gnawed the lower reaches of the American Top 200), under its original title in America and as the grotesquely packaged *In the Beginning* elsewhere, *From Genesis to Revelation* was greeted with curiosity, bordering on pleasant surprise. So many artists of the age, after all, had seen the most embarrassing skeletal remains hauled out of their career-long cabinets…one only had to remember how Decca's Deram subsidiary mortified fans of David Bowie by reissuing his six-year-old "The Laughing Gnome" in 1973 while early 1974 saw T. Rex's Marc Bolan launch legal proceedings to halt the release of his own mid-'60s strivings.

Genesis only added to the uncertainty that preceded the album's reissue with its own disparaging remarks about naïve youth and amateurish fumblings, even condemning the stereo mix (which was all Decca intended reissuing) as having very little whatsoever in common with its plans for the record's sound. Yet Genesis had nothing to be ashamed, or even embarrassed, about. Its makers' youth is apparent, but that is not a bad thing—youth permits an artist to indulge in an earnestness, even pretension, that age and experience quickly wring out of him, and *From Genesis to Revelation* emerged vastly ambitious and brightly precocious, and if elements are preposterous, they are enjoyably so.

> "An eight-minute thing…of which 30 seconds got on the record."

The so-repetitious reissues of the album that have followed over the years have done nothing to reduce its pleasure—beginning with the 1976 *Rock Roots* repackaging, any number of bonus tracks have been appended to the original album, including all four non-LP single sides, plus a clutch of early demos.

But still they cannot overshadow the 13 tracks that comprise the original *From*

Genesis to Revelation. True, the concept itself is not necessarily obvious from the music. Nevertheless, one can enjoy the journey from the horn-punching, finger-snapping "When the Sour Turns to Sweet" and the moodily atmospheric and effects-laden "In the Beginning" through to a dynamic remake of "The Silent Sun" and the brief closing coda of "A Place to Call My Own"—cruelly abbreviated from its original grandeur, to be sure, but a warming and evocative finale all the same.

The production and the arrangements did hearken to the recent work of the Bee Gees, the effortless stream of so-melodic hit singles and albums that saw them once compete with the Beatles for the title of pop's most skillful tunesmiths: such Brothers Gibb compositions as "New York Mining Disaster 1941," "Words," and "Massachusetts" are clear role models as *From Genesis to Revelation* drifts along. But even there, one could only marvel at the young musicians' tenacity. It is, after all, one thing to *try* to emulate the most noteworthy talents of the day. It is quite another to actually succeed.

Comparisons between *From Genesis to Revelation* and the albums that followed are senseless. Even *Trespass*, a sophomore offering that was constructed at least in part from material written and demoed around the time of their debut, was recorded almost two years later, and that can be an eternity in the life and experience of a young musician. But Gabriel's tones are already darkly distinctive, and the vocal and musical harmonies that wash behind him, too, indicate the musicians' intent. Experienced for the first time today, *From Genesis to Revelation* is not, by the standards the band's future would impose, anything like the Genesis you may be expecting. But it could scarcely be anybody else, either.

With their studies taking necessary precedence over any promotional activities, it was spring 1969 before Genesis members were able to reconvene for any period of time, only to discover that any media interest in their music had already come and gone. Decca landed them a performance at the BBC, running through the album's "In Hiding," but the performance was never destined for anything more than a studio training film and has never been broadcast. Another flurry of excitement took place in late May, when the group united at Brian Roberts's new home in Dorman's Park, near East Grinstead, to rehearse and write. There the local *East Grinstead Courier* newspaper caught up with them to wax enthusiastically on the presence of the young recording stars in their midst.

"A lyrical and delicate alchemy of sound drifted across Dormans Park last week when Genesis came to stay. With a curious combination of all-acoustic sounds and vocal harmonies they have so far had three singles released on Decca and one album *From Genesis to Revelation*, all produced by singer and controversial 'pop' columnist Jonathan King."

Somewhat surprisingly, it was Roberts, now working as an assistant cameraman, who dominated the interview, as he documented the group's beginnings. "We all met at school at Charterhouse and began writing together. A group was formed from this. I began to record work and have continued to do so." He also pinpointed a major shift in the group's attitude toward its musical career. "So far all their work has been done from the recording studios. But thinking very seriously of becoming professional, they are looking for the type of work where audiences are prepared to sit down and listen, as on the present college circuits. Their music is essentially for the listener, not the raver."

The days when Genesis was resolute in its refusal to step on stage were fast drawing to an end. Partially, this was because of the failure of *From Genesis to Revelation*—a collapse that was quickly followed by Decca's announcement that it would not be requiring any further recordings from the band. It was obvious that, without live work to let people know the group even existed, the album was never going to sell to more than the proverbial one man and a dog. But, as Roberts pointed out, Genesis's thoughts were also swayed by the birth of an entire new audience for live entertainment—student and college audiences who took the music as seriously as the musicians who made it, and were not going to spoil their evenings by having what looked like "a good time."

Status Quo's Rick Parfitt spoke for every artist playing the college circuit at the time when he remembered, "The places we were playing were the ones where you'd see the geezers with their trench coats on, a pint in one hand, an album under the other arm, sitting on the floor nodding their heads." It was, the *New Musical Express* later pronounced, "the age of cool," in which bands actively discouraged audiences from dancing, shouting, or doing anything but showing gentle, mute appreciation for the labors being undertaken on stage for their benefit.

It is impossible to pinpoint the precise moment when concert-goers stopped hopping wildly around, screaming hysterically at every wriggling bottom. But the catalyst was unquestionably King Crimson, an impossibly grandiose outfit formed from the wreckage of the folk-psych trio Giles, Giles, and Fripp. From the moment King Crimson set foot onstage at the Speakeasy on April 9, 1969, some of the most influential names in rock 'n' rock journalism had flocked to their side; by the time they landed a spot at the Rolling Stones' free concert in Hyde Park that July, they were already the most talked-about band of the year.

Talked about, but not talked *through*. Crimson's music demanded such rapt attention that, when one of its earliest Speakeasy shows was disrupted by members of the Pink Fairies, calling out for old Chuck Berry numbers all night, history *remembered* it. This was a music to be absorbed and admired. It was not an excuse to get roaring drunk and shout for "Nadine."

For Genesis, King Crimson represented a high watermark toward which all of its efforts would now be driven. Both musically and in terms of audience response, the atmosphere of awe and appreciation that was Crimson's to command was precisely what Genesis required for its own music. "We thought they were magnificent," Gabriel confirmed, "doing the same kind of things that we wanted to, but much bigger and better. In the early days, we used to feel that we were rushing things, and we used to think they'd never allow themselves to be rushed…'why do we?' We built Crimson up into giant, mythical proportions in our heads, because they were putting our ideals into practice."

"Geezers with their trench coats on, a pint in one hand, an album under the other arm, sitting on the floor nodding their heads."

As the individual members' personal gig-going revealed to them just how quiet a modern, mature, audience could be, so their doubts and fears over performing live fell away. Duly, the group set about placing those wheels in motion. They recruited old friend (and one-time Anon vocalist) Richard MacPhail as their road manager; they borrowed £150 apiece from Gabriel and MacPhail's parents to fund the purchase of a supremely roadworthy Hammond organ and a Selmer Goliath amp. And they arranged to spend a few weeks at MacPhail's parents' country cottage, Send Barns, near Guildford to rehearse a live set.

The decision to go professional, abandoning their educational courses and throwing everything into the band, was a major step for each of the musicians, and one of them, inevitably, was not prepared to take it. In July, John Silver announced his departure from the group. He'd been offered a scholarship at an American university, to begin in September 1969. Several summertime weeks were then devoured as Genesis sought his replacement, finally settling upon John Mayhew in July, on the eve of their next studio engagement. Returning to Regent Sound on Aug. 20, Genesis had four new songs to demo: "Family," "White Mountain," "Going Out to Get You," and "Pacidy."

It was their first time in a studio without Jonathan King, and the results were patchy, to say the least. But King's departure from the scene was not necessarily a blow. His one-year contract at an end, King's interest in nurturing a progressive-rock act had sensibly lessened as his preferred themes of bubblegum and pop took precedence both in his mind and in the marketplace. Indeed, King was preparing a chart assault that would see him enter the new year with a Top 30 hit of his own, "Let It All Hang Out," and while his former protégés struggled

> "The more records you release under different names, the more chance you have of having hits."

to keep their chins up on the live circuit during 1970–71, King was preparing to mastermind smashes for a host of somewhat more ephemeral talents…the Weathermen, Bubblerock, the Piglets, and St. Cecilia.

From there, the musical genius that he had always insisted was a part of his make-up was revealed to all. Over the next decade, King established himself as one of the most prolific hit-makers in British chart history, in his own (frequently pseudonymous) right and as the proprietor of the riotously successful U.K. record label. Neither was his "discovery" of Genesis a lucky one-off. In 1971, King produced the first hit single by the hitherto unknown Bay City Rollers; in 1972, he launched the careers of Jona Lewie and 10cc.

Neither did his influence end there. Through the 1980s, King became a ubiquitous (if, it must be confessed, somewhat smarmy) presence on British pop culture TV; into the 1990s, he oversaw his homeland's annual assaults on the Eurovision Song Contest and didn't do too shabbily there, either. Today, King is perhaps equally well known for the indiscretions that landed him a seven-year prison sentence for child sex offenses in 2001, but it would be equally criminal if the failings of his private life should ever obscure the triumphs of his public career. Pure pop music…bubblegum, if you will…has produced precious few geniuses. King, however, is incontrovertibly among the greatest of them all.

King and Genesis never had a falling-out—the producer once smiled, "They were far too polite for that!" Rather, both parties simply recognized their innate incompatibility. Genesis wanted a career, King wanted hits, and both parties had determined that the two were not necessarily inclusive. "The more records you release under different names, the more chance you have of having hits," King explained. "A band name is a brand name, and if a DJ or a record buyer doesn't like their last record, they won't want to like the next one. But if you don't like the Piglets, you might like Shag, and if you don't like that, then what about Sakkharin?" Genesis, on the other hand, was simply Genesis.

In September 1969, Genesis made the planned relocation down to Send Barns to spend two weeks rehearsing. They were accompanied, inevitably, by a newly purchased copy of King Crimson's just-released debut album, *In the Court of the Crimson King*, a disc destined to take up permanent residence on the turntable, just as its so-distinctive cover, the broadly grinning moon face of the Crimson King himself, was hung on the wall of the rehearsal room to remind Genesis of the standards to which they now aspired.

More than 30 years from its release, it is difficult to comprehend just how staggering *In the Court of the Crimson King* was and just how absolutely revolutionary its blending of cold, hard metal and so gracefully flowing folk, arch improvisation, and art-school classicism was.

The actual mechanics of King Crimson's music were not beyond Genesis's imaginings. Indeed, Peter Gabriel describes a very similar mélange when he described "going to one of the record companies [and playing our tape]. They'd say, 'This sounds like a folk bit, a rock bit, a hymn…they shouldn't be together, they're all separate genres of music.'" Where Fripp and company raised themselves above such petty pedantry was in the seamless melding of those (and other) styles into a whole so cohesive that it wasn't simply impossible to state where one began or ended, it was difficult to even identify the components in the first place.

Quite simply, *In the Court of the Crimson King* was unlike any music anyone had heard. Even the Moody Blues, Procol Harum, and Keith Emerson's the Nice, the three bands whose vapor trails had so far taken them closest to what would become the progressive-rock ideal, were doing little more than rewiring their wares around the same traditional musical maypoles as had fired every other hero of the rock 'n' roll era.

Other-worldly, ultraweirdly King Crimson may have been from another planet by comparison with any of its so-called peers, as Mellotron flirted with flute and sax, Robert Fripp's guitars conjured new thresholds of sound, and Greg Lake's near-ethereal vocal hung disembodied over all, washing lyricist Pete Sinfield's poetry into plains that mere pop and rock had never even dreamed. But, as they labored beneath the watchful eye of the Crimson King, Genesis believed their music was eminently capable of traveling just as far.

To suggest that Genesis reinvented its sound in the wake of *In the Court of the Crimson King*, of course, is to deny the evidence of the music they had recorded and released a full year before that album was issued. It is true that Gabriel took up playing the flute at least partially in emulation of Crimson's Ian McDonald. However, where King Crimson's influence hung most heavily was in persuading Genesis to take chances where it may once have remained secure; to listen to where a piece of music *wanted* to go, as opposed to where it ought to go; to unlearn, in other words, all the conventions of pop songwriting and musicianship that it had hitherto held so dear.

Close to a year later, the *Trespass* album would document just how far Genesis had journeyed in that direction. However, evidence also exists of the band's most immediate travails, after roadie Dave Rootes borrowed a tape recorder from a friend. Mike Rutherford and Anthony Phillips, still the most prolific of the two basic songwriting teams in the band, decided to take advantage of their location to demo some of their most recent compositions.

The remainder of Genesis was not involved (Richard MacPhail threw in some tambourine), and the recordings themselves are primitive, to say the least. But still the tape allows the modern listener to grasp at least a sense of the sheer adventurousness that flowed through the band's veins at this time. One of their pair's efforts, titled "F Sharp" (after the key it was played in), would subsequently lend itself to Genesis's "The Musical Box," and another track, "D Sharp," was later reborn as "The Geese and the Ghost," the title track to Phillips's first solo album. The music itself, Phillips confessed, left something to be desired…he described the rhythm, in particular, as appearing "a little vibey." But there was no questioning the quality, or the timelessness, of the music itself.

Around the duo's endeavors, Genesis continued assembling a concert repertoire, knowing that, in just a couple of weeks on Sept. 23, it would play its first-ever "public" concert, at a dance in Chobham, Surrey, hosted by one Mrs. Balm, a genteel event that left them with absolutely no clue as to what the real road held in store for them. "When we first went out on the road," Gabriel admitted a couple of years later, "we thought we'd just get the music out and play behind a black curtain, but it wasn't working out."

Genesis played its first-ever professional concert at Brunel University's Acton annex on Nov. 1, 1969. It was, Anthony Phillips later shuddered, "a disaster for me." Preparing to take the stage, he restrung his guitar, unaware that one of the machine heads was loose. The first break in the first song, "the string…slipped." He was certain that everyone was watching and suffered savage pangs of self-consciousness for the remainder of the evening. In fact, it is unlikely whether anyone even noticed. Banks, his organ pumping through that Selmer Goliath amp, had his foot down on the pedals so hard that it's unlikely whether any other instrument was even half-audible. "But they seemed to like us," he reflected.

The group followed through with a string of similarly appointed shows at Twickenham Technical College, the Kingston Hotel, and Eel Pie Island, all within the southwest environs of London, and further afield, too, at venues in Birmingham (they played the Christmas dance at a teacher training college!) and Manchester in mid-December. It is said that the road can go on forever. As Genesis took its first tentative turns up and down and around Britain's highway system, in an age when motorways were still a dream awaiting fruition and the shortest route between point A and point B normally detoured via X, Y, and Z, the band realized that the old cliché only begins to tell the story.

CHAPTER THREE

A MOST CHARISMATIC MAN

With Richard MacPhail at the wheel of the beat-up old McDougal's bread van that was the band's sole means of transport, and the musicians themselves armed with a picnic hamper that they would happily unpack by the side of the road, Genesis was just one more name on a live circuit that was already creaking beneath the weight of countless up-and-sometimes-coming hopefuls.

The psychedelic diaspora—the explosion and outward growth of the myriad talents thrust into being by the musical freedoms of the previous couple of years—was in full force, and every other group appeared to have a new sound to spurt forth. Keith Relf's Renaissance, the folk-tinged classicists that emerged out of the old blues-wailin' Yardbirds, was taking its first steps out, astounding audiences with a brew that was as far from "Shapes of Things" and "Psycho Daisies" as it was possible to move. The Groundhogs were melding hard blues with heavy rock; Black Sabbath was heavier still.

> The head-banging hairy who was watching them had already decided they weren't loud enough.

There was wild fusion from one-time jazzman Keith Tippett, mantric revolution from the Edgar Broughton Band, wired folk from Magna Carta, stoned space freakery from Hawkwind…and some were just so far out that even their names barely began to suggest what may happen on stage: the Spontaneous Music

Ensemble, which genuinely was spontaneous; Eclection, who were deliberately eclectic; Acoustic, which was acoustic; and the Incredible String Band, which was, indeed, incredible.

Genesis, were any passing critic to have attempted to bundle them up into any of the musical movements swirling through the last days of the 60s, fell wholeheartedly into the lighter, lusher end of the spectrum, a bag that was confirmed by the handful of support gigs they were handed as December drew on. A step up to the main hall at Brunel University, in Uxbridge, saw Genesis opening for Fairport Convention, as the folk-rock legend took its first steps back into action following the departures of Sandy Denny and Ashley Hutchings; nearby Twickenham Technical College, meanwhile, paired them with Piblokto, the endearingly eccentric vision of Pete Brown, one-time lyricist for Cream.

Jonathan King, watching paternally from the sidelines, admiringly said, "I'd already decided that I wasn't going to carry on working with the band, but I was very impressed by their dedication when they first started gigging, carrying all their gear out to the sticks and setting up to play auditions for snotty little university social secretaries, who would then decide whether the group was good enough to entertain the students for an evening."

Such auditions offered a frequently dispiriting experience for the quintet, as they ran through their best paces, knowing full well that the head-banging hairy who was watching them had already decided they weren't loud enough. But, slowly, Genesis began to get the hang of it, opting not to showcase a selection of songs from its repertoire, in the hope that one or other may prove the charm, but to condense, instead, every weapon in its musical arsenal into one single number, a version of the newly written "The Knife" that was capable of stretching out to nigh-on 20 minutes.

A hard, intense, and, with Phillips' guitar and Banks' keyboards resounding behind Gabriel's shrieking vocal, dramatic performance, the advent of "The Knife" marked a major shift in Genesis's musical approach. Hitherto, there had always been something "polite" about their music, a reliance (some said *over*reliance) on harmonies, acoustics, and mood. "The Knife," though it sacrificed none of these qualities, added volume and anger to what had once been understated and sinister while its portrayal of life under a totalitarian government, and the fate of those who would rebel against the "order" of things, was similarly a lot more topical than Genesis had ever proven before.

Although "The Knife" was written and recorded some months before American National Guardsmen made headlines around the world for gunning down four antiwar protestors at Kent State University, still the song's unrelenting vision of a riot and its consequences would strike a chord within the same outraged souls who applauded Neil Young's "Ohio" or the Broughtons's "American Soldier Boy." However fleetingly (and no matter how satirical they later claimed the intention of "The Knife"), Genesis found itself officially allied with the "revolution." And the irony of their backgrounds, four scions of the most privileged class in British society, public schoolboys with the accents to prove it, was surely not lost upon them.

If "The Knife" represented a new frontier for Genesis, however, the remainder of the material being worked upon as 1969 drifted away remained firmly rooted in the landscapes mapped out by their debut album: "Visions of Angels," widely applauded in its early state as one of the group's most accomplished numbers, was originally written for *From Genesis to Revelation*, as its plaintive subject matter makes plain. Where the group was stepping out of its initial mold was with its willingness to experiment, embroider, and, more important, extend its songs beyond the three-minute (or so) range that Jonathan King and Decca preferred, to twice, even three times, that length.

Once again, little of Genesis's output from this period, be it live recordings or studio demos, has been made available either officially or otherwise. The liner notes to its 1997 *Archive* box set speak tantalizingly of Genesis's early live shows abounding with such titles as Anthony Phillips's "Stranger," "Jamaican Longboat," "Digby of the Rambling Lake," "Grandma," "I've Been Travelling All Night Long," and "Little Leaf," a harmonic duet by Rutherford and Banks. But the songs themselves remain undisturbed on the shelf.

"Masochistic Man," "Stumble," "Black Sheep," "Key to Love," and covers of the blues classics "Crossroads" and "Sitting on Top of the World," all present in Genesis's very first live shows, have likewise vanished. And, while other early compositions would eventually see release, they did so in very different form to what thrilled (or otherwise) audiences in 1969–70.

Described by Rutherford as "the first thing we wrote as a band," the 45-minute-long "The Movement" enjoyed a handful of live performances before being systematically rendered for later songs—both "Stagnation" and "Get 'Em Out by Friday" had their genesis within "The Movement." Elsewhere, the alcoholic nightmare of "Twilight Alehouse" finally became a B-side in 1974, and "Let Us Now Make Love" would be rerecorded by Anthony Phillips for his 1986 album *Ivory Moon*, with the composer's liner notes recalling a typical Genesis performance of the song.

"This was one of the most popular Genesis songs in the early touring days. [But] few of the quiet, sensitive songs survived on the road, and it was eventually dropped from the set. Apart (of course) from Peter Gabriel's idiosyncratic vocals, Mike Rutherford and myself used to play 12-string guitars, and Tony Banks would swap from organ to my Stratocaster through a Lesley speaker for the [instrumental] sections." For his own version, however, Phillips "returned to how it was originally written, in September 1968, on piano."

What modern fans may describe as the "obscurity" of this repertoire did nothing to hold Genesis back, however. Of course, there were the shows where everything that could go wrong did…the night Mike Rutherford, at that time prone to play cello on stage, found himself raising an audience member's skirt every time he bowed; the evening when the band took a south London stage to find just one person standing in the audience to see them…"Any requests?" asked a nonplussed Gabriel.

There were far more nights, however, when the five not only made some money, but they made friends as well. Early in 1970, Genesis found itself opening for another public school lad, Marlborough College graduate Nick Drake, an enigmatic singer-songwriter whose crippling shyness restricted his live performances to a mere handful of concerts and whose entire career was spent in an obscurity that would not even begin to shatter until years after his death. Certainly Genesis paid little attention to his performance, as Anthony Phillips later regretfully confessed. Drake, however, both watched and enjoyed Genesis's set, approaching Phillips afterward to tell him that the song "Let Us Now Make Love" was "dangerous."

Another early ally was a producer at BBC Television, working on a proposed documentary about painter Mick Jackson. Having caught Genesis live in late 1969, he approached them about contributing some soundtrack material to the program, a clutch of songs that—though they were never used by the BBC—would resolve themselves into three future Genesis classics: "Looking for Someone," "Anyway," and "The Musical Box." Although the original session tape has since been rediscovered, following three decades in obscurity, a fourth number, "Peace," remains unheard.

Former Yardbirds bassist Paul Samwell-Smith, now carving a niche for himself as producer of the recently resurgent Cat Stevens, was recruited to produce the session at the BBC's studios on Jan. 9, 1970, and Gabriel later enthused, "It was excellent. He really *heard* the music." Genesis's attempts to lure Samwell-Smith into working with them on further projects were always politely rebuffed, but the experience was not wholly in vain. Work on Cat Stevens's next album, *Mona Bona Jakon*, was underway at Olympic Studios, and Samwell-Smith invited Gabriel down to the sessions, to add flute to the song "Katmandu."

Poor Peter. Samwell-Smith detailed, "[He] came into the studio, very young and very, very nervous. He almost couldn't play the flute because his lip was shaking, and his hands were shaking. I had to go out and tell him, 'Don't worry, it'll be alright.'" After the guest was gone, however, his very audible fear became something of a standing joke among the more experienced musicians in the studio—Gabriel's hard pants of breath were recorded and spliced into a track of their own, for the studio to laugh at later. (Gabriel would reunite with Cat Stevens, or Yusuf Islam as he is now known, at the 46664 World AIDS Day Concert in December 2003 to perform Stevens's hit "Wild World.")

> "You could never say that any of them had too much to say for themselves back then."

Around the same time as this adventure unfolded, another opened as Genesis found itself a booking agent—London club specialist Terry King. One of the network of truly great, well-connected concert promoters on the capital circuit at that time, King had barely taken Genesis on board when he arranged for them to make their first-ever appearance at one of the city's most prestigious niteries, the Marquee Club, on Feb. 4, 1970.

The billing itself was not ideal—the group would be warming up the crowd for the blues-busting Keef Hartley Band. Undeterred by such a mismatch, Genesis arranged its live set to build up to their own heavyweight blues number, the driving "Going Out to Get You," and the assembled denim and long-haired onlookers were still applauding when King offered the group a return engagement, two weeks hence, on Feb. 19. And this time, they would be lining up alongside a headliner whose audience was already primed for the kind of music Genesis would be offering them, Rare Bird.

All too often overlooked as modern historians ponder the birth of progressive-rock, Rare Bird were one of the brightest lights among all the pioneers, a treasure-trove of symphonic keyboard-driven rock, soaring melodies, and anthemic harmonies. Formed in London in late 1969, twin keyboardists Graham Field and Dave Kaffinetti, bassist Steve Gould, and drummer Mark Ashton, Rare Bird initially attracted attention for daring to play rock without the benefit of a lead guitar—even Keith Emerson and the Nice originally employed the mercurial Davy O'List in that role.

Nevertheless, that novelty swiftly proved among the least of Rare Bird's attractions, and in October 1969, the band played its debut Marquee show—the first of a dozen it would play over the next year and the beginning, too, of a miraculously fast-moving few months. By the end of the month, Rare Bird had a record deal, with the newly launched Charisma Records label; by the end of the year, they had a self-titled debut album in the stores, and the same week as this latest Marquee show, their first single, "Sympathy," entered the British chart.

And now it was Rare Bird's turn to spread some magic around. From the side of the stage, Graham Field watched as Genesis ran through a set that climaxed with a positively pulsating rendition of "The Knife," convinced that he had discovered a new act for Charisma's still infant roster. Field's enthusiasm fed back to the label, and, finding Terry King equally ready to sing this new group's praises, Charisma founder Tony Stratton Smith was quick to check the newcomers out for himself.

Peter Gabriel had already made a call to Charisma, only to be told by the secretary that the label wasn't interested. Now, however, the mood had changed somewhat. "I met them for the first time at a gig in Eastbourne," Stratton Smith remembered. "[Then] there were a few phone conversations with Peter [Gabriel]; he was very much the group's spokesman at the time." Laughingly, Stratton Smith recalled a group who, almost literally, wouldn't say "boo" to a goose. "[Peter] was certainly the most outgoing of them all, although you could never say that any of them had too much to say for themselves back then."

Personally convinced that Genesis should be Charisma's next signing, Tony Stratton Smith nevertheless laid his own beliefs open to the rest of the Charisma staff, arranging for Genesis to more or less audition for the label at their next London concert on March 3, at the first of seven weekly shows at Ronnie Scott's club in London. No sooner was the show over than Stratton Smith was striding triumphantly toward the dressing room to sign the band to Charisma. The applause of his staff was still echoing around the club.

Bluff, hail, and hearty, as they say, a bear of a man who looked as though he could snap your wrist with a gentle handshake, Tony Stratton Smith is one of the most legendary figures to have bestrode British rock of the early '70s. A sports journalist by trade, Stratton Smith covered soccer and cricket for a succession of regional and national newspapers during the 1950s, contributing to a number of annual publications and ghostwriting short autobiographical features for a wealth of the day's greatest players—Brazilian Pelé, Scot Denis Law, and Spaniard Alfredo Di Stefano are among those who placed their trust in Stratton Smith's pen.

Stratton Smith decided to change careers in 1962. Having spent part of the summer in Chile, covering that year's World Cup soccer tournament, Stratton Smith found himself warming more and more to the prospects of spending the rest of his life on a sunny beach. Moving to Rio de Janeiro, Brazil, he seemed set to do just that when he was introduced to Brazilian composer

"Signing anything that looked like it could tune its own 40-piece orchestra."

Antonio Carlos Jobim, who introduced him, in turn, to the lucrative world of music publishing. You hear a song, you buy it from its writer, and then you sell it to the world. It sounded so simple.

Stratton Smith returned to London, but he quickly learned that the game was not all it was cracked up to be. Few, if any, of the copyrights he purchased—for what were generally regarded as extraordinarily generous amounts—ever recouped even a fraction of their initial cost, but Stratton Smith remained fascinated by the music industry. In 1963, in partnership with Lee Gopthal, the entrepreneur behind what became the Trojan Records reggae empire, Stratton Smith formed the Beat &

Commercial Records distribution company, itself destined to become one of the key players on the U.K. music scene of the next decade.

Stratton Smith also returned to writing, and in 1965 he published what would remain his most impressive work, a biography of Elizaveta Pilenko, Mother Maria Skobtsoza, the Russian intellectual and radical who entered the Orthodox Church as a nun in 1932 and died in the gas chamber at the Ravensbruck death camp on Good Friday, 1945—just days before the Red Army liberated it. Its somewhat florid prose ("The sun rose like a golden votive lamp over the concentration camp") notwithstanding, *The Rebel Nun: The Moving Story of Mother Maria of Paris* was, until recently, its subject's only major English-language biography.

Stratton Smith was also one of several journalists with whom Beatles manager Brian Epstein discussed writing his autobiography, the book that became 1965's *A Cellarful of Noise*. Departing to the Netherlands for a few days, the pair quickly agreed that the book was not likely to happen (it was eventually written by the Beatles' press officer, Derek Taylor). But Epstein saw something else in Stratton Smith, a latent hunger and an untapped ability that echoed his own in the months before he discovered the Beatles.

Through Epstein, Stratton Smith was introduced to a new group—Paddy, Klaus, and Gibson—formed in Liverpool by bassist Klaus Voorman, a close friend of the Beatles since their days in the meat grinder of the Hamburg Star Club. Initially, Stratton Smith saw the trio simply as musicians who could regularly demo the songs he was still picking up in his guise of part-time music publisher; having learned from Epstein, however, the even greater riches that could be gained from actually managing a pop group, he was soon buying into the trio's existing management contract with would-be entrepreneur Don Paul. As 1965 progressed, Stratton Smith's world of contacts within the Swinging London club scene saw Paddy, Klaus, and Gibson rated among the fastest-rising Most-Likely-To's of the year.

Enter, once again, Brian Epstein—who bought out both Tony Stratton Smith and Don Paul's interest in the band later in the year ("once we'd groomed them to his standards," Stratton Smith later mused). Undaunted, however, Stratton Smith returned to Liverpool and scooped up singer Beryl Marsden. The pop-art freak-beaters the Creation and the Kubas followed her into his management stable, and over the next two years, all three would bring Stratton Smith a certain degree of success—among the earliest engagements he landed the newly renamed Koobas was a berth at the Beatles' 1965 Christmas concert, while a record deal with Pye saw the band's "Take Me for a Little While" single come close to a little chart action.

In 1967, Stratton Smith took over the management of the Nice, the virtuoso quartet with whom organist Keith Emerson first established his name and reputation. Still escaping its earliest incarnation as the flamboyant backing group behind singer P.P. Arnold, the Nice's popularity was never in doubt, and Stratton Smith's handling of the group's career quickly brought him to the attention of another of the era's most remarkable performers, the anarchic rock/comedy troupe the Bonzo Dog Doo Dah Band.

It, too, sold records in a manner that Stratton Smith's earlier clients had never dreamed of—the Bonzo's "I'm the Urban Spaceman" rose to No. 5 in Britain in fall 1968; the Nice's eponymous third album went Top Three a year later. And Stratton Smith's mercurial mind began contemplating the next stage in his career, launching his own record label.

By the late '60s, the near triopoly enjoyed since time immemorial by the majors EMI, Decca, and Pye had been punctured again and again. Closest to home, so far as Tony Stratton Smith was concerned, was Immediate, the label formed by Rolling Stones manager Andrew Loog Oldham back in 1965 and home to the Nice throughout their career. The first of this new wave of independents to take on the Goliaths and win, Immediate was not only scoring regular hits with the Small Faces, Twice As Much, Humble Pie, and P.P. Arnold, but they had proved eminently capable of hitting the No. 1 spot as well—Chris Farlowe and Amen Corner both brought Immediate memorable chart-toppers.

Immediate opened the door; other independents (nominal or actual) were swift to push through it. The success of the Beatles' Apple; producer Larry Page's Page One; Track Records, helmed by the Who managers Kit Lambert and Chris Stamp; entrepreneur Giorgio Gomelsky's Marmalade; Chris Blackwell's Island Records; Robert Stigwood's Reaction; and Lee Gopthal's Trojan all indicated that not only was there life aplenty beyond the storied walls of the established record companies, but there was also an opportunity for growth—personal, financial, and musical—that could never be countenanced by the gray old gnomes who ruled the traditional industry roost.

Key to Stratton Smith's deliberations, too, was the haste with which those major labels were themselves attempting to update their image, launching their own "progressive" record labels and, as he put it a few years later, "signing anything that looked like it could tune its own 40-piece orchestra."

Decca had somehow abandoned the once-ambitious Deram to more mainstream pleasures but were quick to re-establish the company's credentials with Nova, soon to bring Steve Hillage's Egg to the cognoscenti's attention. Pye launched Dawn, with such off-kilter delights as Demon Fuzz and Comus; Fontana ignited Vertigo, home to Dr. Z, Caterpillar, Affinity, and Ben; EMI established Harvest and scooped up the Greatest Show on Earth, the Edgar Broughton Band, and Barclay James Harvest. The difference was, although each of those labels chased (and usually caught) the underground dollar, their very affiliation with the mainstream, "the Man," rendered them suspect in a world where artistic endeavor did not necessarily march hand in hand with the bottom line.

Stratton Smith visualized a label that would operate with precisely the same integrity as its artists. He called it Charisma because that was what it had.

Charisma was modeled, Stratton Smith told new signings, on Tamla Motown, with the record label an umbrella that sheltered an in-house management company, Mother—overseen by Fred Munt, a former roadie for the Bonzos; a publishing wing, Mooncrest, under the eye of Mike DeHavilland; and a booking agency, presided over by Paul Conroy (future Chairman of the BRITS and CEO of Sony U.K.). Later, Charisma would move into book publishing and movie production as well.

Even the label's distribution was a part of the family, as Stratton Smith linked with Beat & Commercial, the company he and Lee Gopthal had co-established six years earlier; many of the new label's releases would be advertised in tandem with that company's releases, on the newly founded B&C label, home to the similarly themed underground sounds of the Wild Angels, Dry Ice, and Atomic Rooster. (Charisma and B&C singles would also share the same CB numbering prefix until 1972.)

Operating out of offices set above what artists delightedly referred to as a dirty book shop on Brewer Street (the heart of London's pornocentric Soho district), a winding staircase with one room on each of its three landings, the infant Charisma was never more than a one-man show, but the staff with which Stratton Smith surrounded himself exuded a fierce sense of community. Fred

Munt's wife, Gail Colson, was Stratton Smith's personal assistant; her younger brother Glen ran the Charisma press office; her assistant, Jan, was married to Greenslade keyboard player Dave Greenslade. But it was Stratton Smith, as Glen Colson told *Mojo* magazine, who "signed all the bands, and we just sort of ran around listening to him. He was out every night until five in the morning. I was into Jimi Hendrix at the time [easy to forget, but Hendrix was still alive at this time], so I didn't think much of Genesis. But he just said, 'I like the look of these guys. I'm going to sign them.'

"Strat wanted one of everything. He wanted a classical band, a jazz band, a rock band…which used to confuse the shit out of everybody that worked with him. Because you'd come in one day, and he'd have signed something that you knew nothing about, like Monty Python or John Betjeman. But he just wanted to sign acts that were the best of their kind. That was always his dictum."

Charisma's earliest signings remain the label's best-known and best-loved, as Rare Bird were followed by Van der Graaf Generator, a group Stratton Smith had been managing since Koobas bassist Keith Ellis joined them in late 1968. Their second album (but first for Charisma), *The Least We Can Do Is Wave to Each Other*, was Charisma's second LP release, in January 1970.

"Tony Stratton Smith believed that rock music could, and should, be more than teenage fashion fodder."

Lindisfarne, a folky club act hailing from the northeastern city of Newcastle, and Audience, fronted by singer-songwriter Howard Werth, were next. And then came Genesis, whose discovery and signing, Stratton Smith insisted, "was all incredibly fast. I think I met them in the middle of February, and we'd signed by the beginning of March.

"There are certain bands you see just once, and they get so many areas of your mind stimulated. They had it all going that night. In a way, I think the timing of it was right. I was hungry for a band I could really be proud of, and they were looking for a manager they could rely on. Honestly, I think they were just relieved to have a label that wanted them so badly; I was pleased simply to have grabbed them before anybody else saw them."

In fact, he was a little slow in that respect. At least three other labels had already spotted Genesis by the time Charisma blustered in ahead of them: Warner Brothers, which gave the group what Gabriel called "one of those 'come back in two years' routines"; Threshold, the newly launched plaything of the Moody Blues; and Island Records.

Island's interest grew largely out of the enthusiasm for Genesis spilling out of one of the label's own acts, Mott the Hoople. "[Mott] were good to us," Gabriel reflected. "They were fresh from Hereford and got Guy Stevens [at that time, Mott's record producer] involved." Stevens constantly promised to bring Island into the picture—unfortunately, as Gabriel put it, "He was never the most together of people, and his interest took a while to be followed up." Too long, in fact.

Dale Griffin, Mott the Hoople's drummer, remains full of admiration for the early Genesis, still laughing at Mike Rutherford's habit of wearing "half a dozen knitted pullovers at gigs, peeling them off layer by layer as the evening progressed," and remembering the bemusement with which audiences greeted Gabriel's habit of playing (or, rather, walloping) a bass drum while he sang.

"They were a very nice bunch of chaps, very talented and well-educated and well-mannered—a lot like Queen were when we first encountered them. Mott the Hoople and Genesis were wildly different bands musicwise, but I know we Motts all enjoyed listening to the Gens at the gigs we shared, and we got on well socially, too."

> Mike Rutherford...found himself raising an audience member's skirt every time he bowed.

Despite Mott's championing of Genesis, hindsight doubts whether a deal with Island would have benefited the group much. Despite the undeniable cachet of its reputation and strength of its roster, Island was less than prolific when it came to actually "breaking" new acts—through 1970 and 1971, the label developed a voracious appetite for new talent. Yet Island's biggest names at the end of that span remained the same handful who had ruled the roost at the beginning of it, and almost all of those who filed through in the meantime had either broken up or departed.

Threshold was an even less likely proposition, despite its proprietor's natural empathy for Genesis. The Moody Blues' own albums notwithstanding, Threshold had no more weight in the marketplace than any of the other artist-driven labels that would arise during the 1970s—from the Rolling Stones' eponymous concern, through to Emerson, Lake, and Palmer's Manticore, Deep Purple's Purple, and George Harrison's Dark Horse, the headliner alone sold the records. Other signings were essentially there to make up the numbers at the office Christmas party.

Charisma, too, was tiny—all but insignificant in the greater scheme of the early-'70s music industry. But its handpicked staff and roster boded well for anybody lucky enough to be invited into the setup; they were promised that whatever happened (or did not happen) to an artist's career, it would happen in the company of friends.

"Tony Stratton Smith was a rarity in the entertainment business," Peter Gabriel later acknowledged, "a man of passion and a crusader. He believed that rock music could, and should, be more than teenage fashion fodder, and his love for the Best of British determined the character of the Charisma label."

Stratton Smith returned the compliment, acknowledging that Genesis was perhaps the most singular group of musicians he ever worked with. He made no bones of the fact that Van der Graaf Generator was his personal favorite of all the groups at the label—Stratton Smith once singled out the band's frontman, Peter Hammill, as "the most talented lyric writer I ever worked with. In those early days, I thought 'this is it!'" Genesis, on the other hand, was to remain…not aloof but at least a little standoffish, and from the outset, Stratton Smith reflected, "They maintained a semiformal relationship with me. They always made an appointment, never just dropped in from the street. They were polite and liked all their affairs handled in a business-like manner. They were never one of the lads."

Glen Colson agreed, "They were very polite people. They all sounded like Prince Charles. They'd say, 'One does this, one does that. One buys first editions here. Blah-de-blah.'" Some of the office staff found Genesis's obvious breeding a little hard to take, particularly when paired with their equally obvious impecuniosity. But Stratton Smith appreciated their taciturn demeanor and insisted that he would not have wanted it any other way. "You run a record label, you get used to all sorts of people wandering in, wandering out, wandering off with the photocopier. But I can truthfully say that, in all the years I worked with them, I never once picked up the phone to hear somebody say, 'It's about Genesis…I think we need to have a talk.'"

Peter Gabriel acknowledged that same truth while remembering the band's earliest days from the Milton Keynes stage in October 1982. "The wild times we used to have," he deadpanned, "when we would creep into a Holiday Inn bathroom, all of us in the dead of night, unwrap a bar of soap and leave it unused the following morning."

CHAPTER FOUR

AND THEN THERE WERE FIVE

Genesis was back at the BBC studios on Feb. 22, when the group was invited to record a session for DJ John Peel's *Night Ride* program. That in itself was no major achievement—with four or five different groups a week filing up to Maida Vale to record for the show, it was harder for a band *not* to receive such a summons. What was remarkable was the panache with which Genesis pulled off its broadcast debut.

As was standard for any artist undertaking its maiden BBC broadcast, this first session also served as the group's audition tape, and a veritable baptism of fire it was. With just 45 minutes at their disposal, groups were expected to set up their equipment, sound check, and then record as many songs as they could for delivery (in an unlabeled box) to the Talent Selection Group, an eight-strong gathering of BBC staffers and producers, who then delivered their opinions. A "pass" would free the session for broadcast; a "fail" would see it consigned to the dumper.

Genesis passed. Somehow cramming five songs into the allotted space, the band was rewarded with an "enthusiastic pass" by the selection committee; their delight in the music's "intriguing tone colors" was further enhanced by producer Alec Reed's insistence, "I rate this group very highly."

That said, the session did not pass entirely trouble free, as Anthony Phillips got into a row with one of the recording engineers over the sound of his 12-string guitar. He had worked hard to develop his own unique sound with the instrument, only for the engineer to complain that it didn't sound like a 12-string at all!

The group also had difficulty deciding what songs to showcase. "The Knife" and "Twilight Alehouse," concert spectaculars that they were, both seemed logical contenders but would also require more time than the group had at its disposal. They opted instead for the less dynamic but more easily accomplished lineup of "Pacidy," "The Shepherd," "Looking for Someone," "Stagnation," and the song that all concerned were convinced should be their next single, "Let Us All Make Love."

It would be some six weeks before the session was finally broadcast on April 1— the first day of a month that would see similar performances from such fellow up-and-comers as Mott the Hoople, Slade, and Sandy Denny's Fotheringay. By that time, however, Genesis's career had advanced considerably. Genesis had opened concerts for acts as far afield as Canterbury art rockers Caravan and the born again hard rockers of Deep Purple, and March 11, 1970, saw Genesis play its biggest gig yet, when it was booked to open for David Bowie at the Roundhouse.

> "Gabriel has a touch of evil about him when he gets onstage. He reminds me of Jagger at times."

Bowie was still rejoicing in the success, at the end of 1969, of his "Space Oddity" single—his days as the glam-strutting superstar Ziggy Stardust were still some distance away at this time. But Bowie's eye for performance and experimentation was as sharp as it ever would be, as he renamed his band of the time as Hype and demanded each of the members take the stage in outrageous costume.

With former Jimi Hendrix bassist Noel Redding's Fat Mattress also on the bill, Genesis took the stage early enough in the evening that few witnesses to the show, including many of the journalists present to see the headliner, even caught the set.

Genesis, on the other hand, hung around for the entire concert and, watching as Rainbowman (Bowie), Hypeman (bassist Tony Visconti), Gangsterman (guitarist Mick Ronson), and Cowboyman (drummer John Cambridge) flashed and flirted for a performance that would, with lashings of benevolent hindsight, later be termed the birth of Glam Rock, they could not help but be intrigued...not necessarily by the possibilities of dressing up so garishly for their own concerts but by the ease with which the clutch of seemingly disparate songs that was then Bowie's set could be so seamlessly melded into a whole by the power of visual suggestion alone.

Rock 'n' roll, after all, had grown hideously image free in recent years, reacting against the uniformed smartness of the British Invasion era by dressing down as ferociously as the Beatles, Stones, and Kinks once dressed up. Not that the new look was any less of a uniform than the old, but denim, T-shirts, and tatty jackets seem a lot less calculated and, certainly, a lot more natural, than tailored suits and matching trousers.

Now here was Bowie exploding that everyday drabness with an explosion of color, style, and groovy fabrics, and, though it would be several years before even Bowie was ready to build further on the foundations he laid that night, still he had proven what was possible, both to himself and, though nobody would have suspected it at the time, to at least one member of the evening's opening act.

Again, it would be a few years, and a couple of further lineup changes, before even Peter Gabriel was ready to act upon any of the lessons he learned at the Roundhouse. But certainly his dreams commenced their gestation there, and Tony Stratton Smith was already well aware of what they had the potential to create. Discussing Genesis with a *Melody Maker* journalist, his description of the Gabriel stage presence was soon to become a near-headline in the paper. "He has a touch of evil about him when he gets onstage. He reminds me of Jagger at times."

Despite such praise, Genesis remained unhappy about the need to gig. Stratton Smith once revealed, "They had some astonishing attitudes, foremost among them the belief that they would never make it as a live act. Genesis really felt that they would be writers, spend as much time in a recording studio, and remain a mystery beyond that." But their live presence continued to pay dividends.

One Phil Collins, drummer with the unknown and intensely underachieving Flaming Youth, later recalled browsing enviously through the gig guide in *Melody Maker* and spotting Genesis's name everywhere. He'd never seen or heard the band, but still he wondered, "How come they're getting all this work, and we aren't?" Little did he know that, within a matter of months, he would have first-hand experience of the answer to that question.

In fact, according to Gabriel, gigs were still "very sparse" at this stage. But the Ronnie Scott's residency anchored an ever-growing date list, with Genesis regularly washing up at "places like…Farx at Southall, a club in Godalming, and a gig, I remember, at the GKN Social Club annual binge somewhere in Birmingham.

That was for the apprentices, who preferred reggae, so we didn't go down too well." Even worse, the show ended too late (or the band was too tired) to drive back to London afterward, and they were forced to spend a cold, uncomfortable night on the social club floor.

"If you're only getting £30 for a gig, and the transport is costing £15, there isn't much left for hotels, particularly when you're using that money for the week's food bill," Gabriel reasoned. Birmingham was not the only night they spent on a floor although, as time passed, they also became acquainted with what Gabriel shudderingly described as "some pretty rough guest houses." One, that lived for years in Genesis's private mythology, "was so damp that the bedclothes were actually wet. The rooms were like dormitories, sleeping eight people and using all army surplus stuff for the bedding. It was a lorry driver's place, I think."

On April 13, 1970, the group made its debut at the legendary Friars Club in Aylesbury, a venture that, less than a year after its inception, had firmly established itself as one of the key venues on the entire progressive-rock circuit. Any number of venues around the country, clocking the current obsession with progressive music, had taken to launching weekly Prog Nights for the delectation of the handful of hardy locals drawn to whet their curiosity over this radical new musical force. But Friars was the real thing, a club devoted almost exclusively to the music and presenting it so successfully that David Stopps, Friars' owner and promoter, literally had his pick of bands.

"The Who often had some very strange bands supporting us, but Genesis really were one of the strangest."

Genesis, then, were just another bunch of unknown aspirants who may or may not have been any good, and no one can say what may have happened had he been answering his telephone the day Richard MacPhail called to ask if Friars was interested in booking them. As it happened, however, Stopps was out, fly-posting the neighborhood with details of Friars' forthcoming attractions, and it was his mother who took the call. Stopps laughed, "She ended up having this long conversation about vegetables, cheesemaking, and honey...with Richard. When I returned, she said, 'This very nice man...phoned up from a band called Genesis...and I think you should put them on.'" So he did.

The band collected a £10 fee for their troubles, but they also won Stopps' undying support; he continued booking Genesis into Friars for as long as their status allowed them to fit safely into the club and was in turn rewarded for his loyalty when the group, superstars now, returned to the venue in 1980 for a semisecret warm-up gig before their next London show.

The gigs kept coming. On May 8, 1970, Genesis opened for the Who at the University of Kent, as the headliners toured the world-beating set that would soon be preserved on the *Live at Leeds* album. Looking back from 30 years on, bassist John Entwistle joked, "We often had some very strange bands supporting us, but Genesis really were one of the strangest."

The group (and its battered old bread van) landed a welcome respite from the traveling in May, when they headed back to Godalming, and the shadow of Charterhouse, for two weeks of rehearsals at the Angel Inn. The purpose of the hiatus was twofold. A serious rush of gigs was looming on the horizon, beginning with a major London show at the Lyceum Ballroom on June 6. More important, however, work was also set to commence on their next album, *Trespass*.

Charisma was a family, and Genesis had now been absorbed into its bosom. In the studio, the group would be joined by producer John Anthony and engineer Robin Cable, veterans already of the label's catalog; in the design department, the group was introduced to Paul Whitehead, a young Londoner who had spent three years as an in-house designer at United Artists (his first commission was a Fats Domino LP) before John Anthony introduced him to the Charisma setup.

Designing a series of incredibly striking sleeves for the very best acts Charisma could throw at him—Van der Graaf Generator, Trevor Billmus (1970's grossly overlooked *Family Apology* LP), Lindisfarne, and the solo Peter Hammill included—as well as a magnificent portrait of Stratton Smith for the company Christmas card, Whitehead, in his own words, "quickly became known as the painter and designer who works with rock bands, a nice niche to be put in, I thought." It was his work with Genesis, however, that Whitehead considered his greatest achievement—the three LPs he wound up designing for them, *Trespass*, *Nursery Cryme*, and *Foxtrot*, remain "some of the most successful collaborations I have ever had working with musicians. They created the music, and I made original paintings that reflected exactly the contents of the records."

Moving into Trident Studios, London, Genesis was faced not only with the pressures of recording an album that would justify Charisma's (and, now Whitehead's) faith in them, but also one that would do justice to the vast stockpile of material at their disposal and satisfy fans who would doubtless be disheartened to find their own particular favorites omitted from the disc.

"They had an incredible amount of material they wanted to record," Stratton Smith recalled, "which is why we sent them back to Godalming, to try and work out for themselves which numbers were worth recording, and which ones they could put aside." Too many groups leave such decisions until the last minute—by which time the studio clock is already ticking. Secluded from all such pressures, Genesis quickly found that the album's ideal contents all but selected themselves.

Out went those *Night Ride* highlights "Pacidy" and "The Shepherd," and out went the song the band had once imagined might make a new single, "Let Us Now Make Love." "Twilight Alehouse," an in-concert spectacular though it was, was removed from the equation when nobody in the group actually proved keen to try to recapture its live sense in the studio; its absence would also permit the group to program the album in such a way that its closing number would appear as the climax, both physically and emotionally.

Two songs were in with a shout for that position, "Going Out to Get You" and "The Knife." Both were live favorites; both had their armies of adherents among the group's growing audience. But, though nobody remembered how the final decision was arrived at, few would deny that the correct choice was made. The brutal blues of "Going Out to Get You" was shunted to one side; it was "The Knife" whose incisive cuts would slice through the last eight minutes of the LP.

Although Genesis had long since agreed that songwriting credits should be shared equally between the band members, the two separate songwriting teams that had come together in the last days of Anon, Rutherford–Phillips and Banks–Gabriel, remained unchanged, and it was the former pairing whose sound would dominate the sessions—songs such as "Stagnation" and "White Mountain" grew directly out of the demos Rutherford and Phillips had been recording together for three years, and they stood in marked, moody contrast to the heavier efforts that their bandmates were contributing to the party—"Looking for Someone" and, inevitably, "The Knife."

It was a remarkable, and a remarkably successful, balance; the two teams' musical instincts both complemented and countered one another's inclinations, possessing Genesis with an almost symphonic range of styles and textures. Yet it was also a fraught union.

Recording the album, Tony Banks reflected, "really [was] a labor of love. We were living, eating, and sleeping our music. It was an immensely satisfying period for us, when we were…determined not to make a compromise of any kind. We wanted to achieve the same kind of success, in the same kind of way, that bands like Family had the reputation for—just making a name by playing to people and avoiding exploitation and individual trips."

Only drummer John Mayhew, it seemed, offered any kind of a weak link in the chain of their ambition. Already married, and as happy plying his trade as a carpenter as he was playing drums, he had never truly adapted to life in a working rock group. "He was not a good learner," Gabriel mused while Banks elaborated, "everything he played was taught to him by the rest of us. I don't think his heart was in it."

But Anthony Phillips, too, seemed to be undergoing some kind of crisis. For some time, he had found himself a victim of stage fright, an affliction that was only exacerbated by the knowledge, borne of so much experience, that nearly every show Genesis played would, at some stage, fall foul to technical gremlins. The little fiends were everywhere, as the band's ambitious soundscapes found themselves having to adapt, on a nightly basis, to new environments, different stage setups, and different equipment.

Every new club brought with it a new problem, and that was before the instruments themselves started acting up, as they so frequently do. In later years, with Peter Gabriel almost as well known for the peculiar stories he would tell during Genesis concerts as he was for the songs that each of them bled into, the singer admitted he originally started inventing these sagas as a means of buying time for his bandmates, as they strove to solve the latest electric conundrum to benight their performance.

For Phillips, however, such solutions offered little relief to the frustration and fear he was experiencing every night. Essentially, said Tony Stratton Smith, "Anthony was in relatively frail health and couldn't stand up to touring." It was time to take matters in hand. "He and the band had to make a decision"—and the decision, Phillips was adamant, was that he should depart.

Fear was not the guitarist's sole motivation. "I couldn't really work within that close format. Four composers are a very tight, very tight knit unit. It's a hell of a strain if it's all of you writing because everything has to be split four ways. You want it to sound one way and somebody else wants it to sound another way. You compromise for a while but after a certain amount of time it really becomes too much and you just say 'I've got to have it this way—I can't go on.' I was getting very displeased with a lot of the product, and it just got to me to such an extent that I just had to quit."

Describing himself as exiting "in a cloud of dust," Phillips continued, "I remember I was listening to Sibelius when I had one of those strange revelations, that I was terribly limited. Here was this one man, invoking these incredible effects…" and here he was, strumming away with a low-key rock band. "I suddenly felt so narrow as a musician. My guitar playing was limited, and I couldn't play the piano at all. So I set to it." Over the next four years, "a self-imposed exile," as he put it, Phillips would study piano, classical guitar, and orchestration. "You can call it my student period."

Years on, Phillips did concede some misgivings over his decision. "I have qualified regrets about leaving, because it would have been great to be involved in some of the music that came later. In an ideal world, of course, it would have been lovely to have been part of that music. [But] the group wasn't working as a unit when I was in it, so somebody had to leave, and it happened to be me. [So] I can't really have many regrets because it was necessary for the longevity of the group."

Genesis was traveling home from another show, rattling around the back of the transit van that had recently replaced the bread truck, when Phillips dropped his bombshell. He played his final show at the King's Arms pub in Haywards Heath on July 18, 1970, and the only consolation for his bandmates was the knowledge that six weeks stretched ahead of them before their next show.

John Mayhew followed him out of the door, and in later years, the remaining members admitted that they came close to jacking everything in there and then. Mike Rutherford confessed, "The idea of carrying on without Ant seemed ridiculous." On the eve of the release of their sophomore album, Genesis found itself in the unenviable position of having little more than half a band to promote it with.

Uncertain whether Genesis would ever recover from the double severance, Charisma could not, nevertheless, have been more supportive as the band wrestled with the dilemma. The album's release was pushed back to October 1970, and a fresh bout of auditions was announced via the pages of *Melody Maker*. "Tony Stratton Smith requires drummer sensitive to acoustic music…." Days later, on Aug. 24, Charisma received the news for which it had been waiting. Genesis had found its new drummer.

"I can't really have many regrets because it was necessary for the longevity of the group."

Born on Jan. 30, 1951, Philip Collins was possibly better suited to a career in acting than he was music. Certainly his training was all in that direction; he was a prodigious child actor who flickered through a succession of minor roles in major productions. He was a crowd extra in both the Beatles' *Hard Day's Night* and the epic *Chitty Chitty Bang Bang*. He was involved in the Childrens' Film Theatre production of *Calamity the Cow*, and at 13, he took over from Tony Tanner as the Artful Dodger in London's long-running West End production of the musical *Oliver!*

It was a six-month engagement, and his mother June recalled, "When he got the part…in *Oliver!* he was at Chiswick Grammar and the headmaster said if he wanted to do it, he had to leave. I said, 'It's up to you,' and he left. I didn't push him, I didn't have to. All three of my children [Collins has a brother, Clive, and sister, Carole] have known exactly what they wanted to do. I didn't interfere, just let them do it. I don't think it's any good pushing children."

Behind the many scenes he graced, however, the boy nurtured a different dream. From the age of five, Collins was banging away at a drum kit—his first was a gift from his uncles—and, by the time he reached his mid-teens, he was already playing and, unusually for a drummer, singing in a band called the Real Thing. He told *Sounds*, "I was a big fan of [mid-60s freakbeat heroes] the Action, and…they used to do Motown covers, the only band I ever heard who did them as well as the originals. So that's what my group did as well. I was playing drums and singing 'Uptight,' 'Land of a Thousand Dances,' 'Loving You Is Sweeter Than Ever.'"

The Real Thing went nowhere, but the brash young Collins was not concerned about that. Hanging out at London's Speakeasy nightclub, a favorite haunt of so many of the capital's musicians, Collins rarely failed to introduce himself to anybody who looked even halfway useful to his ambitions. "He was a hustler," the Move's manager Tony Secunda once remarked. "Always chatting people up, always pushing himself forward to do anything they needed." When keyboard player Brian Chatto passed through the club one evening and let it be known that he was putting together a band, it was inevitable that he would be pointed in Collins's direction.

Chatto's dream was one of the multitudes of acts being formed (some may say "manufactured") during the late '60s, specifically as a vehicle for various teams of songwriters. It was a practice that was long entrenched in the "poppier" end of the music industry, with the masterminds behind Chatto's group, Ken Howard and Alan Blaikley, having already proven their worth via such hit acts as the Herd (featuring the young Peter Frampton) and Dave Dee, Dozy, Beaky, Mick, and Tich. Flaming Youth, as this latest confection was to be titled, was the duo's attempt to prove that they could write for "older"

"Various sorts of jazz-tinged arrangements of songs in the odd bit of time signature jiggery pokery."

audiences than their past efforts had deemed them. Both the Herd and the readily acronymed DDDBM&T had broached some surprisingly mature, not to mention intellectual, themes during their moments of fame, only to be undone by the media perception of their bubblegum images.

Flaming Youth, if photographs of the quartet are to be believed, was unlikely to breach that particular trust. The theme of its recorded debut, however, probably would—*Ark Two* was a concept album, based around the songwriters' vision of a full-scale exodus from planet Earth (occasioned, naturally, by some vast global catastrophe).

As a theme, the tale was considerably less overdone in 1969 than it is today, and Flaming Youth spent two weeks sequestered within De Lane Lea Studios in London, recording what ultimately emerged as a surprisingly enjoyable (if not startlingly original) album. Certainly it landed some pleasant reviews—*Melody Maker* labeled it "pop album of the month"—and Flaming Youth enjoyed a well-attended launch party at the London Planetarium.

"Live, we were [even] better," Collins averred. "We were doing various sort of jazz-tinged arrangements of songs in the odd bit of time signature jiggery pokery. It was a pretty good group really." The album failed to sell, however, and while Howard/Blaikley retained their faith in Flaming Youth, even setting to work penning material for a new album, the group itself was fast crumbling.

Collins was already auditioning far and wide when he saw the *Melody Maker* ad. "I was a professional auditioner for about six months. I played in the Cliff Charles Blues Band for a few months, playing shuffles all night. That was good fun. I went for the audition for Vinegar Joe—didn't get it—and Manfred Mann's Chapter Three I went for—didn't get it."

When Bill Bruford quit Yes that same summer, Collins was among the first applicants to fill his boots, his personal confidence that he may be offered the job bolstered by the knowledge that Bruford was his personal greatest idol and the one player in whose percussive footsteps that Collins had deliberately followed. Besides, Yes in general and Bruford in particular already numbered among Collins's friends—the Yes man even employed his young acolyte as a drum roadie on occasion, and Collins recalled, "We used to hang out and listen to records together. He turned me on to players like Tony Williams and Billy Cobham, which, of course, was to later affect my own drum conception."

Collins was also among the cast of dozens who filed along to the 24-hour party that was the recording sessions for George Harrison's then-gestating solo debut album, *All Things Must Pass*. "I got a call one night from the manager of… Flaming Youth. He asked me what I was doing and if I wanted to do a session. I said, 'I just got out of the bath, man. I'm watching TV.' He said, 'Well, it's for George Harrison. They need a percussion player at Abbey Road.' So I'm screaming at the cab driver, who wants to give me a tour of north London, 'Get me to the bloody studio!' I got there and Ringo's chauffeur let me in. I was totally starstruck. Ringo was playing drums; Harrison, guitar; Klaus Voorman, bass; Billy Preston, piano; Badfinger, guitars; Maurice Gibb, keyboards; and Phil Spector was producing. Mal Evans, the old Beatles road manager, was sitting in the corner. This was like a dream, you know."

However, Collins also admitted that this magical moment of stardom wound up on the cutting room floor. "[Producer] Phil Spector kept saying, 'Just drums and guitar,' and 'Just drums and piano.' Every time he said 'drums,' I thought he was talking about me. I'm not a conga player; my hands were getting red and blistered. I'm thrashing away about an hour later, after having gone through all the combinations of instruments, and he says, 'OK, let's have the percussion playing this time as well.' My hands at this point were completely shot, and they didn't even have my mike on."

The moment Collins saw the *Melody Maker* ad, he sprang into action. The wording itself did not identify the group in question, but Collins at least knew Stratton Smith by sight, and running into him at the Marquee that same evening, Collins demanded point-blank to know whether it was worth his while auditioning. Stratton Smith assured him that it was, and that weekend, Collins and Flaming Youth guitarist Ronnie Caryl found themselves journeying down to Peter Gabriel's parents' home; reading on through the *Melody Maker* advertisement, Collins noted that a 12-string guitarist was also being sought.

Caryl would not be offered the job—personally overseeing the guitarist auditions, Mike Rutherford later admitted he was too busy trying to find a replacement for Phillips to seek out somebody who may be able to bring something else to Genesis. There would be no such problems for Collins.

CHAPTER FIVE

MIGHTY HOGWEED IS A VEG

On paper, Phil Collins was far from the ideal match for his new bandmates. As roughly hewn as the Carthusian contingent were sharply polished, as happy with a vast, shaggy beard as his colleagues were comfortable with neatly groomed 'staches, Collins was a beatnik to their Laureates and, King Crimson notwithstanding, was not even especially fond of much of the music that Genesis most admired, the bulk of the Prog crew included. "ELP. Moody Blues and the Floyd…I don't like any of those groups," he growled a decade later. "So it anger[ed] me and frustrate[d] me when we got compared to them, because…well, we've got a lot more substance and a lot more balls, and we're constantly questioning ourselves much more than any of them. And we've tried—and succeeded—to develop over the years, we've changed our music, because we keep our ears to the ground more than, say, the Moody Blues."

But, from the moment he sat down at the drum kit, Gabriel was adamant, Collins behaved as though he knew precisely what he was doing, a quality that is often in frighteningly short supply as a band wades through the makeweights who habitually attend auditions. Without even waiting for Collins to finish, Gabriel, Banks, and Rutherford already knew that the search was over. "As soon as Phil came in, everything lifted," Gabriel agreed. "He's an extremely gifted musician, and I remember when Phil sat down at the audition, just the way he sat down I knew he was going to be good."

Collins's arrival in the band also placed him in that unenviable position known to, but not necessarily enjoyed by, every musician who steps at "the last minute" into a combo whose immediate future has already been scheduled. The release of *Trespass* was now just weeks away, and the arrangements that Collins now found himself learning were set in stone long ago, by John Mayhew and even John Silver. Great swathes of *From Genesis to Revelation* remained in the set, and even the handful of unreleased songs that had a place in the repertoire were built around percussive patterns laid down by the newcomer's predecessors.

Equally disconcerting was the discovery that, in Peter Gabriel, Genesis already had a drummer of sorts. The singer had long since drifted away from his early love of drums, but he still retained that bass drum at the front of the stage, and he was not averse to playing it when he felt the occasion demanded. The fact that his idea of "playing" now tended to involve a few hard, but rhythmic, kicks only added to the drama.

Collins's first days with the group were spent rehearsing, and he quickly came to understand the musical dynamic that dominated the band. King Crimson remained an overwhelming presence over their aspirations, but so did Family, the vaguely avant blues-rockers whose latest album, *A Song for Me*, had joined Crimson's newly released sophomore set, *In the Wake of Poseidon*, on Genesis's turntable. Affectionately, Collins detailed how Rutherford used to "thrash away at the 12-string" in rough emulation of Family guitarist Charlie Whitney. He acknowledged, however, that it was clearly a productive procedure.

No matter that their second album was still awaiting release, over the next few weeks much of the material destined for Genesis's third LP was sketched out as well.

Born out of the now abandoned "The Movement," "The Return of the Giant Hogweed," a somewhat convoluted epic designed to replace "The Knife" as the traditional set closer, had been around since Gabriel first read the newspaper reports, the previous year, that warned southern English gardeners that a veritable plague of the virulent weed was suddenly poised to infest the best-kept estates. It took only a little more imagination to visualize the plants tearing themselves out by their roots and then striding across the countryside, killing "with their hogweed hairs."

The swirling "Fountain of Salmacis," with its Tony Banks–fuelled retelling of the old Greek legend of Hermaphrodite; the homespun philosophy of "Seven Stones"; and the light-hearted punning and absurdity of "Harold the Barrel" all needed no more than the slightest embellishment to be deemed complete.

"The Light" was a song that boasted Collins's first-ever stab at lyric writing and was eventually reborn as 1975's "Lilywhite Lilith"; there was "Twilight Alehouse," and of course, there was "The Musical Box," a composite of musical passages that dated back to Anthony Phillips's day but that had now developed into an epic saga of sex and the supernatural that was inspired, Gabriel later revealed, by childhood visits to his timber merchant grandfather's country home at Cox Hill. There, the formal gardens stretched out to encompass goldfish ponds, a rose garden, squash courts, and the croquet lawn upon which little Cynthia would scythe off Henry's head with her mallet.

One early break from this routine came when producer John Anthony, in the studio now with singer Colin Scot, began calling around his own circle of friends and associates in search of guests musicians to help out at the sessions. Scot remains a true obscurity in the eyes of modern rock historians; in 1970, however, he was at least as well known as many of the other players recruited for his album, a litany that included Genesis's Gabriel and Collins, Van der Graaf Generator's Peter Hammill and Dave Jackson, King Crimson's Robert Fripp, Yes vocalist Jon Anderson, and Strawbs' pianist Rick Wakeman. (Soon to be united in Yes itself, this was the latter pair's first experience of working together.)

> A veritable plague of the virulent weed was suddenly poised to infest the best-kept estates.

All filed in from the recesses of the progressive underground, and the ensuing *Colin Scot with Friends* album remains one of those legendary treasures of an age when rock 'n' roll truly could be considered a community of like-minded souls, gathered together in an arena where ego, commerce, and corporate policy are all a long way from the sheer joy of actually making music together.

Though much of it drifts along in a period folkie vein, skewing between Scot's self-composed material and well-selected offerings from the Bonzo's Neil Innes, Davey Johnstone of the Elton John Band, and Martin Hall, more than a handful of moments are sublime eloquence: Harvey Andrews's antiwar "Hey! Sandy," the closing "Here We Are in Progress," looped by a so-characteristic Fripp guitar line, and "Do the Dance Now, Davey," ushering in side one with a clutch of notes that could have fallen from Genesis's still-gestating "The Musical Box."

Collins' first shows with Genesis took place in the English midlands, as the band set about breaking in its new look around some of the less-limelit corners of the U.K. gig circuit. Further attempts to plug the void left by Phillips's departure had failed; on stage, guitar duties now fell alongside the keyboards in Tony Banks's province, with Rutherford throwing in whenever his basslines permitted. It was a less than satisfactory arrangement, but it was the best they could do for now, and from most unbiased accounts (and even a few biased ones), it really wasn't bad. "I liked the four piece, but I know Tony didn't," Collins later confessed.

Back in London at the end of August, Phil Collins found himself setting up on a Marquee stage he had hitherto only ever stood in front of, gazing enviously at the nightly succession of musicians who were permitted to walk those historic boards. For Genesis, it was its fifth appearance at the club in as many months and its third as headliners—the strangely folk–themed Amazing Blondel was opening the show for them, and Roger Noakes, an acquaintance of that act from their earliest days, remembered "hanging on" to watch the headliners, on the strength of that one track on the *Wowie Zowie* compilation.

The croquet lawn upon which little Cynthia would scythe off Henry's head with her mallet.

"They started slow; for a long time, through at least the first half of the set, they were just another sort-of acoustic, sort-of moody prog band. They reminded me a lot of King Crimson's quieter moments, although I do remember thinking that someone needed to remind the drummer [Collins, of course] that he didn't need to get quite so excited all the time…he was crashing away, and it was really a distraction. As the set went on, though, you noticed the tempo picking up, the energy levels rising, and suddenly they were into 'The Knife' and all hell broke loose on stage. I'd never seen a band structure their set so dramatically, and I went away *so* impressed."

Noakes was not alone in his assessment. Tony Stratton Smith, having spent weeks of uncertainty wondering whether the group would ever recover from the recent departures, was equally thrilled and admitted, years later, that there was a time when he personally believed Genesis could remain a four-piece group. "They were writing, they were demoing…." The songs "Moss" and "Wooden

Somewhere behind a forest of drums, future superstar Phil Collins was aching to escape.

Mask" both entered the band's set during their four-piece days, and there was even talk of releasing the latter as a single, after Charisma's first choice, *Trespass*' "Looking for Someone," got no further than a few promotional copies mailed to DJs and journalists.

With *Trespass* now in the stores and accumulating at least a few more press reviews than its predecessor, Genesis's need to plug the empty space on the stage was growing more and more pronounced. The album itself would later be revealed as selling little more than 6,000 copies, but as the group toured, it seemed that every one of those 6,000 purchasers was coming along to the shows and wondering why things didn't sound *quite* as powerful as they could.

Looking to deflect such comments, Ronnie Caryl, rejected at his original audition, was nevertheless invited along to play one show at Princes Risborough (close to the Aylesbury Friars' stronghold) on Oct. 6, 1970. The closest Genesis came to a permanent solution, however, was when Friars promoter David Stopps recommended the group listen to a local guitarist, the Farm's Mick Barnard. They listened and, for whatever reasons the prevailing conditions demanded, offered him the job.

Although the group would continue looking for a full-time guitarist, Barnard arrived just in time for Genesis's first-ever television appearance, on the BBC's *Disco Two* rock show, the short-lived predecessor to the better-known *Old Grey Whistle Test*. The band would be performing just one number, "The Knife," and Gabriel alone would actually be *performing*—Musicians Union regulations of the time demanded that his bandmates be restricted to simply miming their parts...or, in Collins' and Barnard's case, their predecessors' parts.

> The Killer would turn off the electricity at the mains and come looking for them in pitch darkness.

It was a disaster. Gabriel revealed, "The backing track was the same as the album, but I did the vocal on top, and I was very nervous on that occasion. I don't want to do TV again for a long time. It was a shocking performance, and I'm not trying to excuse it. I'm just not an animal, a performing animal being put through his tricks, how the sound engineer saw it.

"You should have a say in shows like that. You should have some control like you do with an album sleeve. We're not performers to be manipulated by those people.

I think the BBC has a condescending attitude to pop and pop musicians. It's only entertainers who are required to give a good performance every night, to put on a show. To try and get a BBC producer to understand what you want to do in a program. The whole problem is that they don't believe the intricacies of sound balance make a difference to us. They think it's a fuss about—nothing." Genesis would not appear again on British television for another seven years.

Happier outings quickly followed, however, including a rousing near-hometown reception for Barnard when Genesis played Aylesbury College, part of the still-escalating diary of pub, university, and town hall shows that would take them through to the end of the year, and a climactic free all-nighter at the London Lyceum on Dec. 28. Barnard was also a guest at Tony Stratton Smith's home in Crowborough, near Tunbridge Wells, as the band continued winnowing down material intended for their third album.

A sixteenth-century farmhouse with sloping floors and quaint little rooms, the setup was a welcome refuge for most of Charisma's artists and a creative one, as well. According to Stratton Smith, one of Van der Graaf Generator's favorite pastimes when visiting was a game called Killer. First, he explained, they'd draw straws to see who'd be the Killer; then, having all dropped a tab of acid, the rest of the company would retreat to the furthest recesses of the house to find a hiding place. Then, the Killer would turn off the electricity at the mains and come looking for them in pitch darkness.

> "Someone needed to remind the drummer that he didn't need to get quite so excited."

Genesis's behavior was somewhat more refined, but the creativity was no less unbridled. Among the contributions that Barnard cemented into the band's future repertoire were the guitar sequence that closes "The Musical Box" and a handful of the finishing touches to "Twilight Alehouse," two songs that, although both would develop further before being consigned to vinyl, hallmarked what Gabriel referred to as the group's strongest musical quality.

"There is a lot of freedom in the music. Nobody has to compromise too much. In our writing we are trying to do something that hasn't been done before, and that is to write a combination of sections that match." The fact that two guitarists already had made identifiable contributions to "The Musical Box," and a third would soon be adding his own, amplified the success of that experiment.

Gabriel was also enthusiastic about the effect the guitarist, in tandem with fellow newcomer Collins, had on the *Trespass* material: "The addition of Phil and Mick [has] made me more rhythm conscious." The Lyceum show, however, would mark Barnard's final major appearance with the group. A few days earlier, as Genesis perused the latest issue of *Melody Maker*, their eyes were caught by a "musicians wanted" advert placed by Stephen Hackett, searching for players who shared his determination "to strive beyond existing stagnant musical forms." Gabriel made contact immediately.

Exactly one day older than Peter Gabriel—he was born on Feb. 12, 1950—Stephen Hackett was just recovering from the demise of his last band, Quiet World, following the release of its debut (and only) album, *The Road*.

Formed by the British-born, South African–bred brothers John, Lee, and Neil Heather, Quiet World was among the first acts signed to Dawn, the progressive-rock offshoot of Pye Records, releasing *The Road* that summer in 1970. Discussing the album on the occasion of its CD remastering in 1999, label manager John Schroeder remembered it as "a lot of little musical things that were very catchy, changes that were very clever, and, at the same time, [they had] this story going through it…a story on life, on love, on the value of love in its various ways. It's a journey of love from an embryonic stage right the way through to Man"—and one could only wonder, once Hackett was confirmed as Genesis's new guitarist, could any other band on Earth declare that every one of its members made their recorded debut with a concept album?

Hackett described Quiet World's sound as a mixture of musical cultures—a precursor of World Music, in fact: "the black and white races, as it were," merging to create a hybrid, a true "sound of the streets. I still use it as an influence." His opinion, expressed 30 years later, that the album itself may now sound dated is negated, however, when one compares all that Quiet World achieved with dabblings taking place elsewhere on the progressive scene.

At a time when both the Incredible String Band and the Third Ear Band were taking their own musical excursions ever deeper into foreign cultures, *The Road* is certainly no more (or less) a child of its times than *Trespass* and may even have shared many of the same reference points. It certainly utilizes similar musical textures, with Hackett's already stylish guitar playing not only predicting elements that he would later bring to Genesis, but also unknowingly echoing moments that Anthony Phillips had already bestowed upon the band.

The Road was completely ignored upon release—Schroeder described it as "ahead of its time" but also acknowledged, "I don't think it was promoted at all." There was also a problem of perception. "Pye was far too associated with pop and budget records for Dawn to be taken seriously as an underground label." Although the company was responsible for a string of releases that, today, are recognized among the finest of all progressive style issues of the day, Dawn's only major success came with the jugband pop of Mungo Jerry, and when Quiet World split soon after *The Road*'s release, few people even at the label seem to have noticed.

> "Is that an electric guitar? Is that an electric piano put through a fuzzbox?"

Late in 1970, then, Hackett decided to put the entire experience behind him and placed his ad in *Melody Maker*. A few days later, he and his brother John met with the members of Genesis and then trotted on down to the Lyceum show. More than 30 years later, Steve Hackett still remembers how he was immediately entranced, both by the group's material and by the means by which they delivered it.

Back in June 1969, the Hacketts caught King Crimson at the Marquee Club, and both still marveled at the spectacle. For John, "pinned to the back wall by the colossal sound of…King Crimson playing '21st-century Schizoid Man,'" the moment where "the sax player lifts up a silver flute and out floats the most beautiful sound I've ever heard" was the moment when he abandoned his guitar lessons and took up flute instead. For Steve, meanwhile, it was the sheer dexterity of the group that remained with him. "Very loud…and very precise. At first, it was difficult to tell if I was hearing guitar or sax…it was difficult to tell quite what was what."

Genesis possessed that same quality. "What attracted me to the band when I first joined them was the fact that it was possible to work with a number of 12 strings that might sound a little like a harpsichord…is that an electric guitar? Is that an electric piano put through a fuzzbox? When you've got a guitarist playing in a pianistic style and a keyboard player who wants to bend, this was cutting-edge stuff in the 1970s. Now, of course, with the amount of sounds everyone's got [from computer technologies], nobody knows what the sound source is anymore, and we can all be fooled. Back then, though, it was a challenge, and Genesis were really intrigued by it."

Hackett brought more than an eclectic ear to the performance, though. "I started off playing harmonica at the age of four, and God knows what kind of sounds came out at that age. Then I started playing guitar at 14 and switched from a single-line instrument to chords, you know? That opened up a whole new vista."

As a songwriter, he possessed a romantic streak that was, by pop music standards, as unconventional as it was all encompassing. Let other bands write about holding hands and falling in love, he smiled—as though daring Genesis to even try to do that. Hackett's tastes were for songs "that had less to do with the mating ritual and more in common with romances of other kinds—times, places, situations, stories."

He also introduced an imagination whose roots were buried within his love of classical music but that viewed the challenges of past masters from a completely opposite viewpoint than Anthony Phillips. He, after all, quit because he wanted to pursue the perfection he heard from other players. Hackett, on the other hand, sought to translate the moods and techniques (as opposed to other rock musicians' obsession with the grandiosity) of one musical form into another.

One of the first of these lessons he brought to Genesis, he said, was "tapping with the guitar, which you first hear on *Nursery Cryme*. I was trying to sound like a keyboard player at the time, I was using an idea from J.S. Bach, and I was trying to play it on guitar, and the only way to play it on guitar was to make a jump that the fingers can't do, and access a wider range on the fret board in the same way that a keyboard player can do, go from bottom to top in one movement. I thought 'Why should guitars be limited like that? Let's see if it'll work.' And, when I first came up with that, I couldn't play the technique in time at all. It's a technique that only works on electric guitar, it doesn't work on acoustic guitar." But it has, he laughed, become one of *the* staples of modern rock guitar.

"I'm not classically trained," Hackett said. "I've just been an orchestral groupie for years, following around classical people. I like watching them, I like listening to them, I like learning from them." But he had no intention of emulating them.

Back in 1965, he remembered, "I first heard Segovia play Bach, and I thought, 'Well, he's done all those Bach pieces and he's done them all wonderfully, and he did them in the 1920s. So, I could either spend all my life trying to get these pieces together, or I could try and write in a wide range of styles and occasionally sketch in a classical style.'" That, he now perceived, was the opportunity that Genesis was extending to him.

Watching Hackett's absorption into the group from the sidelines, Tony Stratton Smith believed there was just one major hurdle for the newcomer to overcome— the mountainous shyness that he shared with Peter Gabriel. "The two must have connected in dumb show," Stratton Smith reflected. But he didn't care about that. The point was, they had connected. Over the next few years, Gabriel and Hackett would form a creative partnership that was itself to push Genesis to heights they had scarcely dared dream of.

CHAPTER SIX

PLAYING OLD KING COLE

The group's commercial standing, such as it was, did not enter into the incoming Hackett's calculations. Indeed, he later insisted, "When I first joined the band we literally didn't have two pennies to rub together. It was a case of, if I broke a guitar string, we used to have to save up or auction something, whatever. Yeah, things were very different obviously, and it was very much a shoestring operation when I first joined the band."

Although *Trespass* had outsold *From Genesis to Revelation* by some six to one, that still equated to no more than 6,000 copies shifted, and though Genesis's live reputation was certainly building, still there were a lot of empty spaces when they played live, as Hackett quickly discovered. His first show, at University College London on Jan. 15, 1971, was a nightmare of nervousness and the group's traditional array of malfunctioning equipment (Hackett's fuzzbox included), but it was one of the group's better-attended outings. But, back on the road over the next few days, as far afield as Blackpool and Derby, the darkness of the clubs did little to conceal the emptiness of the dance floor.

That gray scenario was to shift suddenly on Jan. 24, 1971—that is, nine days into Hackett's career as Genesis's third guitarist. The previous month fellow Charisma hero Van der Graaf Generator issued its third album, the leviathan *H to He Who Am the Only One*, a record that the band's sax player, David Jackson, later described as "challenging, just about playable." Confident that Van der Graaf Generator's cult following would at least sustain the album in the marketplace, Tony Stratton Smith began brainstorming ways of either increasing its catchment area or using one act's following to help build that of certain other Charisma acts.

Just weeks earlier, Marc Bolan and T. Rex had announced that their next tour—the first since "Ride a White Swan" brought them their first major British hit—would go out with specially reduced ticket prices, a mere two shillings (10 pence, or about 20 cents) each. There was no way the venture would make a profit. Shrewdly, Bolan relied upon the audience repaying their largesse via increased record sales. Stratton Smith saw the same opportunity and set about arranging his version of the outing, a 27-date British tour that would see Van der Graaf Generator, Lindisfarne, and, bringing up the rear, Genesis, go out at a cut-rate six shillings per ticket. Taking its name from the common nickname for the shilling, a *bob*, the so-called Six Bob Tour was to open at the London Lyceum on Jan. 24.

> "They would usually treat our set like an extra-long intermission and go to the bar."

For Genesis, the tour served up the biggest venues it had ever visited, the 1,000 to 2,000–seater theaters that then pocked the British landscape (before they were all knocked down and turned into parking lots and supermarkets—the Kinks' "Come Dancing" paints that portrait with alarming accuracy), and as it snaked around the United Kingdom, the tour established a bond, particularly between Genesis and Van der Graaf Generator, that would never be broken, both among the musicians and their fans.

Like Genesis, Van der Graaf Generator were prone to regular equipment mal-functions, with Hugh Banton's organ, bewildered as it was by the constant adjust-ments and alterations its owner made to its innards, the most sickly of all patients. Tony Banks affectionately wrote, "The first image that comes to mind when recall-ing Van der Graaf Generator is David Jackson and his two saxes; the second is of Hugh Banton with his head deep inside the organ, trying vainly to get the thing working again."

With their repertoire built around sing-along folk songs and charmingly collo-quial humor, Lindisfarne fit less comfortably into this mutual appreciation so-ciety—vocalist Alan Hull later explained, "Personally we got on great, and there'd always be a huge Lindisfarne contingent in the crowd, singing along with every song. But you could always sense the serious Van der Graaf fans shifting restlessly in their seats, and the Genesis crowd, small though they were, would usually treat our set like an extra long intermission and go to the bar."

Such audience reservations notwithstanding, the three bands were all but inseparable through the duration of the tour, both onstage and off, as they journeyed crammed cheek to jowl into the tour bus. Peter Hammill detailed the traveling arrangements: "Lindisfarne were at the back with the Newcastle Brown [ale], Genesis were at the front with the picnic hampers, and we were in the middle with the dope." Upon arrival at each evening's venue, the three would sound check and then retire to their dressing rooms. But "the bands were always checking each other out," Hammill continued. "We were always trying to blow each other off, a friendly rivalry of course."

He spoke for each of the performers, too, when he estimated, "Out of every five shows, there would be two average, two execrable, and one absolutely fantastic." For *Melody Maker* journalist Michael Watt, covering the Lyceum gig, it was Genesis that ran away with the honors that first night. "It would be insidious," he wrote, "to single out any one of the bands for future success, but at Sunday's concert…Genesis emerged with the greatest honors and audience acclaim. They are harder and more incisive than the delicacy of [*Trespass*] would suggest, and…Peter Gabriel, frantic in his tambourine shaking, his voice hoarse and urgent, is a focus for all the band's energy."

Neither was that the only occasion upon which Genesis apparently came out on top, although Van der Graaf Generator's Guy Evans wryly added, "There was always a PA issue. The fact was that somewhere in the budget, VdGG was always a bit shorted on the PA side. We got old microphones, and we never had a mixer. Genesis had two Audiomasters. I'd like to bring that up with somebody at some point…."

Tony Banks's memories of the tour itself were more modest. "As the most junior band, [we] were given the easier task of opening the show. If we didn't go down well, we could say that the audience were not all in yet or that they were not warmed up." Of the others on the bill, "Lindisfarne always had a great reaction…[their] greater immediacy made them easier fare for what was normally an enthusiastic crowd, but one not that familiar with any of the music. Nevertheless,

Van der Graaf were normally able to win the audience over with their more complex, but distinctive music, building up to a climax with 'Killer.'"

Indeed, it was Lindisfarne that, against all odds, emerged as the tour's most potent superstars-in-waiting, both in terms of the amount of money Charisma was willing to put behind its subsequent promotion and the quantities of records shifted over the next 12 months. By October 1971, the Newcastle-based band's new *Fog on the Tyne* album was on course to become Charisma's first-ever U.K. chart-topper (dragging its predecessor, *Nicely Out of Tune*, into the Top Ten in its wake); by the new year, their "Meet Me on the Corner" and "Lady Eleanor" singles were both Top Five bound. For Van der Graaf Generator and Genesis, on the other hand, their most immediate rewards would come from further afield, across continental Europe.

Genesis's first overseas shows took place while the Six Bob Tour was still under-way. Taking advantage of a four-day break in the itinerary in early March, the band flew to Belgium to play Woluwe St. Lambert on March 7. The following day took them to Brussels, where they were guests on television's *Pop Shop*, a local variation on the *Don Kirshner's Rock Concert* format, with one or two acts a week playing condensed versions of a regular live show.

Genesis's performance included a little bit of everything—a couple of songs from *Trespass* ("Stagnation" and "The Knife"), a few live favorites ("The Light," "Twilight Alehouse," "Going Out to Get You"), and two new songs, "Happy the Man" (a Mike Rutherford riff that, with the addition of a Lindisfarne-esque sing-along chorus, was the latest in Genesis's well-meaning attempts to write a hit single), and "The Musical Box."

Back home again, wrapping up the last dates of the Six Bob Tour but still working around an only marginally less hectic live schedule, the group then returned to the studio to begin work consigning their latest material to tape. Building around the imagery of "The Musical Box" (a theme that also inspired artist Paul Whitehead's sleeve design), the new album was to be called *Nursery Cryme*. But, looking back, it was the recording sessions themselves that sometimes seemed criminal.

Paired again with *Trespass* producer John Anthony, the band was fast coming to the conclusion, as Mike Rutherford put it, that he wasn't "strong enough." Fully aware of Genesis's studio inexperience, he complained, "You either have a producer who is a strong personality, and you sit back and you let him give his interpretation of the music, or you have someone who's very much with you and helps you, [who] doesn't have much say beyond guiding you. John was in the middle."

A year earlier, in an interview with *Melody Maker*, Gabriel described Anthony as "our cohesive force. Left to ourselves, we [are] a drag with insufficient technical knowledge. As a band we'll always need a producer." But Anthony was also "[just] another member of the band, rather than the one with all the power, the one who dictates what we want and what we don't want. The group did all the arrangements, and we considered the type of sound we wanted before we went into the studio." In fact, as it turned out, Genesis was uncertain about the producer since the beginning—*Trespass*, Rutherford insisted, "really suffers…because the production is not worthy of the songs. John's a fine producer, but it turned out that he wasn't right for us. He got a soft sound on our stuff that wasn't what, in retrospect, we wanted."

"We…weren't happy," Phil Collins agreed. "There was a lot on tape that wasn't coming across, and a lot more that wasn't even getting down on tape. We spent a lot of time, ten weeks, rehearsing the numbers for it, and when it was finished, the sound just wasn't what we wanted."

Internally, too, there was some discord, as Steve Hackett discovered that he was not immediately able to contribute all that he may have wanted to the proceedings. The Crowborough rehearsals at the end of 1970 had seen the band all but nail down the form and content of their next album, and Hackett found himself now simply reworking lines that past Genesis guitarists had already nailed into place.

Hackett would make his mark on "The Musical Box" by suggesting they add the sound of a real musical box to the song, but

The horrific saga of a beheaded child returning to taunt his killer in the guise of a lecherous old man.

he acknowledged there was little else for him to do beyond play the songs as they were designed to be played. He would, however, be able to squeeze in one major contribution that both helped shape the album and would, with hindsight, help shape Genesis's eventual future, "For Absent Friends."

"That was the first song I wrote for the band," Hackett explained. "And it was also the first song to have Phil singing lead on it. Phil and I collaborated on that and we co-wrote…I wrote the music, then Phil sat down, and we co-wrote the lyric." A plaintive, homely tale of two old folk just going about their day, "For Absent Friends" would be positioned between the two epics that would otherwise devour the vinyl LP's first side, "The Musical Box" and "Return of the Giant Hogweed," a positioning that could easily have seen it get utterly swamped.

Instead, the charming little interlude of normalcy that lay between, respectively, the horrific saga of a beheaded child returning to taunt his killer in the guise of a lecherous old man and the 50s B-movie tale of a race of overgrown plants wiping out the human race, punctured both the pomposity and the absurdity of those grander conceits. As Genesis's reputation began to grow, so did awareness of their decidedly non–rock 'n' rolling background. A suddenly proven ability to pull back from what a few critics were already referring to as their exclusive, classical background and see life as it really is was one that would ultimately pay grand dividends.

"It was an album that I was very, very happy with at the time I'd done it," Hackett mused later. "I'd done some session work beforehand but nothing really that I felt was 'me' and made a decent contribution to, so I was very happy with the album. I was ecstatic in fact. It took quite a long time to put together really, because Phil and myself were new members at that particular time and we went out into the country to do it—complete seclusion, and then we recorded for three weeks, I think. It was a nice start really."

In concert appearances notwithstanding, "The Musical Box" received its first major public airing on May 31, 1971, when BBC DJ Bob Harris broadcast a session the band recorded for him three weeks earlier. Because of the length of the pieces—they also aired *Trespass*' "Stagnation"—there was room for just two songs in the session, but it was an impressive venture regardless, no doubt drawing a few more ears into the group's orbit.

Confidence was growing all the time, with Peter Gabriel, in particular, loosening up a little more at every show. A year earlier, he scarcely moved on stage. Now he was ready to fling himself into any number of contortions, and the sheer excitement of watching Genesis increased correspondingly. "When you mount the platform live, you must go at it with the attitude that it doesn't really matter," insisted Steve Hackett. "You say 'I'm just going to go up there and have fun.' The moment you start thinking, 'I'm in a concert hall, everyone's looking at me, oh my god, my trousers might fall down,' you're lost. And that's what was so great about Pete. He'll hang himself upside down, he's not afraid to burst into a sweat…or break a leg. Literally."

On June 19, 1971, midway through a frenzied performance of "The Knife" at Aylesbury Friars, Gabriel took a running leap from the rear of the stage, soared across the audience clustered across the dance floor…and then crashed to ground, breaking his ankle. Utterly unaware that anything untoward had occurred, the audience was still cheering his derring-do as the stricken singer was carried back to the stage to complete the song on his hands and knees and then remain crouched stage-center as his colleagues filed back to the dressing room. "He was just lying there…he had gone all white and was complaining that he couldn't get up," Tony Banks remembered. Finally, the St. John's Ambulance Brigade carried the groaning singer away while promoter Dave Stopps took to the microphone to make the immortal announcement, "The artist has left the building…and gone to the Royal Bucks Hospital."

Shaken but clearly not overly stirred, Gabriel was back in action just three days later, his plastered leg less an inconvenience than a magnificent stage prop. One night, at Friars' Bedford venue, he appeared onstage with a broomstick as a crutch; at others, he rolled on in a wheelchair and left uncomprehending members of the audience bewildered by the fortitude of this apparent cripple. "I really hammed it up," Gabriel laughed. "I really played the wheelchair freak. But it really misfired with quite a large percentage of the audience because I was making a few jokes about the state I was in, and they were thinking, 'Poor guy, he really is crippled.'" The wheelchair taught him, however, just how important visual elements could be to a rock band—a lesson that, like the Roundhouse gig with David Bowie a year earlier, would be filed away for further consideration.

> "I'm in a concert hall, everyone's looking at me, oh my god, my trousers might fall down."

August 1971 saw Genesis make its debut at an event with which it would, over the next few years, become all but synonymous. The 11th National Jazz and Blues festival was taking place in Reading for the first time that year—previous events were staged in nearby Richmond, Windsor, Sunbury, and Plumpton, before complaints from each town's locals forced it to move on.

It was, though few knew that at the time, a fortuitous relocation. Over the next years, the Reading Festival would become the dominant force in British rock—the showcase not only for their greatest bands of the age but also the birthplace for innumerable superstars of the near future. How ironic that festival organizer Harold Pendleton was invited to this new location only because the local council, looking to mark the 1,000th anniversary of its town's foundation, believed it was indeed a jazz and blues festival, a billing that the event had outgrown back in the mid-'60s.

Neither would Pendleton revert to such forms for Reading's benefit. Charisma Records was represented not only by Genesis but also by fellow Six Bob Tour mates Lindisfarne and Van der Graaf Generator, plus Bell & Arc and Audience. Arthur Brown, Rory Gallagher, Wishbone Ash, Medicine Head, Osibisa, Renaissance, and folkies Ian Matthews and Ralph McTell figured elsewhere on the bill.

Genesis's set took place midafternoon on the second day of the festival, Saturday, June 26, but despite their lowly billing, the band's performance was later highlighted among the high points of the entire event, so much so that Pendleton would summon Genesis back to Reading for each of the next two festivals. In the meantime, Genesis marched onto another of the legendary festivals of the age, taking up a wee hours slot at an event that offered (and delivered!) nonstop live music from midnight on Friday to dawn on Monday—the Weeley Festival, close by the seaside town of Clacton.

There they again joined the Six Bob Tour crew among the supporting cast while King Crimson, the Groundhogs, Status Quo, Barclay James Harvest, and Rod Stewart's Faces also piled in to watch as T. Rex, now riding its third monster hit in six months, proved itself to be the hottest act in the land. Played out in front of a raucous teenybopper audience that may not even have registered the other bands on the bill, T. Rex's reception has since prompted critics and historians alike to reflect on Weeley as the weekend when the entire British rock scene was riven in two to disgorge—in one direction, the pop heroes of the day, and, in the other, the underground heroes who would be facing off against them. Genesis, with a live set that was now comprised wholly of epic numbers, was under no misapprehension of which camp it was numbered within.

Gigging through the fall and secure in the knowledge that it was now capable of selling out most of the clubs in the land, Genesis confidently expected sales of *Nursery Cryme*, released in mid-November 1971, to reflect its rise in stature. Instead, with Charisma's traditionally limited promotional budget now concentrating on Lindisfarne, the album again flopped badly—so badly that, by Christmas, its sales had yet to surpass the 6,000 or so accrued by *Trespass*.

It was a shocking disappointment; more than that, however, it may well have spelled out-and-out calamity for Genesis, as Tony Stratton Smith suddenly found himself forced to make some tough very decisions—or, rather, to confirm his willingness to make them.

Genesis was not the label's only underachievers. Van der Graaf Generator, Audience, Bell & Arc…everybody, in fact, that was not Lindisfarne, had singularly failed to actually make the label any significant amounts of money, and voices within Charisma's financial wing were loudly raised against Stratton Smith approving any further investment in any of them. Genesis, however, was certainly among the worst offenders, as Stratton Smith later recalled. He was told, point blank, that unless he dropped the group from the roster, he risked losing everything. His reply, perhaps, sums up everything that was gallant about both the label and its founder. So far as he was concerned, there was little difference between the two alternatives.

"I said to a certain lawyer, 'If Genesis leave Charisma, then so do I.'" He had, he told author Johnny Rogan, "a kind of clairvoyance about them. I knew this was a band of incredible quality. You had to give them time to grow." And besides, Genesis was precisely "the kind of artiste" for whom he'd "built the label" in the first place. "I never had a moment's doubt."

Stratton Smith made a similar guarantee on behalf of Van der Graaf Generator, but even he knew that there had to be an end to the spending. Early in the new year, both Genesis and Van der Graaf Generator were curtly informed that they would be receiving no more "capital investment," as David Jackson put it, because they were not considered "a viable group"—a peculiar phrase that prompted Jackson to rejoin, "When were we officially viable? I missed out on that period."

In fact, viability was just around the corner for both bands. February 1972 saw Van der Graaf Generator head out on its first-ever Italian tour and reach No. 12 on the local chart with the newly released *Pawn Hearts* album. Simultaneously, *Trespass* rose to top the Belgian chart, and weeks later, as Genesis prepared for their first visit to Italy, it was with *Nursery Cryme* on its way to No. 11. Elsewhere in that same country, AOR balladeer Ornella Vanoni was about to tackle the *Trespass* highlight "White Mountain" for her latest LP *Un Gioco Senza Età*, and another local hero, singer Rita Pavone's brother, was planning his own trip inside the Genesis songbook.

Neither the Belgian nor the Italian markets meant much in terms of major sales, but still the Italian tour in April saw Genesis playing before some of the largest and most enthusiastic audiences it had ever seen. In Belgium, meanwhile, Genesis recorded another concert-style TV broadcast for *Rock of the Seventies*, highlighting three songs from *Nursery Cryme*—"Musical Box," "Return of the Giant Hogweed," and a truly mesmerizing "Fountain of Salmacis," plus the song that continued to get away, "Twilight Alehouse." (Recorded for *Nursery Cryme*, "Twilight Alehouse" was again dropped from the final running order.)

Such continental advances notwithstanding, cash flow remained an issue. But there were always solutions, no matter how makeshift they may appear. Desperate to upgrade the equipment it had been using, it seemed, forever, Genesis befriended Flash, the indeed flashy band formed by guitarist Pete Banks following his less-than-glorious departure from Yes in 1970. Banks already knew Phil Collins well—"He used to watch Yes play at the Marquee club," the guitarist explained; now, he remembered, "There was this kind of thing between the roadies, where the Flash roadies would hire out equipment to Genesis, and vice versa. They had a good thing going. I'd often show up at a Genesis gig, just to see how well our equipment was working!" Further vindication of the group's (and the equipment's) live prowess was delivered in March, when BBC Radio aired an entire Genesis concert in the Saturday evening *In Concert* series.

In May 1972, Charisma, curious to discover whether Genesis's ever-growing live success could possibly translate into the notoriously more fickle singles market, delved into the vault in search of a possible hit. They found a ripe contender in the hitherto-shelved "Happy the Man" sing-along; unfortunately, they also discovered they had seriously misjudged the group's ability (or, even, readiness) to cross over in such a fashion.

For all Lindisfarne's chart success, mid-1972 was the height of glam rock in Britain, a period that may have permitted the occasional progressive-rocker to gnaw at the Top 30 but that was dominated otherwise by the strains of David Bowie, T. Rex, Slade, the Sweet, and Gary Glitter—acts who, though purists decried their reliance upon theater and costume, had nevertheless constructed a universe around themselves in which everything was larger than life. Building upon that tentative step into costuming that he undertook at the Roundhouse two years before, Bowie had not simply redesigned his own career, he had designed his own rock star, Ziggy Stardust. But, if the members of Genesis had any thoughts of joining in with that circus, they kept them strictly to themselves—even Peter Gabriel, who was watching developments even closer than most. "Happy the Man" may have been in the record stores, but the band scarcely paid it any attention, even in concert, and the release passed unnoticed by even many of the group's fans.

Unbowed—even unsurprised—by the single's failure, Genesis pressed on, preparing for its appearance at the Great Western Express Festival, in Bardney, near Lincoln, on May 28.

The four-day festival was blighted from the outset, as the prophecies of dire weather—less a prediction than a certainty in England in May—were matched every step of the way by sundry locals' attempts to halt the event

> *Melody Maker* rechristened it "the festival they couldn't stop."

through the legal system. As the weekend drew nigh, *Melody Maker* rechristened it "the festival they couldn't stop," although there remained an awful lot at stake as the event unfolded. A cast of organizers that included the former British Ambassador to Washington, DC, Lord Harlech, and actor Stanley Baker faced the possibility of being jailed, should the festival fail to live up to its guarantee of peacefulness.

In keeping with festival fare the world over, the bill was the usual mixed bag of acts, albeit one that makes the modern nostalgics' eyes tear over. Nazareth, Focus, the Incredible String Band, Atomic Rooster, Slade, Humble Pie, Stone the Crows (making its first live appearance since the onstage death of guitarist Les Harvey—

Yes's Steve Howe stood in for him), Budgie, Skin Alley, and Capability Brown head-lined the Giants of Tomorrow stage, and Roxy Music made its official live debut on that Saturday.

The festival program introduced many of the bands—Genesis's entry, written by journalist Geoff Ward, included the hope that "the first [sic] major festival appear-ance" by "the adventurous Genesis" was a success "because, as a band that's been going six years (though only three years as professionals), they have much to offer that's impressive."

The group's thoughts were already turning toward its next album, and the Italian tour saw the quintet cement a new showstopper into their repertoire, a moodily swirling Mellotron-fired piece titled "Watcher of the Skies." It would eventually become the ideal concert opener; at Lincoln, however, "Watcher of the Skies" began its live life midset—and it struck an odd chord indeed, as an already rain-swept mud bath was hit by the heaviest downpour yet. Clearly, the watcher was not watching too closely.

The song itself was inspired, Banks explained, "By my liking of science fiction... a combination of Arthur C. Clarke's *Childhood's End* and Marvel Comics' *The Watcher.*" The Mellotron, meanwhile, was an instrument that both Steve Hackett and Banks had long coveted for its "sound and power." Banks explained, "It was Mike Pinder of the Moodies who first really brought home to me its real value...you listen to the Moodies' early albums and...[he's] always there providing just the right touch at the right moment." "Watcher of the Skies" was awash with such moments, and the number quickly became an integral part of the Genesis experience—and even survived one American journalist's insistence on comparing it to the Band's "Chest Fever."

Wet but wonderful Lincoln was followed by the band's return showing at the Reading Festival in August. Again Genesis was low on the bill—the group received £175 in payment for its appearance; the headlining Rod Stewart and the Faces pocketed the then-massive sum of £4,000. Nevertheless, it was an event whose pay-off would prove to be worth far more than that. Billed halfway through the first evening's entertainment, below Curved Air and Mungo Jerry but above Nazareth and the Pretty Things, Genesis had just 40 minutes at its disposal and resolved to scale the showcase toward the most frenetic side of its nature.

Typically, the band's arrival on stage was followed immediately by a major equipment malfunction…"Talk among yourselves," was the first greeting from stage to audience. But once the show started, Genesis was unstoppable, making up for the time they'd lost with the breakdown by helter-skeltering through one of the fastest renditions of "The Knife" on record and then barely pausing for breath all the way through to "The Musical Box." In-between times, there was room for just two other numbers, a brutal "Twilight Alehouse" and a stirring "Watcher of the Skies," but still Genesis rendered a fieldful of Friday-night festival-goers spellbound and speechless, even before it reappeared for a triumphant encore of "The Return of the Giant Hogweed." When the reviews of the festival appeared in the following week's music press, Genesis's victory was writ large over them all.

"Talk among yourselves."

CHAPTER SEVEN

DRESSING FOR THE OCCASIONAL

Triumphing alongside Genesis at Reading that year was String Driven Thing, one of the handful of new talents signed to Charisma over the past 12 months (Spreadeagle and Capability Brown were among the others) and already widely predicted to be the next one to break out in a major fashion. What was all the more remarkable about String Driven Thing's Reading appearance was that it was only the band's second show since signing with Charisma, which, in turn, meant it was only its second since being hauled out of the Glaswegian club circuit it had hitherto graced.

Originally formed at the tail end of the 1960s by the husband-and-wife singer-songwriters Chris and Pauline Adams, plus percussionist John Mannion, the group released just one album, 1970's *String Driven Thing*, before fading from view. The trio relaunched the group two years later, adding multi-instrumentalist Colin Wilson, and signing with Charisma after pulling the name out of the phone book. Visiting London, Chris Adams "found myself with time on my hands, so I went into a phone box and looked through *Yellow Pages* for record labels. 'Stratton Smith Enterprises' jumped out at me, so I phoned and got through to Mike DeHavilland. He told me to come right round."

Little more than a week later, Stratton Smith and DeHavilland were in Glasgow, watching the band run through its paces at Burns's Howff, at that time *the* music pub in Glasgow. "He was long haired, affable, with a softly hoarse voice and a rascally laugh," Chris Adams remembered. "He also exuded a quiet *gravitas* that made him the ideal person to run a label called Charisma. We liked him immediately, and happily, he liked us."

String Driven Thing signed, and soon after, Charisma put them on the road. The group's first show was in a tiny community hall in Tunbridge Wells, close to Stratton Smith's Crowborough retreat; the second was the 1972 Reading festival, and opinions are still divided over the reasoning behind that, as Chris Adams explained. "One school of thought might have seen it as a bold move on Strat's part or a vote of confidence in our ability, another would view it as sheer lunacy to expose us at this stage to the glare of 60,000 fans and the world's music press."

Either way, the gamble paid off, and, with String Driven Thing's first Charisma album (another eponymous set) ready for release, Stratton Smith paired String Driven Thing with Genesis, as that band continued its scouring of the U.K. concert circuit. Chris Adams continued, "I remember at our first college gig with them, a member of their crew called Adrian was erecting lights. This was at a time when gantry lights at gigs was virtually unknown, as was the art of rigging. Suddenly there was a huge crash, as a car headlight came crashing onto the stage. Luckily no one was killed, but Adrian continued as if nothing had happened, stiff upper lip firmly set."

Chris Hewitt, one of String Driven Thing's longest-standing associates, explained, "Tony [Stratton Smith] saw Charisma as a family of bands and the idea of the Charisma packages touring together was part of that philosophy." Peter Gabriel happily shared that attitude and, although Chris Adams described the singer as "approachable, [but] painfully shy," Hewitt continued, "Gabriel liked String Driven and the fact they got loads of encores as support to Genesis did not bother him."

Phil Collins, on the other hand, routinely "kicked up a fuss about String Driven stealing the thunder from the Genesis sets," a manifestation of that same uncompromisingly competitive spirit that has historically divided the little drummer boy's audience into two very separate camps—of undiluted love or unmitigated hatred, refusing to acknowledge that any mere support band should have the right to fight Genesis for the evening's plaudits.

For now, Collins was left to seethe in silence; besides, offstage he and the support act got on famously. Adams explained, "The public school background...made the [others] very difficult to get to know. [But] we got to know Phil and Steve quite well. Phil would give Pauline cracked cymbals for a percussion rack, and Steve and I had shared a drink. I'd had a few polite words with Mike Rutherford, but as for Tony Banks, even in a shared dressing room there was not even eye contact. This could have been natural reserve, although it came across less as shyness, more aloofness. Given this, there was never any chance of jamming together, and while SDT would go for a drink after each show, Genesis always went straight back to their rooms."

Genesis was playing its last few shows before retiring to the studio to work on its next album. Conscious of their discontent with John Anthony, Tony Stratton Smith suggested they look further afield for their next maestro, beyond the realms of the British prog scene and into the untapped territory of Americana. Bob Potter had worked alongside Bob Johnson with the likes of Bob Dylan and Simon and Garfunkel and, in Tony Banks' words, was recruited in the hope he could prevent things from becoming "too arty."

It was a step too far. The first day in the studio, as Potter sat down to hear the material his clients had so far gathered, Banks opened with the introduction to "Watcher of the Skies," doomladen, stately, atmospheric…and, so far as Potter was concerned, awful, a shameless borrowing from the theme to *2001*. And that was that. "We didn't hit it off too well," Collins admitted. "He didn't like the way we did things, and *vice versa*. He decided he wouldn't do it halfway through some of the takes."

Genesis returned to Charisma; the label went back to the drawing board and finally came back with Dave Hitchcock, the knob-twiddler behind the last couple of Caravan albums. Accompanied by a couple of engineers, Tony Platt and John Burns, the group had finally found what Collins called "the right combination. Enthusiastic and energetic. We all got a real lift when they came in." Finally, work could begin.

The basic shape of *Foxtrot*, as they christened the new album, was already falling into place, with "Watcher of the Skies" and "Get 'Em Out by Friday," a horrifying glimpse into a future where town planning and genetic engineering march hand in hand to economize on space, already scheduled as side one's *pieces de resistance*. Impressive, too, was a short guitar sketch offered up by Steve Hackett—for all its brevity, and despite all that he has accomplished in the years since then, "Horizons" remains one of the guitarist's best-loved compositions, not only by fans but by the artist himself.

Clearly modeled in part on Bach's first *Cello Suite in G Major*, "'Horizons' was the first piece, I think, I ever wrote in its entirety, that was used by Genesis." It was founded in the guitarist's long-held love of the classical composer Sibelius, and he explained, "Those sweet little pieces that are self-sufficient, that can be played in one go on one guitar, have always appealed."

The bulk of Genesis's attentions, however, were for the most audacious step the group had taken since *From Genesis to Revelation*, as the band stepped into all but uncharted waters and visualized a single, side-long track that would sum up every facet of the band's abilities and interests, the gargantuan "Supper's Ready."

> "Those sweet little pieces that can be played in one go on one guitar have always appealed."

Such an offering was not necessarily "unusual." Van der Graaf Generator accomplished a similar feat in 1971, when it unleashed "A Plague of Lighthouse Keepers" across one half of their *Pawn Hearts* album. Pink Floyd had made several journeys into extended soundscapes, and Emerson Lake and Palmer's "Tarkus" consumed a full 50 percent of the album of the same name. Steve Hackett, however, remains adamant that "Supper's Ready" was "conceivably the longest continuous piece of rock music that anyone had ever done at that point.

"There were a number of bands who were involved in long-form rock, Yes and King Crimson, ELP, but there was also a tremendous amount of improvisation involved in that." Genesis, contrarily, opted not to allow its improvisational skills any more rein than necessary, and Hackett, for one, was convinced that the project was doomed, even as he marveled at the brilliance, skill, and personal satisfaction that were to be bound up in the number. "We worked on a piece that was 30 minutes long. And when we first wrote that, and performed it live, I really thought that the game was up and we'd be sussed for the imposters we were. I didn't think people would buy long form rock, and I don't really know why they liked it, to be honest.

"I felt we'd outstayed our welcome by the time we were five minutes into that piece. Lyrically, you couldn't really pin it down. There was the gobbledygook factor and all the rest, and in the middle of this long piece, you had the occasional thing that were mini-pop songs, like 'Willow Farm'…which, funnily enough, was one of my favorites. That was one of the strongest segments; it was Beatlesque, very catchy. I thought that was the band playing at its best. Because it was pastiche, it was possible to do that with gusto in most situations."

The remainder of "Supper's Ready," however, filled him with dread. But his fears were not realized. In fact, as Hackett subsequently admitted, "The reverse was true. We were hailed as beings from another realm, that managed to come up with this magic stuff, and so my instincts were entirely wrong." Indeed they were. Though it utilized musical passages that dated back as far as 1968 (the "Eternal Sanctuary Man" section was composed by Banks around the time he started university), "Supper's Ready" remains one of Genesis's best-loved and best-executed vinyl performances, and it was destined to make an immediate impression in concert as well.

There was still something missing, though, as Hackett and Gabriel made clear to their bandmates. The guitarist explained, "We were at our strongest alliance at that point, Pete and myself, and we refused to do ["Supper's Ready"] live, unless we had all the bells and whistles. On record, it's an incredibly complicated piece, and we said, 'No one's going to buy this long piece of music unless it's got everything, unless it has got the sound effects, and the whistles, and the *all change* in the middle of it.' With a piece of music like that, you've got to be able to *deliver* it. You can't go out expecting people to listen to this thing like a recital, and they're not going to go to the bar."

"I really thought that the game was up and we'd be sussed for the imposters we were."

Of course, such innovations cost money, both to purchase and to transport, and there would be plenty of arguing as the pair strove to make their point. The days of the band and its gear simply piling into the old bread van were long gone—so, too, was the transit van that replaced it. Now, as Gabriel proudly informed *Zig Zag* magazine, the group traveled "in two hired cars…we have a lorry for the equipment and a lorry for the lights." That fleet would only grow even more impressive if Hackett and Gabriel's latest schemes were put into action.

There was also the matter of the band's stature. Although Genesis's next British tour, coinciding with *Foxtrot*'s October 1972 release, would see them playing the theater circuit for the first time, still the group was barely making ends meet. The majority of its shows that fall remained nominal support gigs, as Lindisfarne crowned the most successful year of its career with its own monster outing and took their labelmates along as "co-headliners."

Nevertheless, by the time the tour opened, rehearsals had shaped "Supper's Ready" into a form that not only equaled but was occasionally capable of surpassing its vinyl counterpart; and Gabriel had taken the step that absolutely none of his fellows or associates were expecting—that which would finally catapult Genesis out of the footnotes on page three of the music papers and onto the front pages themselves.

A handful of concerts were organized in the days before the tour kicked off, to give some final fine-tuning to the now *Foxtrot*-heavy live set. It was, the band admitted, a fragile operation. Great swathes of Genesis's traditional live show were shunted aside to make space for the new material, and when Gabriel stepped out at Aylesbury Friars on Sept. 2, the second night of this mini-tour, he had a very special request to make of the audience. Warning them that they would barely recognize a single song, he asked that they turn normal convention on its head and applaud only if they actively hated anything they heard. Appreciation, on the other hand, should be registered with catcalls, jeers, and as much booing as possible.

"He just walked on halfway through, and I thought 'bloody hell....'"

Needless to say, by the time Genesis left the stage, the entire audience was howling boos and hisses...and the musicians were beaming their heads off. What a strange spectacle that must have made for any latecomers to the show and for anybody who attended certain future concerts. "It backfired slightly when we got a section of boo boys following us around," Banks laughed. "Full of good intentions, but somewhat disconcerting. We weren't looking for that reaction every night!"

At the Dublin National Stadium on Sept. 28, however, Gabriel had something else up his sleeve. Nobody paid any attention to him slipping offstage during the long instrumental interlude that bisects "The Musical Box"—it was what he always did. When he returned, however, audience and band alike could not help but gape. Where once had stood Peter Gabriel, unremarkably clad in jeans and T-shirt, there now towered a vision, a lank figure in a long, red woman's dress, surmounted by a fox's head.

"He just walked on halfway through…" Phil Collins grimaced. "And I thought 'bloody hell….'"

"There was a gasp when I came out," Gabriel agreed. He had never worn more than he needed to in the past; he had propelled the songs by the force of his presence alone. Now, however, he was not simply a man singing a song. Now he himself was the performance.

The fox itself was adapted from a similar vision that dominated the new LP sleeve, which in turn drew its inspiration from a recent TV commercial for Fox's Glacier Mints, in which a polar bear sits on a glacial-looking mint, to the angry bewilderment of a passing fox. The original design for *Foxtrot* was intended to restore the fox to its rightful place on the ice cube. Talking it over with designer Paul Whitehead, however, Gabriel and Hackett had other thoughts. "We wanted it to be a fox changing into a woman," Gabriel told *Sounds*, "because we're both attracted by the idea of a change…."

Even Hackett, however, never imagined the fox coming to life before his very eyes and reflected, "I thought it was wonderful, the first gig that he did that. I seem to remember that we used to run things through the band, we used to call it 'composition by committee,' although playing composition by committee doesn't really work, and artistic direction by committee doesn't really work because the corollary is, 'What do you think of this idea?'—and, as soon as you start doing that, you're lost. So I was full of admiration that he'd run with the ball…."

There were some dissenting voices, including—perhaps surprisingly—Phil Collins. "In the beginning, I thought the visuals were a bit strange," he admitted in 1974, on the eve of Genesis's most costumed extravaganza yet. "I wasn't sure if it was my cup of tea. I have this sort of puritan attitude to my music…I think music should be played simply. But I am the drummer with the band and that is what the band does, so you go along with it and get into it. I'll probably end up with a jazz band one day."

Gabriel explained, "You've got your stuff and you want to get it over as best you can. Rather than put all the paraphernalia of props and costumes on 12-bar blues, we write the material and then see how best we can get it across. We try to get some of the lyric content across visually; I act out some of the characters in the songs." But when critics (primarily American ones, for whom any man who wore a dress was a glitter-rocking teabag faggot) subsequently tried to tar Genesis with the same Glammy brush as the then all-conquering Alice Cooper, David Bowie, Gary Glitter, and so forth, Gabriel was quick to reject their accusations. Costuming of some sort was no stranger to rock 'n' roll, after all, all the way back to Elvis's lamé, the Beatles' suits, and the entire universe of expanding consciousness that had reigned supreme during the psychedelic era.

That latter was precisely the mood that Gabriel was intent on re-creating, as he relived in his mind the evenings that his teenaged self had spent at the legendary UFO Club in London, the world-within-a-mixed-media world of lights, sound, and film that was climaxed in so many minds by the appearance of the Crazy World of Arthur Brown, their eponymous singer's head a ball of living flame, and his two bandmates hunchbacked demons cavorting at the beck and call of the self-professed God of Hell Fire. "We [are] more like the 1967 groups," he agreed, "the Crazy World of Arthur Brown and the like." But even beyond Brown's pyrotechnic exertions, "we are trying to get a fantasy theatre of music which hasn't really been done before."

What Gabriel didn't let on, was that the red dress and fox's head were simply the appetizer. He had far greater extravagances in mind, with far more dramatic gestures and apparel.

On Oct. 14, as the tour touched down in Kingston-Upon-Thames, *Foxtrot* became Genesis's first-ever U.K. chart entry. Weeks later, it was hovering at No. 12, a peak that transformed Genesis overnight from unknown nobodies most familiar from handbills hanging in student unions to one of the most potent "newcomers" on the British rock scene. Lindisfarne, on the other hand, was lost in the ensuing tumult, as Stratton Smith's long-established policy of using his headline act to help break the support group backfired spectacularly.

Watching from afar, String Driven Thing's Chris Adams remembered how "friends of mine returned from a Lindisfarne/Genesis gig raving about the little-known support act whose lights and stage show had totally overshadowed the top act. [Tours like that] are good sense if you only manage the support band, but how do you placate the headline act who have had to resort to turning the house lights on during their own set to try to diminish the Genesis factor?" You couldn't. Piling on top of whatever tensions already existed within a band for which success had come far too quickly, that tour, and the constant overshadowing by Genesis, played a major part in the group's eventual discorporation, and within six months, the headliners had shattered, to struggle on instead as two very separate groups, a half-strength Lindisfarne and the half-formed Jack the Lad.

Throughout Genesis's earnest courtship of Britain, and the conquest of Europe that unfolded alongside it (*Foxtrot* followed *Nursery Cryme* into the Italian chart, peaking at No. 15), few of the band's attentions were focused in any one direction. They were aware that their albums were being released in America, for example, but neither local audiences nor Charisma's U.S. distributors, bubblegum supremo Neil Bogart's Buddah label, seemed at all concerned with taking the relationship any further—indeed, Buddah seemed not to have even known *what* to do with a band like Genesis, so far did they fall from the label's traditional catchment area of bubblegum pop, Melanie, and novelty songs. As news of *Foxtrot*'s international success fed into the label's New York offices, however, Buddah announced that maybe there was a place for Genesis in the American heart.

DJs Scott Muni and Alison Steele, at New York radio station WNEW, had long been champions not only of Genesis but of the Charisma stable in general, airing even the longest cuts from the albums (including "Supper's Ready") at every opportunity. As the station's annual Christmas party concert hove into view, a benefit for the United Cerebral Palsy Fund, the idea of importing two Charisma groups, Genesis and String Driven Thing, for the occasion began to take shape.

Genesis was firmly opposed to the entire plan, as Stratton Smith revealed. "[They] were against it at first and rightly so; it was a difficult thing for any band. But I had a problem. Genesis had already arrived at a point in their presentation that it took them so long to set up and strike the set to maximize their show that they could never be a support group."

A single concert was organized at the most prestigious venue available, the Philharmonic Hall in New York City—an event, not to mention a $16,000 extravagance, that British music paper *Sounds* described as "the biggest make-or-break attempt since Brinsley Schwarz played the Fillmore East three years ago."

On that occasion, a planeload of U.K. writers flown over for the occasion were witness to nothing more than an embarrassing flop. Brinsley Schwarz weren't ready for the show, and New York certainly wasn't interested in the band. This time around, however, there was interest. Far beyond WNEW's catchment area, journalists and DJs were pricking their ears up at the mention of both Genesis and String Driven Thing. While Genesis dispatched Richard MacPhail and the road crew over to New York a week before the show to make sure everything ran according to plan, Buddah set about arranging to fly in journalists and DJs from all over the United States (and beyond) for the occasion.

"The biggest make-or-break attempt since Brinsley Schwarz."

All was nerves as the party set out—Gabriel was so concerned that the American authorities would open his luggage and pull out his foxy dress that he asked Pauline Adams to carry it through in her own suitcases. Barely had the bands touched American soil, however, than problems began mounting up.

As part of his scouting activities, MacPhail arranged for the two groups to play a warmup show at Boston's Brandeis University, the evening before the New York concert. But the carefully laid plans were swift to go awry. Arriving in Boston, Genesis discovered the one thing nobody was able to predict. Although they had all the necessary equipment to convert their British equipment to work with American electricity, the change in voltage completely upset the workings of Tony Banks's keyboards. They still worked, but they did so in ever new and unexpected ways.

The show, while not a disaster, was still carried off on a wing and a prayer, and while all concerned believed that a full sound check the following day would iron out the problems, they reckoned without the presence of the Philharmonic Hall's traditional occupants. Leonard Bernstein, no great fan of rock 'n' roll since Keith Emerson and the Nice ritually dismantled his "America" in 1968, was rehearsing the Philharmonic Orchestra that day, and he wasn't going to surrender the stage to a bunch of hairy Englishmen.

"We couldn't take over the hall until 4 o'clock," Peter Gabriel shuddered, a timescale that left the band with just four hours before show time and very little time for a sound check—"The first time in two years that we haven't done a [proper] sound check before the gig. On top of that we were using strange equipment and the whole thing had become quite absurd."

In fact, Genesis had around an hour on stage before the show started, leaving String Driven Thing crammed into a final few frantic minutes with the stage still full of crew and the audience baying at the doors. Suddenly, Chris Adams remembered, Genesis roadie Adrian yelled "in his best commanding officer voice, 'Right! Everyone off stage!!' I thanked him gratefully, thinking we were about to get a few precious minutes. He blinked at me and frowned. 'That includes you!!'"

Sound check was not Genesis's only concern. Worryingly, Gabriel had succumbed to a throat problem after spending a night breathing the unfamiliar dust and dryness of the hotel's ventilation system, and things were only going to get worse. String Driven Thing played a blinder of a set, and while the audience showed no sign of being anywhere near sated, still Genesis knew the pressure was on for them to perform.

Introduced by an emcee whose praise included a reminder that none other than Keith Emerson had ranked among Genesis's biggest fans since he guest-reviewed "The Knife" for *Melody Maker* in 1971, the band launched into what *Sounds* writer Jerry Gilbert called "one of the best versions of 'Watcher of the Skies,' I have heard." There were, however, problems—it would not have been a major Genesis gig without them, and Mike Rutherford spoke for each of his colleagues when, coming off stage at the end of the concert, he threw his bass to the floor, convinced that the group had blown it, furious that they had just performed a concert that was scarcely half as good as it ought to have been, as they knew they were capable of enacting.

He was not to know, not immediately anyhow, that there were moments that the audience would remember far longer than the irritating buzz from Rutherford's amps that drowned the opening moments of "Supper's Ready"…and those were the moments by which an ecstatic crowd judged the concert: the point midway through "The Musical Box" when Gabriel stepped out of the darkness in his fox's head and a long red dress; the point when he produced a camera, walked to the very lip of the stage, and began taking pictures out at the audience; even the sequence, again during "Supper's Ready," when his ailing voice finally failed him, and he was forced to let Hackett and Banks take over the microphone as the number moved toward its climax.

Gabriel alone attended a postshow reception at the Inn at the Park; the rest of the band, apparently, was too dispirited to show up. But while Genesis only registered the flaws, a spellbound New York acknowledged everything but. As Tony Stratton Smith put it, "I told them afterwards, 'I know you weren't 100 percent, but they don't know, and 75 percent of you is better than they'll get from most bands.'"

"The final ovation was tremendous by any standards," *Sounds* concluded. "The reaction was genuine, the crowd wanted more, and that's an extremely rare sight for a little-known British band making their debut in New York. And so Genesis came back to do 'The Knife,' after which the house lights were quickly up." And slowly the roaring filtered out of the auditorium, to the dressing room where the band were still deep in self-recrimination; to the street outside, where passers-by clocked the ecstatic concert-goers and asked them precisely what had taken place that night; and all the way to the uppermost echelons of Buddah, where company boss Neil Bogart was suddenly discussing Genesis's prospects in tones he'd scarcely employed since the days of the 1910 Fruitgum Company.

Still reeling, the band flew home to learn that ever-more exaggerated word of their mighty triumph had preceded them. The Atlantic Ocean was an awful lot wider in those days than it is now, the gulf between America and Britain an unfathomable void across which rumor flew faster than fact, and the mildest whisper could become an echoing bellow. Thus, a well-received sold-out show became, in the eyes of the British media, the first step toward a new British Invasion, with Genesis the once unfathomable advance guard that had shredded all of Uncle Sam's defenses. Suddenly, people who may never have looked twice at its record covers were reading reports of Genesis's American breakthrough and were demanding their own chance to catch the band, before the Yanks took possession of them forever.

"I liked [New York] more than I'd expected to," Gabriel acknowledged. "I have this vivid memory of the streets looking like a futurist painting, with steam hurling out of the holes in the road and tremendous energy and speed hurtling from all quarters, but the visit was over so quickly that we didn't have time to have a good look round. I managed to go to the Museum of Modern Art, but that was about it."

CHAPTER EIGHT

SELL IN ENGLAND BY THE TON

Suddenly, both bands were on a high. String Driven Thing were even pushing for a hit single, as the maddeningly infectious "Circus" became one of the underground smashes of the era; audiences were ecstatic; and Stratton Smith was planning his next move, the launch of Charisma's German division. Immediately after the New York show, Genesis, Lindisfarne, and String Driven Thing headed for Hamburg to take part in the launch party. On the night, however, Genesis was conspicuous by its absence. "Adrian fell asleep on a train somewhere in Switzerland," Chris Adams remembered. "The coach with all their mikes and stands was decoupled from the train and shunted into a siding."

Home again, Genesis kicked off the new year, 1973, with a low-key show at the Greyhound in Croydon, moving onto a string of European shows and TV performances (excellent footage exists of a show at the Paris Bataclan on Jan. 10), before returning to Britain for its first full headlining tour of the United Kingdom, kicking off at the Lanchester Arts Festival at the beginning of February. Two nights later they were in Bristol; then on February 9, they were in London—and all hell broke loose.

After such a rocky start, Genesis had grown happily accustomed to Gabriel's fox-headed femme fatale and were gleefully conspiring to add fresh visual dimensions to the live show—stage-shaking explosions at the climax of "Supper's Ready," an ever-more grandiose light show, and, to be unveiled at the London Rainbow, huge sheets of white gauze that draped over the PA system to billow out with the sound and transform the old wooden stage into something approaching a fairyland. But, as the group rehearsed for the gig, there was no suggestion that tonight would be any different from the nights that had gone before. A well-oiled machine was rolling along without a hitch.

Sound check, too, came and went without any untoward happenstance, and as the musicians walked out on stage for the opening number, buffeted by the swelling tones of "Watcher of the Skies," even then it was business as usual—until one of them glanced in Gabriel's direction and found the singer's head bracketed by a monstrous pair of bat wings.

Steve Hackett had pushed hard for the band "to have a light show and a Mellotron; then Pete came in with the fox's head." Tonight, however, he had opened his wardrobe as wide as it would go, "and suddenly we were able to present the whole thing. I was very happy with the show that we did at the Rainbow, where he came out with all these costumes for the first time. He didn't ask anyone what they thought; that was what he was wearing, and it was absolutely fine. The same numbers we were playing on stage that people had walked out for, and gone to the bar for, the same numbers, the same songs, 'Watcher of the Skies,' 'Friday,' 'Hogweed,' suddenly people were sticking around for the whole show, in case they missed something.

The singer's head bracketed by a monstrous pair of bat wings.

"It was just the best thing, because it just made it look so good and people went nuts. Suddenly, the band had a future. We didn't try it out in the provinces first; Pete just went for it at the biggest gig we had; he just went for it, and it made all the difference. Suddenly we were getting the front covers, and that was the tipping point for Genesis, as far as I was concerned."

Indeed it was. Breathless accounts of the Rainbow show were splashed across the following week's music papers. "The band's new stage act," *Sounds'* Jerry Gilbert reported, "transcends just about everything that has come under the portrayal of surrealistic art in an eminently tangible rock form," with Gabriel "the personif[ication] first [of] the surrealist evil that lurks within *A Clockwork Orange* and then the sweet bizarre innocence of Lewis Carroll's Alice."

Even before such wordy pronouncements hit the printed page, however, word of

Genesis's absolute transformation had made its way through a grapevine of fans spread up and down the country, so that every night's audience was split equally between those holding their breath in anticipation of what they were about to receive and those who received it first but still couldn't believe their eyes.

Gabriel's visual antics were not confined to the performance itself. Offstage, too, he now sported a distinctive look, a great stripe of baldness razored through his scalp that left passers-by split in their opinions. "Some people will react negatively to anything that's different," the singer chuckled. "And others will think, 'Poor boy, he's been in a car accident [and] had his brain taken out.'" As for the truth of the matter, Gabriel concocted a veritable library's worth of reasons for having half-shaved his head, anything from "a cheap gimmick," to the ful-

> "'Poor boy, he's been in a car accident [and] had his brain taken out.'"

fillment of a clairvoyant's claim that he was a Mohican in a past life—or, at least, in a negative version of it. A true Mohican haircut, as the punks of several years later reminded us, shaves the head, but leaves a single strip of hair.

Building on the success of its New York partnership, String Driven Thing was once recruited as the support act. Unhappily, it was a booking that the group was patently unable to make the most of, after Chris Adams was hospitalized with a collapsed lung. "I walked into the local A&E with chest pains, was diagnosed as having a 'spontaneous pneumo thorax' and told I could take to bed and let it reflate slowly over a month, or they could cut through my chest wall and let the trapped air out, allowing the punctured lung to reflate.

"As we were due to start the tour in ten days, I chose the latter. So, still ambulatory, I was taken into a man's ward, where curtains were drawn round the bed, I was given a local anesthetic, and two doctors then took it in turns to bore a hole through my chest with a drill and bit.

"It took them almost half an hour and, when a tube was fed into the cavity, my screams must have traumatized my fellow patients, who had watched me walk in unaided a short time before. Sad to say, though, not one of the Charisma 'family' came to see me, and though we did make it on stage to open at the Rainbow, it was a gig we would never have been asked to do." Adams's nightmarish experiences would become the inspiration behind String Driven Thing's next album, the magnificent *The Machine That Cried*; in the meantime, String Driven Thing pulled out all the stops to ensure, like so many Charisma support bands before them, the headliners were going to have a hell of a time trying to come out on top. "That tour was our first with drums," says Adams, "and as it progressed, the reception got better and better, 'til we reached Essex University, where a student sit in was in full swing. Grahame was on fire that night, and after the obligatory encore, we made our way to the shared dressing room, but as we sat down, the Convenor burst in to say the crowd was going mad. We went back on and hit them with 'It's a Game,' our proverbial showstopper. Back in the dressing room, and now half-changed, the same guy appeared again, saying we'd have to go back on to prevent a riot. There was a long strained silence; then Gabriel gave his strange, horsey laugh. 'On you go,' he said, genuinely pleased that the 'Charisma Support Act Syndrome' was still alive and operational."

Meanwhile, the trans-Atlantic phone lines were humming as Buddah and Charisma talked daily to plan the two bands' next move, a return trip to America, to confirm what they had threatened in December. Further ammunition was heaped into that bandolier at the end of February, when the syndicated U.S. radio program the "King Biscuit Flower Hour" arranged to record and broadcast highlights of two Genesis shows (in Manchester and Leicester) to help herald the group's return.

> "Gabriel gave his strange, horsey laugh. 'On you go,' he said."

Genesis's first American tour commenced with a return visit to New York, this time at Carnegie Hall, on March 2, 1973. But, though String Driven Thing was again lined up to support them, things did not go as planned.

"Even though 'Circus' was the *New York Times'* single of the year, and the people at Buddha were very excited about the band, it was deemed by Fred Munt that we should now start to pay our dues"—a time honored rock tradition that translated into spending as many weeks a year as possible grinding around the domestic college circuit in a van. There would be no more trips to America.

To this day, Adams is uncertain whether the group was being punished for some unknown transgression—threatening Genesis's supremacy from the lowly support slot perhaps, or if they were simply rising too fast for Charisma's liking, queue-jumping the label's own sense of order. But when Adams approached Stratton Smith to complain "about our total lack of confidence in his 'manager,' he hummed and hawed and did nothing." By the end of the year, with the critical response to *The Machine That Cried* pushing String Driven Thing toward its highest plateau yet, both Chris and Pauline Adams had quit the band they formed.

Neither was Genesis having an easy time of it in the United States. From a triumphant New York homecoming, the tour zipped up and down the East Coast, venturing into Canada for a handful of shows and returning to both Brandeis University and the Philharmonic Hall. However, whereas a one-off show with the full weight of the world promoting the hell out if it is easy to sell out, 16 gigs in a string of disparate markets is a somewhat tougher proposition.

From the outset, it was acknowledged that Genesis would not be able to take the usual route toward American hearts, by landing a never-ending chain of prestigious support acts. Even among the most confident of headliners, precious few would willingly set themselves up to be blown off stage by a warmup act with Genesis's reputation. The group opened for Woodstock veteran Richie Havens in Chicago on March 20, and Steve Hackett recalled another show supporting Lou Reed. But hopes of landing further such shows never came to pass, and plans to recruit an opening act in every city they passed through also fell apart when the group members realized they were scarcely earning enough money to feed themselves, let alone another set of mouths. Night after night, then, Genesis was frequently the only name on the evening's bill, and the sad truth was, few people in Miami, Philadelphia, Sherbrook, Pittsburgh, Montreal, or wherever had ever heard of them.

The nights that went well, however, were magical, and Genesis returned to Europe for a handful of summertime shows across France and Germany, before wrapping up with its third consecutive appearance at Britain's Reading Festival. Headlining Sunday, the final night, hoisted above the likes of Rory Gallagher, the Faces, Cockney Rebel, and Status Quo, the band was rewarded with a warm, if slightly puzzling, review from *Melody Maker*'s Michael Watts. Introduced as "a group who use theatrical effects as well as thoughtful electronic music in the style of groups like Pink Floyd," Watts continued, "they played safe by rendering what we have heard before. 'The Musical Box,' 'Supper's Ready,' and 'The Return of the Giant Hogweed' pleased both myself and the 25,000 audience and was an effective climax to three days of sunshine and friendliness."

Headlining Reading confirmed Genesis's preeminence in British rock circles; memories of the American tour seemed equally adamant that the advances it had made so far would hold the group in good stead for the future. "I don't think anybody believed that they were just going to walk into America and become superstars," Tony Stratton Smith mused. "It was nice to think that, and Buddah Records certainly gave them that impression, but deep down we all knew it was going to be a long hard slog."

It was to try to alleviate some of that prospective burden that Stratton Smith proposed Genesis's next album should be a live recording. He had arranged for the *King Biscuit Flower Hour* tapes to be handed back to Charisma for mixing (by engineer John Burns) and was pushing hard for the band to sanction a double live album, one that would showcase its current concert set for all who demanded their own souvenir of the concerts and preserve it for all time, in advance of the changes that would inevitably be wrought by their next album.

"A Marcel Marceau album that is absolutely silent, with clapping at the end"

In the meantime, such a release would allow them more time in which to plan for that album, rather than have to ride the annual merry-go-round of tour/album/tour that had hitherto consumed the group's time. It would also serve as a one-stop introduction to the best of Genesis for anybody curious to hear the group but nervous about shelling out for a regular album.

Genesis refused. No matter the quality of the *King Biscuit* tapes, still there was the knowledge that Genesis had played, and would continue to play, better concerts. To preserve any one (or two) night as representative of them all was to do both band and audience a disservice. Besides, it was less than a year since Phil Collins was loudly quoted, in *Record Mirror*, insisting there would never be a live Genesis album. "In the studio there is always the temptation to put a lot of extra instruments and sounds into the songs which we couldn't possibly hope to re-create on stage, but nevertheless we still take a lot of time getting an album together. We'd never do a live album because of this. There would be too much going on to make a good live recording."

Stratton Smith persevered, however, and slowly a compromise was reached. The full-price double album would instead be slimmed down to a budget-priced single disc. Gabriel's between-song stories and interludes would be excised, so, too, would the sidelong performance of "Supper's Ready." Even the sound of a rapturous audience would be suspended, as Gabriel waxed eloquently over the virtues of "a Marcel Marceau album that is absolutely silent, with clapping at the end" and then complained, "You can spend far too much time listening to clapping."

Instead, the mundanely titled *Genesis Live* would showcase only those songs whose presence in Genesis's live set was demanded by all who heard them and would continue to be so—"The Knife," "The Musical Box," "Get 'Em Out by Friday," "Return of the Giant Hogweed," and "Watcher of the Skies." Other numbers would come and go. But those five were all but permanent fixtures. Neither did that relative brevity harm it. Priced indeed at a budget rate, *Genesis Live* rapidly became the group's fastest-selling album yet and, in September 1973, broke the group into the U.K. Top Ten for the first time.

Stratton Smith's concerns for the group's future welfare were not groundless. After four years of road management, Richard MacPhail departed in April 1973 to concentrate on the environmental concerns that had always lain close to his heart, and the loss of his calming presence immediately opened a void within the band.

Although Genesis had already taken the decision to begin writing and rehearsing toward a new album, when it came time to actually start work, the warm democracy that had once been the hallmark of the sessions was replaced with a bristling fractiousness that not only swept up present-day grievances but also rounded up slights that dated back a decade.

In the past, Genesis had always entered the studio with at least elements of its new album in place, whether the songs were broken in on stage in the months before the recording sessions began or not. "I don't like recording material before we've had a chance to work it on the road," Gabriel told *Sounds* in 1973, "because it never quite works out as we intend it to." Steve Hackett, meanwhile, once documented a dispute whose gist was "you broke my ruler in 1963"; "ah yes, but you pinched my sweets in

1964." As these battles consumed the group's three most vocal songwriters, Gabriel, Banks, and Rutherford, Hackett and Collins simply melted back onto the sidelines to watch and wonder where it would all end. Or if it already had?

Ultimately, such ruptures were never serious enough to endanger Genesis. They were, however, destined to irreparably hamstring the work in progress. There was a long period of time during which the only fresh number in the group's arsenal was "The Battle of Epping Forest," an epic penned around a newspaper story Gabriel read about a gang fight that took place in Epping Forest, on the outskirts of east London—an old-fashioned "gentleman's bout," in which the two sides agreed up front not to utilize firearms. Although critics could point out that the song's lengthy cast of combatants was little more than an excuse for Gabriel to adopt an increasingly wild range of voices and characters, still the song has a gripping grittiness, and it would readily emerge as one of the gestating album's key numbers.

Other material slowly piled up, breaking through the assorted writers' blocks, but the group had to reckon with other distractions. Steve Hackett remembered,

"What do you think you are doing; you are disturbing the livestock!'"

"We were rehearsing in this house near Chessington Zoo and…we used to get these irate neighbors who used to come over and say, 'You're playing too loud! What do you think you are doing; you are disturbing the livestock!' It was one of those sort of things basically full of interruptions, really. It was a very weird album."

Hackett's solution to the in-fighting was to throw himself deeper into the writing and recording process than he ever had before, until his contributions were not only impossible to ignore, they frequently outpaced the efforts of his bandmates. The signature "Dancing with the Moonlit Knight" was built around one of Hackett's ideas, and the magnificent "Firth of Fifth," described by Hackett 30 years later as "my interpretation of Tony's melody," is the guitarist's pick for "my best known electric guitar solo with the band. It'll always be twinned with me, and I still enjoy playing it. It's a great melody for guitar; I've played it many times."

Hackett was also responsible for salvaging one of the songs that didn't make it through the long-standing policy of "composition by committee," Gabriel's "Déjà

Vu." Abandoned early in the sessions, Hackett nevertheless loved the number so much that, more than two decades later, he prevailed on Gabriel to complete it for inclusion in the guitarist's own *Genesis Revisited* album.

"The band was not happy," Tony Stratton Smith confirmed. "There was never a point when I thought they might actually break up, but there were occasions when I thought we might lose either Phil, who was clearly losing patience with the amount of time it took to decide anything, or Steve, who just seemed very insecure trying to state his case to the united front of Pete, Mike, and Tony. They disagreed with one another constantly, but they always ganged together when somebody else weighed in against one of them…." The manager recalled one occasion when the Carthusian contingent was clearly at loggerheads, two against one, over some matter or other. "But when they put it to a vote, and Steve and Phil voted with the majority, the other pair promptly switched sides, and Steve and Phil were outvoted three to two."

The very title of the album, too, says something for the mood within the band. In common with the remainder of the western world, Britain was not in an especially happy state in 1973, battered by the oil crisis and lurching toward recession. Into this potpourri of social despair, the country then proceeded to stir some individual wrenches of its own, compounding the global disarray with a succession of evermore damaging strikes, crippling inflation, and punishing unemployment.

The government of the day had already thrown up its hands in despair and was simply awaiting the next general election, early in 1974, to put it out of its misery. Yet the opposition was no better prepared to take on the task than the government itself, and everywhere one looked, another slice of English life was being sacrificed at the altar of commerce and greed…the country truly was being parceled out to the highest bidder, and whether Genesis intended the simile or not, still *Selling England by the Pound* remains the most aptly titled album of the year.

External influence collided with internal instinct. Phil Collins has since criticized the album, pinpointing it as the peak of a bandwide need to prove what great musicians they were. "Albums like *Foxtrot* and *Selling England by the Pound* may sound a little heavy-handed today, yet at the time they represented new musical directions for the band. When we recorded…*Nursery Cryme*, …*Foxtrot*, and *Selling England by the Pound*, the Mahavishnu Orchestra with Billy Cobham were very much in vogue. Their style of playing odd time signatures and complex rhythmic figures influenced our music. Personally speaking, I feel I was trying to do a little too much on those early albums. I was trying to prove to people that I could play. In doing so I wasn't necessarily playing what the music required.

"We were collectively guilty of that as a group. You tend to try to prove what you're capable of musically and make the mistake of displaying that technical ability at every opportunity. Something like that only resolves itself as you gain maturity as a player and as a person. You eventually feel comfortable playing something very simple if that's all the music requires. 'The Cinema Show'…has a very elaborate arrangement and is played in seven."

Neither was there any consensus on material. Tony Banks, for example, pleaded with his bandmates to omit the gently lilting "After The Ordeal" from the album, describing it as the worst piece of music the five had ever recorded while Gabriel fought to excise the closing instrumental passage of "The Cinema Show"— moments that would, once the album was released, be singled out among the most evocative on the entire record. Neither would anybody win these conflicts—rather, like the battle of Epping Forest, the squabbling ended honors even, and the only loser was the album itself.

"The Battle of Epping Forest" and "The Cinema Show" both clocked in at more than 11 minutes, "After the Ordeal" at almost five, the opening "Dancing with the Moonlit Knight" at eight, "Firth of Fifth" at nine, and there were still three more songs to squeeze on. But, in those days of vinyl only, an album was reasonably confined to just 45, stretching toward 50 minutes of music per disc, before the sound quality began to suffer. *Selling England by the Pound* would emerge with close to an hour's worth of music packed into its protesting grooves, resulting in a muddy-sounding disc that needed to be played *very* loud to make much sense whatsoever; it would be the mid-'90s before the record was truly heard to its greatest effect, following its remastering for CD.

Further damage was wrought by Tony Stratton Smith's decision to retire from active management, to concentrate on running Charisma alone. He had been considering such a switch for some time but always had too many bands beneath his wing to execute a clean break. By late 1973, however, Van der Graaf Generator and Lindisfarne had already broken up, and Audience and String Driven Thing were set to follow. Of the artists he most treasured, only Genesis remained on the company's managerial books, and when Stratton Smith stepped back to look at them, he realized he personally had taken the band as far as he could…or, at least, as far as he wanted to take the band.

Genesis had done the hard part; he believed the band was now poised on the brink of enormous, international superstardom. "What they needed [now] was the hard-nosed supertour manager, setting up these tours and logistics and sitting on the record company's neck. That's a particularly time-consuming skill in itself, and I really didn't want to do it."

Orchestrating the continued growth of Charisma, on the other hand, was a challenge he relished. In early 1973, Charisma finally vacated the rabbit-warren homeyness of Brewer Street for plush new offices in Soho Square, and over the next year or so, the label would become home to an entire new generation of up-and-coming names, several of whom seemed at least as precocious (not to mention eccentric) as those who ignited the roster in the first place—the pub rock-reggae combo G.T. Moore and his Reggae Guitars, the Lindisfarne spin-off Jack the Lad, psychiatrist R.D. Laing, and Australian singer-songwriter Gary Shearston. There was a berth for Poet Laureate Sir John Betjeman, a signing that the *New Musical Express* celebrated via a fascinating and deeply humorous interview with the great man, around the time of the release of his first album; there was a solo career for Robert John Godfrey, a keyboard genius who Stratton Smith originally intended to pair with String Driven Thing but who never gelled with his prospective bandmates.

Few of Charisma's new signings were flavored with the same degree of community that marked the original Charisma crowd; there would be no gleefully conjoined audiences for a modern Six Bob Tour–type outing. But anybody fearing that the crusading charisma of the original Charisma had gone the same way as so many of the other early-'70s musical attributes certainly had nothing to fear from these quarters.

Stratton Smith explained to author Johnny Rogan, "I had to make [a] decision, and for me, I made the right choice for my peace of mind. Whether I made the right choice economically is a totally different question, but extraordinary as it may sound, I've never been highly motivated by money. I enjoy making things work, more." Instead, he arranged what, on paper (literally), looked like the most straightforward transition ever, as the band's management was handed over to concert promoter (and long-time Charisma ally) Tony Smith. Forget about the "Stratton," and outsiders may never have realized anything had changed.

"We got into a strange situation where we had [two] managers," Gabriel told *Melody Maker*—Fred Munt who oversaw the day-to-day business and Stratton Smith who was at the helm of all things Charisma. "Roles were not clearly defined, and there was not enough contact between them. So it got a bit messy, and in the end, Tony came in. He travels with us and can be there—on the spot." He was also devoted to the band, musically as well as personally, and can even take credit for nailing perhaps the one comparison with another act that Genesis could truly live with…"the Syd Barrett days of Pink Floyd." There was the same sinister insistence of reality impinging on the unreality of their lyric, the same sense of a unifying internal mythology to the myriad streams and events that the songs approached, and the same overwhelming sense of Englishness to both the lyric and the language. And, as it turned out, the two groups had the same ability to transform the catastrophic loss of their acknowledged frontman to their immaculate advantage.

Stratton Smith's announcement was a blow nevertheless—so was the incoming Tony Smith's discovery that, for all it had accomplished so far, Genesis was still some £200,000 in debt, as it continued struggling to recoup the advances that Charisma had paid them over the years and that it had spent on equipment, lights, and lorries. "We're not a poor band," Hackett laughed as the extent of the debt became clear. "We're a bankrupt one—or, we would be if everyone demanded their money at once." It was especially galling being so deep in the hole, he explained, because the band had recently set its heart on purchasing a quadraphonic sound system.

For Phil Collins, relaxation through the conflicts that had split Genesis into two such disparate camps revolved around absorbing the latest King Crimson album, the behemothic *Lark's Tongue in Aspic*—idol Bill Bruford's first with the group. Crimson's similarly newly established bassist John Wetton continued, "My ex-wife lived with Phil Collins before we met…and she told me that he would addictively listen to *Lark's Tongue in Aspic*, playing it back to back, over and over." And, if his fellows' arguing grew too loud, he'd simply turn it up and up.

He delivered a more pointed commentary on the impasses that dominated the group's creative process by looking outside the band for action, beginning with a guest slot on Flash guitarist Peter Banks's then-looming solo album, *Two Sides of Peter Banks.* Banks recalled, "I phoned Phil up and asked him if he'd play on my album, and he enthusiastically said 'yes.'" Steve Hackett, too, "came down to the studio for a few hours and put some ideas down. Unfortunately, I didn't have a chance to really use him as much as I wanted. His guitar playing is very different from mine…at first [he] reminded me very much of [Robert] Fripp. He would work out certain guitar lines; he definitely wasn't a spontaneous guitarist at that time." One other memory sticks out. Banks laughed, "Everyone got paid standard [union] scale, and Phil always had his little invoice and receipt book for tax purposes. I was always impressed with that."

Other extracurricular activities developed, as Collins joined Mike Rutherford and Anthony Phillips in the studio to cut a track for a various artists collection that Charisma were readying. *Beyond an Empty Dream* was an ambitious set that Stratton Smith described as a collection of modern hymns. With Collins taking another of his then-so-rare vocal excursions, the trio initially intended recording just the one song, "Take

> "We're not a poor band, we're a bankrupt one."

This Heart," for the album, even taking over the chapel at Charterhouse for the occasion. But the session went so well that they quickly turned their attention toward a more fascinating project, a full-blown Phil Collins solo single.

The A-side, "Silver Song," was a number that dated back to Phillips's time in Genesis—it was originally written as a tribute of sorts to drummer John Silver. Backed by a new song, "Only Your Love," the single was recorded in a day and passed onto Charisma soon after. The label, too, seemed enthusiastic, but time passed, and the single remained unscheduled…soon, it was forgotten, lost beneath the weight of other activities that Genesis, individually and collectively, now had on its plate.

For Collins, however, the cancellation of the single remained a blow, without ever becoming a crippling bone of contention—he had already been disappointed in the past, after plans for Gabriel and himself to cut what the singer called "a few pop-type singles" were abandoned. "There are plans for Phil, and I to get some of our friends into a studio," Gabriel told *Record Mirror.* "But I don't think we'd release them under our names."

No sooner had the fate of "Silver Song" become apparent than Collins decided to simply go out and perform without any of the complications of a record deal, a stage show, or even a structured live set. Zox and the Radar Boys was born.

Rarely settling down to any kind of permanent membership beyond Collins himself, Zox and the Radar Boys sucked in a string of heavyweight musicians, all of whom would have agreed that, sometimes, it's fun to simply go out and play. Bill Bruford, Peter Banks, Deep Purple organist Jon Lord, and Steve Hackett all boarded Collins's little dreamboat to play barely announced shows around the London club and pub circuit. "[I have] no idea why it was called [Zox and the Radar Boys]," Pete Banks confessed, adding that he frequently had no clue what the evening was going to demand of him, either. "I'd just sit in with no ideas of what we were going to play, not a clue. It was kind of open-ended really."

Zox and the Radar Boys gigged sporadically through the late summer and early fall, but Genesis business was soon summoning Collins to action—the release of *Selling England by the Pound*, rehearsing for the accompanying tours, and wrestling with Charisma over whether it was time to release a new Genesis single.

CHAPTER NINE

WEIRD SCENES INSIDE THE WARDROBE

The divide between being an album-oriented band and a singles machine had haunted the British rock scene since the late '60s, when Led Zeppelin announced it was too serious an act to be bothered with the rigmarole of chasing regular hits. (At least in Britain—American and Japanese singles success, for a multitude of now-obscure reasons, did not seem to bother them in the slightest.) Other groups were swift to follow Zeppelin's example, either refusing point-blank to release singles from their latest albums or declining to promote those that did sneak out. Even among those bands that were able to score singles success…Deep Purple, Curved Air, Family, and Black Sabbath were all numbered among the album-oriented community…the humble hit 45 was treated as a slightly embarrassing afterthought.

Genesis, through its years of greatest obscurity—which may readily be stretched as late as *Foxtrot*—had never expressed any thoughts on the matter. The band simply wanted to sell records and didn't care especially whether it was 7-inch or 12-inch. Now that Genesis had started to rise, however, the mood shifted. The albums were selling; the concerts were selling out. All a hit single would achieve would be to drag an army of kids into the party, with all the teenybopper paraphernalia that entailed.

Charisma first mooted "I Know What I Like (In Your Wardrobe)" as a single in late 1973 to coincide with the release of *Selling England by the Pound*. The song itself was a masterpiece, tight and concise, with a light-hearted spoken word intro and outro, a chorus that you could swing through trees on, and a spellbinding Steve Hackett guitar riff. But while Hackett acknowledged that Genesis was hoping "to increase our appeal by paying more attention to singles," the band initially refused to countenance such a release, and it would be the following spring before the 45 finally appeared—while Genesis was out of the country, on its latest, longest American tour yet. It was from the other side of the ocean, then, that the band watched in amazement as the peculiar tale of a henpecked gardener breached the Top 40 at the beginning of April and then rose inexorably up toward No. 21.

Genesis was even invited onto television's *Top of the Pops*, at that time the single-most important U.K. venue for any group hoping (or otherwise) for a major hit. But remembering its miserable experience on *Disco Two* four years earlier, Genesis lore insists that the band refused the invite, although the rigors of its stateside itinerary would have made it impossible anyway. What the group did do was nix Charisma's suggestion that a filmed live performance be aired instead and left *Top of the Pops* to fill the void the best it could, by organizing the show's regular dance troupe, Pan's People, to appear instead. "I heard it was quite interesting," Steve Hackett mused. "Pan's People cavorting in lingerie to 'I Know What I Like.'"

The film footage that Charisma had in mind for this momentous occasion was drawn from a specially arranged concert that the band staged at Shepperton Studios at the end of October, 1973, in front of an invited audience of friends, fans, and family. *Tony Stratton Smith Presents Genesis in Concert* captured Genesis at the end of a two week U.K. tour, with *Selling England by the Pound* not only dominating its live repertoire but with its imagery now shoving all of Gabriel's past costumes into history. It featured some of the best remembered, and certainly most photographed, of Gabriel's onstage persona date from this era, and *Tony Stratton Smith Presents*…can take much of the credit for that.

Not all of his costumes were admired by his colleagues, however. The flower head that emerged for "Willow Farm," the bizarre box-like construction that bedecked "Apocalypse," the old man who materialized during "The Musical Box," these were great. But the vast Britannia garb that cloaked "Dancing with the Moonlit Knight" struck Banks as "silly," which suggests that it is just as well that the film itself remains unseen (at least officially—bootleg prints have circulated for years), as Stratton Smith's intended cinema release was canceled at the group's insistence.

The moment in "Willow Farm" when Narcissus
is turned into...a hogweed?

Once again, the uncertainties that came so close to stymieing the *Genesis Live* album raised their rancid little heads, while there was also a fear that a film release, coming on the heels of everything else, could easily leave the band open to accusations of overexposure.

As it was, there was little escape from Genesis that fall and into the new year. A week after the Shepperton Studios shoot, the group embarked upon its latest North

American tour, an outing that peaked with six gigs in three days at Los Angeles's Roxy, days before Christmas. It was the group's first-ever visit to the West Coast, and Gabriel enthused, "We found we had a sort of underground mystique. One guy from a music paper said we were probably the last of the underground bands, and in a way, it seems to have spread on the West Coast, a strange, intense cult thing focused on us."

Gabriel dressed up as Santa for one of the shows, complete with bushy white beard; at another, he took a lungful of helium to aid his vocal effects and wound up with hiccups for two days straight. If Genesis had any misgivings whatsoever about America, the singer admitted, it was that it was growing "harder and harder to get exploding equipment." The live performance had expanded to include some remarkable pyrotechnic effects, but "with all the terrorist things going on [the Weather Underground were very active at this time]…you need a license now. And to get the license you have to be vetted by the police and proved to be a responsible citizen with no left-wing tendencies."

"Pan's People cavorting in lingerie to 'I Know What I Like.'"

Not all went well, however. Looking back on the tour in February 1974, *Circus* magazine sniffed, "Genesis thought they would make it big in 1973, but they were classified as just another glitter band." But Gabriel was not downhearted. "Drag band was actually the classification," he smiled. "[But] the categories change as frequently as the contents of the categories. We read a book called *How to Be Rich and Famous*, and it said, 'Glitter is good for 1973.' What was it for 1974? Whatever it is, we'll be it."

It rather looked as though it would be sufficiently simply for them to be themselves. Returning home from a posttour vacation in Hawaii, Genesis discovered that a projected three-night residency at the Drury Lane Theatre in London had expanded to five, simply to catch up with the initial ticket demand. It was the first time any mere rock group had occupied the grand old pile for such a protracted spell, but Genesis—as its audience never tired of reminding the letters' pages of the music press—was never a "mere" rock band, a point that Gabriel proved as he hooked himself to the wires that traditionally "flew" Peter Pan across the stalls and levitated above the stage. Gabriel adored the venue. "It's a lovely place,

While Hackett tries not to stare, an angelic Gabriel tries out a
new halo.

tremendously moody. You could well imagine it being haunted…but can ghosts buy records?"

From the Drury Lane residency, Genesis swung over to Europe for a handful of shows, and then it was back to the United States and Canada at the beginning of March for a tour that kept them on the road until early May.

Again, America proved a tough nut to crack, with a hectic itinerary regularly pockmarked by long periods where Genesis was unable to actually find a gig—peculiarly, the full six-week outing was not booked beforehand, the idea being that word of mouth would see them adding far more shows than if they sat on the phone at home. It didn't work like that in the slightest, but even this enforced redundancy had its compensations, as Steve Hackett recalled. "That whole *Selling England* period was a tipping point, in that the band had progressed to the level of playing to rival the jazzers; and then we heard in New York that John Lennon liked the album. We thought, 'We can't get a gig in this country; we're sitting around in L.A. not able to get a gig…but at least John Lennon likes it.' And we were able to use that to our advantage."

Gabriel wound up with hiccups for two days straight.

"I Know What I Like" raised the profile even further, but the time that the band members spent on the road together, companionship that was rarely diluted even by visits from family and friends, was taking its toll on the five. Barely was the group home again, in early May 1974, than Phil Collins was confiding to Dutch journalist Armando Gallo that he was definitely on his way out of Genesis, to concentrate on session work and a new project he and bassist Percy Jones were in the process of assembling, a jazz-rock outfit called Brand X.

He was true to at least part of his promise, as well. Throughout 1974–75 alone, Collins was the drummer across the sessions that became former Velvet Underground man John Cale's *Helen of Troy* album ("The first time I've ever seen anybody open a packet and put out a whole gram of cocaine along the guitar case. And then do it, and then go and sing"), Argent's *Counterpoint*, Tommy Bolin's *Teaser*, Jack Lancaster's *Marscape*, William Lyall's *Solo Casting*, Nova's *Vimana*, Thin Lizzy's *Johnny the Fox*, and, most significant of all, singer Eddie Howell's *Man from Manhattan* album in early 1975, a project that the outside world knows better for the involvement of Queen's Freddie Mercury and Brian May on the title track but also bears the distinction of introducing the members of Brand X to one another, as Collins and Jones worked for the first time with guitarist John Goodsall and keyboard player Robin Lumley.

Collins's bandmates, too, were utilizing their downtime to stretch their wings in new directions. Steve Hackett was at home writing and demoing material that he had already decided would see the light of day *somehow*…"Either I'd record it with Genesis, or I'd record it on my own." Mike Rutherford, meanwhile, was reunited once again with Anthony Phillips, this time to demo material that the guitarist proposed would feature on his own debut solo album…to be released a staggering seven years after he first left Genesis. Again, the duo was not averse to looking to the past—several tracks, including the album's eventual title track, *The Geese and the Ghost*—dated back to the demos the pair had recorded together back in 1969.

Gabriel, meanwhile, was deep in conversation with film director William Friedkin, who was convinced that Gabriel's future lay not in music but in screenwriting. The American apparently came across the short story that Gabriel inserted in lieu of liner notes on the sleeve of *Genesis Live* and detected an hitherto untapped talent within those 200 or so words. Working on his next movie, the horror film *The Sorcerer*, Friedkin suggested Gabriel become involved in the storytelling side (German synth-wizards Tangerine Dream had already been booked to create the soundtrack), and that project was to consume much of Gabriel's interest over the next months.

Gabriel's attentions were further distracted by his wife Jill's pregnancy and the touch-and-go birth of their first child, daughter Anne. Fragile and sickly, the baby spent the first month of her life on an incubator—"It was," Gabriel later understated, "quite a black period." Tony Banks agreed. "The birth changed him a lot. And it was difficult for us to accommodate that because, at that stage in the group's career, we still wanted to do as much touring as we could."

Instead, they were at home, filling time as best they could, and it would be late summer before all five members of Genesis were again in the same room together. And though not one of the five would bet on the recent difficulties being surmounted, still they owed it to the band…to their fans…to their record label…to make the attempt.

Intent upon working with as few distractions as possible, Genesis chose to cut itself off entirely from the "outside world" and took over the rambling pile of Hedley Grange, where Led Zeppelin had hatched some of its most shimmering moments—and where, very early on in the process, Genesis decided its next move would be a full-blown concept album, a full circle return to the summer of 1968 and the creation of *From Genesis to Revelation*.

In the years since then, concept albums had taken something of a battering, musically and critically. From the Kinks' serial attempts to epitomize the genre with Ray Davies's increasingly personal journals of insecurity and neuroses; to the four-side sprawl of Yes's *Tales from Topographic Oceans*, a musical reinterpretation of Jon Anderson's latest mystic bedside reading; from the sex 'n' drugs 'n' suicide soap of Lou Reed's *Berlin*; to the apocalyptic pulp sci-fi of David Bowie's *Diamond Dogs*; the very phrase *concept album* was capable of striking genuine fear and horror in the soul of an entire generation of rock fans—the generation that would, within a couple of years, be lighting the first pomp-deflating fires of punk rock beneath the bloated corpse of all that rock 'n' roll had become.

Those flames had yet to be ignited as Genesis convened amid the atmospheric semidereliction of Hedley Grange to begin planning its contribution to this canon. But already the band was aware that it needed to tread carefully through the mine-field that stretched out before it, to conjure an album that not only told its story in song but that made certain those songs were themselves capable of withstanding scrutiny in their own right.

The impetus behind the concept was Gabriel's, the tale of a young Puerto-Rican street tough who, having first encountered the unusual sight of a lamb reposing in the middle of Broadway, is catapulted through a series of increasingly surreal events, encounters, and medical mishaps. Although Gabriel's venture into screen-writing had thus far come to naught, still he was fascinated by the long-form story, and if Hollywood was not yet ready for his literary vision, rock 'n' roll surely was. That Genesis had never previously turned an entire album's worth of lyrics over to one writer was of no concern—as Gabriel was prone to remark, how many great novels can you think of that were written by five different people?

While Gabriel busied himself with the story, his bandmates turned their attention to setting it all to music. There was room for collaboration, of course, although more often than not it occurred when the time came to marry lyric to music. For the four musicians, much of their composition came about through improvisation—musical sequences, as opposed to songs, were hatched and granted titles that are themselves as evocative as any "unreleased" numbers in Genesis's early canon: "Pharaohs" (soon to become "Fly on a Windshield"), "Victory at Sea" ("Silent Sorrow in Empty Boats"), "Sexsong" ("Counting Out Time"), and, best of all, "The Evil Jam" ("The Waiting Room").

There was time, too, to look back to the group's earliest days, as Banks and Rutherford pulled "The Light" out of the memory banks, reworked it to form the basis for "Lilywhite Lilith," and then returned to the aborted 1970 TV documentary soundtrack for the hymnal beauty "Anyway," a song that would readily have graced the *Beyond an Empty Dream* collection.

Moments of sublime majesty evolved. The grinding rock of "Back in New York City," the eerie "The Carpet Crawlers," the surreal "Counting Out Time"—while Gabriel documents his hero's first, unfortunate encounter with the opposite sex, Steve Hackett lets rip a

> "I was trying to play a cross between Django Reinhardt and a hobbit."

guitar solo that sounds, for all the world, like a symphony for kazoos, feeding back through a comb-and-toilet-paper. "It's a guitar played through a Synthi-High Fly," Hackett reported 30 years later, as he awaited the release of a spectacular new 5.1 Surround Sound remix of the album. "I can't remember who makes them—I used to have one; it was very good and it broke. But it was something that made a very off sound. I was trying to play a cross between Django Reinhardt and a hobbit."

If anything distanced *The Lamb Lies Down on Broadway* from its predecessors, however, it was its setting and its language. Assessing the band's stateside impact for *Melody Maker* in mid-1974, journalist Peter Jay Philbin insisted that the appellation most frequently applied to Genesis in that country was "English"—not in terms of mere geography but as a tangible description of its very sound and energy. "The settings, characters, word choices, and puns that populate Genesis's songs exhibit an English consciousness, the height and consistency of which are unique…[an] ultra-Englishness [that] brings an unmistakable brand of personality to material of remarkable universality…" and so forth.

Of course it was an imagery that Gabriel firmly seized upon with the Britannia costume, imprinting it even deeper into the watching psyche, while the group's very love of lyrics was itself an extremely English (or, more accurately, *British*) pre-occupation. At the lowest common denominator, American acts of the period liked to rock and roar, and the less words there were to trip over, the better. British bands, on the other hand, frequently sounded as though they'd swallowed a dictionary and then washed it down with a thesaurus.

The Lamb Lies Down on Broadway eschewed all that. From the opening moments in an early morning Times Square, Genesis had firmly relocated to the other side of the pond, and just one example of Gabriel's lyric provides evidence of the group's success. He grew up in a land where cars have windscreens, and they drive on motorways. But now he was singing of a fly "…waiting for the windshield on the freeway." A great image in a foreign language.

"New York City was a conscious setting," said Gabriel, "because it was important for the main character to be earthy, to have certain blemishes on his character that could be whole and identifiable when taken into a fantasy situation. What fascinated me about New York was the speed of the city, and the fact, too, that class origins broached to an English group would be less credible to an American New Yorker." There was also the possibility that an American audience would react more strongly to an American hero.

With the group recording as the material was written, what became *The Lamb Lies Down on Broadway* was completed in a matter of weeks—a far cry from the years that precocious rockers would soon be lavishing upon their precious recordings, and a far cry, too, from the protracted gestation that Genesis's peers, Emerson Lake and Palmer and Yes, were suddenly prone to bestow upon their creations.

It was this immediacy, even spontaneity, that gave *The Lamb Lies Down on Broadway* so much of its appeal, both at the time and, as Phil Collins confessed, 25 years later. Of all Genesis's albums to date, he said in 2001, *The Lamb Lies Down on Broadway* remained his favorite. "You can't listen to it all in one go, well I can't…but there's a lot of music that was improvised, and I couldn't tell you what was going to happen next, unless I listened to it three or four times. So, in terms of listening to something and being surprised by it, I think *The Lamb* would be my favorite."

Steve Hackett, contrarily, professed himself very disappointed by the finished product. "I felt at that time, there was a lot of things on *The Lamb*…which didn't particularly meet with my approval, and there was a very kind of claustrophobic kind of sound [to it] . . . and a haphazard thing. We had a lot of jam sessions and things which turned into numbers, and, in a way, it kind of lacked the discipline and accuracy which I was after in music."

From Hedley Grange, the entourage relocated first to what Gabriel called "a barn in Wales" to record with the visiting Island Mobile studio, then shifted back to London to mix the album and overlay some of the more intricate effects, including the battery of sound manipulations that the album credits refer to "Enossification"—provided, as the name would imply, by a visiting Brian Eno. "It was really more like gimmicky effects on a couple of things," Tony Banks explained. "He used that Echoplex, and he just wiggled it on the introduction to the whole album. He did the vocal effects on 'Grand Parade' and 'In the Cage.' But he didn't play anything; it was just effects. And it all happened the day I wasn't there. I was ill."

As so often happens in such situations, however, the group's involvement with Eno was not to end there. Eno was recording his own new album, *Taking Tiger Mountain by Strategy*, at the same studio, and when Gabriel asked how the band could repay him for his efforts, the visitor glanced over at Phil Collins and replied, "Well, I need a drummer." Collins laughed, "I got sent upstairs as payment."

Collins and Eno cut just one song together on this occasion, "Mother Whale Eyeless," but "it became a beautiful relationship." The fol-

"He was prepared to waste an awful lot of time and money just to find out what it sounded like."

lowing year, as Eno worked on the follow-up *Another Green World*, he invited Collins along to the proceedings, alongside bassist Percy Jones, this time for three tracks, and Collins later insisted that the Eno experience in many ways fed into what he hoped to achieve with the still-gestating Brand X. "It's the spirit; never mind the quality. Feel the width. I liked his idea of just getting people together and working off the top of your head. In Genesis, we used to know exactly what we were going to record [when] we went into a studio and who was going to play what, whereas with Eno I used to go in there [without any idea of what to expect]."

"I remember one classic; he gave us all a bit of paper, and we made lists from one to 15. Eno said 'No. 2, we all play a G; No. 7 we all play a C sharp'; and so on. So it was like painting by numbers. And it's that kind of bravery…he was prepared to waste an awful lot of time and money just to find out what it sounded like. He used to love me and Percy; we'd go in and run through our dictionary of licks, and he'd record them and make a loop of them. It's the attitude—'I don't really know what I'm doing; I'm not really a musician, but let's have a bit of fun anyway.' I thought that was great, and I still do."

The Lamb Lies Down… was originally scheduled for release in October 1974, little more than a year after *Selling England by the Pound* and just six months after the band came off the road. Such exquisitely balanced timing was not, however, immutable. Eleven concerts around the United Kingdom's largest theaters and stadiums had already sold out when Steve Hackett sliced into the tendon of his thumb, just days before the tour was to open.

The concerts were canceled, to be rescheduled for the following spring, and the tour launched instead in Chicago on November 20—only for the hapless Hackett to then break a tooth on a pretzel shortly before the show. Still receiving electrotherapy for his hand injury, he was now feeling the after-effects of a trip to the dentist as well. Equally damaging, delays at the record company ensured that *The Lamb Lies Down on Broadway* was still to be released as the tour kicked off, with alarming ramifications for Genesis's own intention of performing the new album in its entirety, "a great big lump of music and story," as Gabriel took to introducing it.

No more than three old favorites ("Watcher of the Skies," "Musical Box," and "The Knife") were being held in reserve as encores. Everything else would be new. Hackett admitted, "We were playing two hours of music that nobody knew. Including me. I [was] sitting on stage thinking, 'What's coming next?'" And though Gabriel expressed the wish "I hope the concerts work like a film," he knew it would take a lot more than hope to persuade an audience to treat them as such.

From every angle, the venture was a colossal risk, even for an act that was absolutely secure in its audience's love. The group's ambition was not, in itself, unique—the Who routinely performed *Tommy* in its entirety following its release. The difference was, *Tommy* had already been released. Audiences knew what to expect and already knew they loved it. For Genesis, for whom word of mouth still remained a far more powerful advertisement than the band's music and past reputation, it was truly sailing into the unknown, not only trusting onlookers to accept the new album on its own uncompromising terms, but also to accept that Genesis, too, had changed.

No more flower hats, no more bat wings, no more Britannia. The audience's first onstage glimpse of Gabriel caught him in nothing more outlandish than the leather jacket and jeans that were *Lamb* hero Rael's own uniform; and though the arrival of the megatesticled Slipperman an hour or so into the performance would put even the most bizarre past outfit to shame…a semishapeless mass of latex lumps and warts, from which Gabriel's limbs waved like a panic-stricken anemone and his muffled voice resonated with eerie darkness…still *The Lamb Lies Down on Broadway* demanded more from an audience than many artists would, or had, ever dared request.

Neither was Genesis to wholly succeed with its ambition—or, as it rapidly became clear, Gabriel's ambition. Nobody was happy about the full presentation that Gabriel insisted upon; many of the songs, Banks affirmed, were never conceived as live vehicles, and Rutherford publicly regretted the loss of so many older songs from the repertoire.

Equally disturbing was the very nature of the set itself, with the musicians seated in the shadows, leaving the bulk of the stage to Gabriel and the accompanying slideshow alone. "It was my least enjoyable period in the group," Banks later confessed. "A very fraught tour, the least fun of any tour."

Further pain rained down when it became apparent that audiences were neither especially impressed…nor impressive. As the U.S. tour wound on, ticket sales were sluggish enough to see gigs either downgraded to smaller venues or even canceled outright. American critics unfamiliar with either Genesis or the album professed themselves utterly baffled by the proceedings; fans, still acclimatizing to four full sides of new music, regretted that the tour came to their town so early.

Sales of the album were less discouraging. *The Lamb Lies Down on Broadway* made the Top Ten in Britain, and America pushed it as high as No. 41, a vast improvement on its predecessor's No. 70. And, when the year's statistics were finally tallied, they revealed a quite remarkable year for the group. Both *Genesis Live* and a reactivation of the five-year-old *From Genesis to Revelation* also cracked the *Billboard* Top 200 over the past 12 months.

The American tour at an end, Genesis launched its European tour in Denmark in February 1975, with the rescheduled British dates arriving in April. A BBC broadcast from the Wembley Empire Pool show, though abbreviated to just one hour, remains the most exciting of all extant *Lamb*-era live recordings; the Birmingham show ranks among the most heavily bootlegged; and the entire outing was a lot more successful than the earlier portents suggested. It was with spirits finally rising once again, then, that the group returned to the continent for one final spin through Germany, Spain, and France. What only the band members knew for certain was that it would be their final spin. Peter Gabriel was quitting the group at the end of the tour.

His decision had been building for close to two years, of course; it dated back to that flirtation with William Friedkin during the previous summer and beyond that as well. From the moment he donned his first costume, Gabriel had found himself becoming distanced from his colleagues, not only in the eyes of the group's audience and the press—that, as any frontman will admit, comes with the job—but also in the eyes of his bandmates. Not one of them was casting covetous eyes at his position, of course. But all four could not help but resent the attention that Gabriel commanded so effortlessly; they mourned the long-gone days when he was as anonymous as them and Genesis lived their life "by committee."

Gabriel first broke the news of his departure to the band a little more than a week into the American tour, over dinner during their two-night stint in Cleveland at the end of November. All agreed to keep the news to themselves until the last minute, but it was inevitable that rumor and gossip would slip out, to fuel a few musing headlines in the British music press. Late 1974 was, after all, the season of the high-profile splits…Mick Taylor had just walked out on the Rolling Stones, Mott the Hoople were splintering, and Ritchie Blackmore was preparing to depart Deep Purple. Now, though its tour still had months to run, Genesis looked like adding their name to that grim butcher's list.

Determinedly, the group kept their counsel, staging some of the *Lamb*'s most successful shows during that last run of gigs but well aware that the clock was ticking down fast. As they entered the final burst of concerts in France, every night

A stocking-faced Gabriel contemplates
"The Battle of Epping Forest."

brought a new edge of unpredictability, as the whispers of the road crew seemed set to unleash some new practical joke on the band members. Chris Adams was in the audience at the Paris Olympia to witness what he recalls as "a particularly cruel trick. At the climax of the set, [Gabriel] would run to a high riser at stage right, then the spot would sweep across stage to find him miraculously on the left hand riser. Really, it was a roadie who was wearing the same black costume, but on this [par-ticular] night, the spotlight flashed across to find the roadie standing bollock naked...and, when it leapt back again to Peter, there he was, staring in disbelief at his naked 'doppelganger'"

Yet when the end finally came, it was something of an anticlimax. All tour long, the band members' thoughts concentrated on the final show of the tour, in Toulouse, and the penultimate night, in St. Etienne on May 27, was just another gig to get through. And then the promoter announced that Toulouse was canceled because of poor ticket sales, and Genesis took the stage that night in a state of absolute shock.

"The spotlight flashed across to find the roadie standing bollock naked..."

They got through the performance on autopilot, still without offering the audience any suggetion whatsoever that they had witnessed Peter Gabriel's final show with Genesis…and, possibly, Genesis's final show ever. Or maybe there was one clue. As the band concluded their set, Gabriel produced a trumpet and blew "The Last Post."

CHAPTER TEN

THE ART OF IMPROBABILITY

In June 2000, at the Euro 2000 soccer championships in Holland/Belgium, the Czech Republic took on the world champions, France. The game ended 2-1 France, but for any watching supporters with an eye for irony (and who aren't too fussed about the spelling), one of the biggest headlines of the day came after the half-time break, as the Czech coach rearranged his team for the next 45 minutes. The highly rated defender Petr Gabriel was replaced by Fukal. And more than one old Genesis fan telephoned another to say, "Well, it's not the first time *that's* happened."

Peter Gabriel's departure was, if hindsight be our guide, almost welcomed by his bandmates. Tony Smith later insisted, "I always said you could virtually replace anyone in the band apart from Tony"…a belief that would be borne out by subsequent events. Steve Hackett acknowledged, "Pete's departure was liberating in some ways. A tremendous amount was lost, but the band ran more smoothly, there were less issues to be raised, less costumes…less complicated certainly." But still, he confessed, "The band was in crisis. The entire future was uncertain. You have to remember that Peter was very much the star of the band and, at that point, we hadn't decided internally that Phil was going to become the singer.

Petr Gabriel was replaced by Fukal.

"So, pretty much everyone in the band at that point got involved in separate projects." By the end of May 1975, Collins was preparing Brand X for its launch,

Rutherford was back alongside Anthony Phillips, and Hackett was working on his first solo album, *Voyage of the Acolyte*. "No one," as Hackett put it, "really knew what was going to happen with the band," so they just made certain that something else was going on beyond it.

Tony Banks, too, was considering breaking out with a solo album, writing furiously through that spring and early summer, but held back by the awareness that, if Genesis was to stand any chance of continuing, it was its next album that he should be considering—all the more so since he was clearly the only member of the group who was thinking in those terms. While his fellows busied themselves elsewhere, then, Banks diverted his attentions away from his solo career and began writing toward a new Genesis album.

According to the ever-watchful Tony Stratton Smith, the responsibility and, perhaps, the derailment of Banks's ambitions themselves became a subsequent source of some bitterness—"Nothing serious, nothing that to boil over, but I know Tony was unhappy about it. The problem was, and I believe Tony has said this himself, for much of this period, nobody knew whether there was even a band to be writing for. He was the only person who truly believed Genesis would continue."

The somewhat makeshift nature of the new material testified to this. Although by the time *A Trick of the Tail* finally appeared in spring 1976, there were few achingly empty spaces on the album, and there was little that truly represented a full band effort, either. Both "Mad Man Moon" and the magnificent title track were composed by Banks alone; other songs, including the near-metallic "Squonk," the contrarily gentle "Entangled," and the similarly themed "Ripples" were co-writes with just one other member of the group (Rutherford, Hackett, and Collins, respectively). Banks even revealed that two of the songs were rooted in instrumentals he'd written back in 1968.

"It could have been crap and then we would have been in trouble."

Only the opening "Dance on a Volcano" and the closing "Los Endos" were full quartet compositions—but it was there that Banks, at least, claimed to find the most adventurous music on the entire album. Based around a somewhat dreary demo that was kicking around the studio throughout much of the summer,

"Beloved Summer"/"It's Yourself," "Los Endos" spontaneously developed into another jazz-tinged workout that, filed through a clutch of themes from elsewhere on the album, before pursuing a theme based around the climax of "Supper's Ready" to its most breathtaking conclusion. It was a staggering accomplishment—but the question still remained, would anybody ever get to hear it?

"The first week of writing *A Trick of the Tail* was...key," Mike Rutherford explained. "We went in without Steve who was doing [his] solo album...there was a question mark over what was going to happen, and the three of us went into Churchfield Road [in Acton, west London], and we had a great time. We wrote 'Squonk' and 'Dance on a Volcano.' It just sort of happened and sounded great. But we could have gone in and it could have been crap, and then we would have been in trouble. That was an important week, I think."

Occasional rumors did leak out of the Genesis camp, first of Gabriel's departure, then of the band's struggle to replace him. Collins later admitted that, no sooner had they heard the news than he and his bandmates "were making plans in hotel bedrooms." But what those plans may be, no one could say.

Nor, once the split was made official in August 1975, was either party willing to shed further light upon the severance. Boldly, Phil Collins insisted, "We're going to carry on as if nothing had happened," but even Gabriel's official press statement seemed uncertain, as he spoke of his need for greater artistic freedom, for wider-ranging experiences, for less time spent living the life of a "rock star," at the same time as confessing that he was not *detailing* the reasons why he left but actively still looking for them. Only one determination seemed set in stone as one read through his statement: "There is no animosity between myself and the band or management. It is not out of the question that we might collaborate in the future."

Gabriel also insisted that nothing sinister should be read into the delay in making the announcement, explaining instead that it was agreed upon in the hope that Genesis may have found his replacement by the time the news came out. In fact, there were other reasons for the silence, as Charisma continued clinging to the hope that some kind of cooling-off period might serve to change Gabriel's mind.

B&C, Charisma's parent company, had recently lurched into what the *New Musical Express* described as "crippling bankruptcy," a situation that simply wiped out several of the smaller labels under the company's wing and left Charisma itself gasping for breath. A new distribution deal was quickly arranged through the massive Phonogram combine, but for all the high hopes engendered by the label's most recent signings (space-rock veterans Hawkwind among them), Genesis was the only name on the label's roster that, again in the *NME*'s words, "were worth a financial light." Or, at least, it had been, and Gabriel admitted, "There were considerable incentives made for me to stay." But his mind was made up and, with it, Genesis's determination to continue on without him. Charisma's official statement continued, "They are now looking for a new singer. They have a few ideas, but nobody has been fixed."

In fact, the group had been actively searching for a new singer for several weeks by the time the split was made official; a series of ads running in the back pages of the U.K. music press let it be known that a self-proclaimed "Genesis-style band" were seeking a lead vocalist. They had also started recording, accompanied into the studio by David Hentschel, a friend and occasional sounding board since his apprentice days as a Trident Studios tape operator while Genesis recorded *Trespass*.

The auditions would take place as the sessions continued, with one of its more off-the-wall ideas suggesting that the album be recorded with a succession of different singers, an aural document of the auditions themselves. Unfortunately for posterity, it rapidly became apparent that few of the aspirants were even capable of carrying a tune, let alone helping to carry an entire LP.

Still, the hailstorm of hopeful cassette tapes that arrived in response to the ads would build up some genuinely delightful anecdotes, including one that involved a brightly accoutred transvestite turning up at the studio to perform a song called "I Got the Sex Blues, Baby." How disappointing that Hackett has absolutely no recollection of the event. "That I can't remember. It *must* be apocryphal; I'm sure I would remember. It must be some other band! We would have taken him on just for the novelty value."

Neither, if the rumor mill could be believed, was the transvestite simply a one-off. One George Gabriel ("Would you believe?" asked Hackett. "That was really his name.") offered his interpretation of the Beatles' "Norwegian Wood," but most of the tapes they received, Hackett condemned, were worthless: "You know, put it in, beep, 'Thank you,' off."

"We're not looking for a substitute for Peter who can do that kind of perfor-mance," Tony Banks told *Melody Maker*. "We want a good voice…a stage performer who can jump in at the deep end. Either he's got to have had some experience, or he's got to be a natural because he's going to be thrown on stage in front of sever-al thousand people a night." Unfortunately, even among the proven performers, the group's search for Peter-like perfection proved fruitless.

Kim Beacon, a latter-day member of the String Driven Thing, was recruited after Chris and Pauline Adams left the band; one-time Manfred Mann guitarist Mick Rogers and singer-songwriter Nick Lowe, recently solo following the breakup of Brinsley Schwarz, numbered among the 50-odd vocalists lining up to be auditioned. But Phil Collins acknowledged that the only vocalists they liked were those that sounded so much like Gabriel that it would have been suicide to even try and work with them. Although backing tracks for much of the album were now complete, the band had reached an impasse so far as further advancement was concerned. When Charisma announced plans to release a Steve Hackett solo album in the fall, the pos-sibility that Genesis had completely fallen apart loomed louder than ever.

Recorded during June/July 1975, *Voyage of the Acolyte* had been germinating in Hackett's mind for several years, not necessarily as a solo album *per se* but certain-ly as an outlet for the compositions he was writing that either did not meet Genesis's requirements or songs that were abandoned outright. "There was one piece that Mike had written which we'd rehearsed as a band, round about the time of *Foxtrot*, and I was very disappointed that we didn't use it. So I said to him years later, 'I really like that piece…' and I had a long piece of music…'Would you mind if we put that on the end?' He said fine, he played on it, did a great version of it, and that was 'Shadow of the Hierophant.' I was very pleased with that at the time."

Other pieces dated from the *Lamb Lies Down on Broadway* sessions, as Hackett explained. "Although it was a double album, I think that creatively speaking every-body had surplus material, and in a way, we had kind of narrowed down the field of what material we were going to use. But…I found I was still writing material, but I didn't have an album to put it on."

Phil Collins, too, sat in on the sessions, drumming throughout and supplying vocals to "The Hermit," but any notion that *Voyage of the Acolyte* was little more than Genesis by proxy was demolished by the other contributors. John Hackett, keyboard player John Acock, bassists Percy Jones and John Gustafson, and vocalist Sally Oldfield, plus cello and horns from Nigel Warren-Green and Robin Miller, respectively, forged an eclectic lineup that was a constantly surprising rat's nest of musical convolutions, lush melodies, twisted time signatures, and dramatic sound effects.

Warmly received by the U.K. press, *Voyage of the Acolyte* climbed to No. 26 on the British chart in September, itself an impressive statistic that evidenced just how anxiously audiences were awaiting further developments within the Genesis camp. For the most part, however, the last months of 1975 passed by without any suggestion whatsoever that Genesis may rebound from its decapitation; in fact, it was looking more and more likely that it wouldn't.

> "That was the beginning of a certain type of Genesis song— depressing songs about women."

Brand X was up and running by now, as Collins, Jones, Lumley, and Goodshall, plus saxophonist Jack Lancaster, arranged to continue their acquaintance at Trident Studios in September 1975. There they cut seven long and generally unwieldy instrumental numbers, premiered in December when the group played its first live shows, opening for Jack the Lad at the London School of Economics, before headlining their own Marquee showcase. A full tour was arranged for January, and the Dec. 6, 1975, *New Musical Express* story announcing the outing was at pains to assure fans, "The participation of drummer Collins does not mean that Genesis have broken up, but simply that they are mainly inactive while…deciding whether or not to replace Peter Gabriel in the lineup."

There was, however, one major revelation. "They have already completed the greater part of a new album…with Collins taking most of the vocals, and it could be that they will continue to operate in this manner…."

"I really wanted to have a crack at [singing]," Collins later acknowledged, "but I wasn't about to ask. I wanted someone to ask me. Besides, I'd always sung harmonies before, and I wasn't sure if I had a ballsy enough voice to carry the songs."

Several people had already pointed Collins in that direction in recent months. Among the guests as Collins married long-time girlfriend Andrea Brett—she had sung alongside him in the Real Thing—Yes singer Jon Anderson was one of the first people to suggest Collins should take over from Gabriel; Steve Hackett recalled, "The first song I ever wrote for Genesis, which was 'For Absent Friends' (from 1971's *Nursery Cryme*), was the first that had Phil singing lead." Two years later, *Selling England by the Pound*'s "More Fool Me" brought the diminutive drummer a second showboat, and "that," said Hackett, "was the beginning of a certain type of Genesis song—depressing songs about women."

Now Collins was to step out again, although when he did finally take the initiative, it was impatience, rather than need, that pushed him into action. Rehearsing one of the group's new songs, "Squonk," with Mick Strickland, a singer who had already impressed them enough to be worth a second chance, Collins sat through a singularly *un*impressive rendering, spent the night considering the group's position, and then turned up the next day to announce that he fancied a try.

He'd already been scheduled to sing one of the new songs, the languid ballad "Ripples." But, as they worked verse by verse through the riff-laden "Squonk," and Collins drew on vocal reserves that even he had never been aware of, a lightbulb flashed on above everybody's head. They completed "Squonk" and then tried another song. And another. And suddenly, the entire album was complete. The tapes were rolling throughout the process; song by song, producer Hentschel filed away another near-perfect take for future reference. By the time the band had run out of new songs, all knew that their next album was already in the can—with or without a lead vocalist.

"Gail and Strat were in despair," Chris Adams remembered. "They had spent years trying to break the band, and now, on the eve of what should have been payday, the star had quit." Hearing Collins's first tapes, however, their mood brightened. "When those first tapes with his voice were played, Gail was over the moon. 'He sounds so much like Peter!' Not surprising really, as Phil had double-tracked him on stage and in the studio for years, and though his voice had a quality all of its own, he had learned his mentor's phrasing well.

His own band, Adams continued, "had all been ambivalent about the early Genesis stage act, with the accent on 'repeating the record verbatim.' Gabriel was a huge talent, a strange haunting presence, but sadly he was tied to a bass drum [a hangover from his drummer days], and with Hackett and Rutherford seated, the only movement on stage was the whir of Collins' arms. Boy did he overplay! But then, after he became the singer, suddenly the drums stuck to keeping time!"

Peter Gabriel, breaking his self-imposed silence for a *New Musical Express* interview toward the end of the year, spoke only passingly of his old friends' activities. "From what I've heard, there's some good stuff going on, far better recorded than before. I never felt we captured our live energy on record." Word that the new material was a lot more song oriented had already reached him and he admitted, "I think they're overcompensating for me by doing fewer instrumental passages, which isn't the best idea—though I'll probably be slammed for saying so. [But] as long as Phil does the singing it'll be alright; he sings a lot like me."

Hackett agreed with Gabriel's concerns, acknowledging, "I think the band was falling between two stools, really. On one hand, you had this rock symphonic approach, and on the other, you had the pop-song sensibility that they really embraced after the departures of Peter and myself. But it was the earlier period that attracted me more, the kind of musical odyssey where a song would start out, and you weren't really sure where it would end up after everyone had contributed a little bit to the writing of it. A five-man writing team produces some very strange, quirky, unlikely twists and turns, and I think the idea of the musical journey was made possible by each of us running with the baton, writing almost as if it was kind of a relay race."

A Trick of the Tail encapsulated both the promise and the doubts wrapped up in Hackett's remark, and tapes of the completed album hit Charisma like a landslide. Nobody doubted that Genesis had pulled it off—whatever "it" may be. Long before the album's release, visitors to the label offices found themselves assailed by its strains, tapping their toes to the catchier numbers, and it depended entirely on the office staff's mood whether visitors were actually told what they were hearing—or whether they believed it when they were told.

A decade later, Stratton Smith told *Details for Men* magazine, "I don't think there was a single vote in favor of Phil initially, but that changed within six weeks. As far as the writing went, I took the view—as, I suspect, did other members of the band—that Phil may not be adequate. As regards the singing, I had an extraordinary feeling that we were doing something a tiny bit dishonest, in that Phil's voice sounded so similar to Peter's. I think Phil was a far more skilled actor than anybody had given him credit for, and sitting and playing behind Peter for so long, there was a kind of unconscious wish to do it the way Peter did."

In another interview, he confirmed, "Phil did sound just like Pete. A lot of people said that, but what they didn't realize was, a lot of the time, he *was* Pete...he sang a lot of backup in the early days, harmonizing behind Pete, so what people thought was Peter Gabriel alone was actually the two of them." Removing one-half of the equation was instantly noticeable—for all his subsequent success and the wealth of plaudits that have descended upon Collins in the years since he took the microphone, the drummer's voice possessed little of the power or expressiveness that was (and is) Gabriel's forte; it possessed little, too, of the personality that would allow him to take the most preposterous lyrics and transform them into something of intensely deep meaning.

That failing (if such it is—a lot of people actually prefer Collins's voice) was most apparent on another Banks/Collins co-write, "Robbery, Assault, and Battery." In and of itself, the song should have followed effortlessly in the footsteps of past Genesis story epics "The Battle of Epping Forest," "Get 'Em Out by Friday" and "The Return of the Giant Hogweed." Instead, it was universally proclaimed the weakest track on the album— *not* for any failings within the song itself but because Collins's delivery simply could not convey any sense that he was at all involved in the unfolding drama. It is to Collins's credit, then, that songs such as this were the first to be dismissed from the Genesis arsenal as he settled deeper into his role...the next album's equally execrable "All in a Mouse's Night" sadly notwithstanding.

> "Everything was a lot quicker, because there were [only] four mouths instead of five."

Elsewhere, however, the transition was seamless, conjuring moods that were not too far removed from the peaks of *Selling England by the Pound* while retaining musical structures that dated back to *Trespass*—a new beginning that sensibly drew its impetus from the past. There are few more heart-stopping moments in the Genesis canon, for example, than that unfolding as the near-orchestral coda of "Entangled" gives way to the pounding clatter of "Squonk" while that latter song's semimythological subject matter itself bleeds easily into past Genesis sagas. "A

Trick of the Tail," too, is a remarkable song; it is another mythology but one that is so readily fed into a pop-toned format that, of all the possible futures that *A Trick of the Tail* laid bare, the smartest money would surely (and most accurately) have rested there. "It [was] very easy working with the four of us," Collins told BBC DJ John Peel as the sessions came to an end. "Everything was a lot quicker, because there were [only] four mouths instead of five."

Having confirmed that Genesis could continue to exist in the studio, however, the group still needed to address the live question. Singing drummers, although scarcely a rarity by the mid-'70s (the Eagles' Don Henley and 10cc's Kevin Godley were just two of the principal exponents of the art at that time), were nevertheless bound by considerable strictures, the most potent being the sheer physical gulf that exists between the two disciplines.

Collins was not unaware of the problem. Just as Gabriel's vocal had proven impossible for any outsider to replace, so was Collins's drum style equally individual. There was, Collins was convinced, only one player who could possibly fit into his shoes—the same player that he had set out to emulate during his own musical apprenticeship. The fact that Bill Bruford was now occasionally playing alongside Collins in Brand X eased the transition even further—Bruford recalled one conversation with Collins when, in response to another moan about not being able to find a singer, Bruford suggested, "You sing, and I'll play drums."

There were other points in Bruford's favor, not least of all the massive support that he enjoyed throughout the progressive-rock cognoscenti. His stints with Yes and King Crimson were legendary—so much so that, once he had slipped into Genesis and it hit the road in March 1976, the calls from the audience suggested that great swathes of the crowd had come along simply to be in the presence of the master.

The post-Gabriel Genesis made its live debut in April 1976 in London, Ontario, at a 400-capacity club that—by the time the group came onstage—had somehow contrived to cram nearly 2,000 curious onlookers into the room. For more-than-obvious reasons, the largest part of the set was concerned with *A Trick of the Tail*; for fans hoping to experience even a frisson of the fantasies that had once been Genesis, however, there would be little room for disappointment. "As soon as I'd started, the audience was so warm," Collins recollected of that first gig. "They must have known how nervous we were all feeling. [But] after the first tune everything settled down, and it was fine."

The band had already made it plain that there would be no room for the costumes and disguises of old—Collins admitted that one of his pet peeves about Genesis's past incarnation was the frustrated knowledge that, "watching Peter rushing around on stage in his costumes, a lot of the songs just weren't getting heard properly." Over the years to come, Collins' most extravagant concessions to the songs' visual demands would be to put on a raincoat or juggle a hat.

Yet, without ever threatening to eclipse his predecessor, Collins made a more-than-palatable stab at "Firth of Fifth," "I Know What I Like," "Watcher of the Skies," a monster medley of highlights from *The Lamb Lies Down on Broadway,* and, catching entire audiences off guard on a nightly basis, "White Mountain" from the *Trespass* days, and "Supper's Ready" in its bombastic entirety. Stunning everyone who doubted whether Genesis could ever have pulled such constructions off without the added distraction of Gabriel's theatrics, an audience was now germinating that would soon wonder why they'd ever even needed the guy with the flower-top face mask.

In truth, and the cold light of later days, one would not dare try to compare Collins's interpretations of "classic" Genesis material with his predecessor's; too prone to lapse into silly voices, too likely to litter the lyric with

> "A lot of the early Genesis stuff was surreal sci-fi fantasy escapism, and I can't listen to it."

extraneous "yeahs," "heys," and "ohs," Collins—for all his childhood acting experience—was never going to make the likes of "The Knife," "The Lamb Lies Down on Broadway," or, again, "Supper's Ready" his own.

Listen to Gabriel's version of "The Musical Box"; forward to the brief, pregnant pause that bisects the lyric "now seems so…far from me"; the menace and momentum in that simple silence is simply spellbinding. Collins, performing the same song, scarcely even seemed aware of its existence. It was not his fault, of course; he was neither trained as a singer, nor as he later confessed, was he an especially conscientious one. He later confessed, "Before I started singing, I really didn't care about the lyrics. It was the sound of the voice, the groove of the tune. Then I started singing, and I realized the voice is the thing that communicates to people.

[But] I felt like I was playing a part sometimes, rather than being me. Even singing my own lyrics, I wasn't really me."

Later still, he confessed, "A lot of the early Genesis stuff was surreal sci-fi fantasy escapism, and I can't listen to it. I'm not a big fan of our past. When I listen to an old Genesis record, nine times out of ten, I tend to be embarrassed by it." The idea of actually having to voice those songs, then, was one he resisted, even though he knew there was no choice; "Supper's Ready" in particular, was a task he dreaded. "I was asked to [sing it]," he explained with sly emphasis. "It was *suggested* that I sang it."

Collins's misgivings aside, it is unlikely whether *any* singer could have truly made a success of the mission, so exquisitely built around Gabriel's vocal mannerisms were the songs in question. Yet, what alternative did the band have but to play them, and Collins but to sing them? It would be several years before the post-Peter Genesis would even begin to have sufficient material of its own to fill a full concert, songs that were written with Collins' talents and tonsils in mind, and it would be some time after that before audiences would come along without expecting at least a handful of blasts from the past. In the meantime, then, everyone would just have to make the best of it.

Which, of course, they did. With Richard MacPhail returning to the road crew for the first time in three years, Genesis remained on the roads of North America through April and into May 1976; June and July then returned them to Europe. Audiences on both continents were ecstatic; having been forced to all but write the band off when Gabriel fled, crowd were now witnessing a rebirth that few could have predicted—one that, in some ways, threatened to overshadow any past incarnation.

Though the group would be returning to the studio in August to begin work on their next album, the penultimate shows of its British tour, in Glasgow and Stafford, were both filmed—and, this time, the ensuing movie would not be left to rot on the shelf. As a visual spectacle, *Genesis in Concert* may (as if the point needs to be made again) have suffered in comparison with its unseen forebear, a point that director Tony Maylam seemed curiously aware of as he draped the raw footage with a wealth of extracurricular attractions and footage. But musically, it caught Genesis at the unlikeliest peak of its career so far, and the most successful.

Around the world, *A Trick of the Tail* had become its fastest- and biggest-selling album ever.

"I was surprised how easy it was for us after *A Trick of the Tail*," Tony Banks mused. "People had always behaved toward the group as if Peter was Genesis. We made one album without him, and suddenly it wasn't a problem." Steve Hackett, too, was taken aback by the alacrity with which audiences had accepted the change and the sudden ease with which Genesis's career was apparently unfolding. Whereas Banks remained grateful for that, however, Hackett found it beginning to gnaw at him.

CHAPTER ELEVEN

ANCIENT ASSOCIATIONS
LINGERED ROUND MY HEART

Off the road in early July 1976, the band members' attentions necessarily flew in whichever fresh directions they could. The activities of the previous summer had awakened each of them to the fact that it was possible to juggle both the group and a side career, and Collins and Rutherford, at least, were both to take advantage of the knowledge.

For the drummer (he left the microphone at home), that meant a return to the pastures of Brand X. *Unorthodox Behaviour*, the group's first album, was released in summer 1976, and British Genesis fans of a certain age may well remember how they spent one Saturday afternoon that June, waiting for BBC Radio DJ Alan Freeman to premier one track from the ensuing *Unorthodox*

> "I don't think you'll find I will be using Phil Collins again."

Behaviour album, "Walking on Three"—and how shocked they were at the decidedly un-Genesis qualities of it all. Now the quartet was ready to begin planning its next album, the punningly titled *Moroccan Roll*.

Rutherford, too, returned to former pastures, as he hooked up once again with Anthony Phillips, to determinedly wrap up the ever-elongating sessions for the guitarist's proposed solo album. *The Geese and the Ghost* would finally be released in 1977 through Charisma's Hit and Run publishing wing's eponymous label and quickly emerged an album that allowed listeners to take an alluringly

Collins does the Conga, 1977.

sideways peek into what may have been Genesis's future, had he not departed following *Trespass*.

Rutherford dominated the ranks of co-conspirators, but there were credits, too, for Steve Hackett's flautist brother John and for Phil Collins, summoned from those earlier sessions to handle "Which Way the Wind Blows" and "God, If I Saw Her Now." If those pastures were familiar, however, much of *The Geese and the Ghost* pursued avenues that Genesis had all but abandoned following Phillips's departure—gentle acoustic melodies that may or may not resolve themselves into larger vistas, an astonishingly esoteric arsenal of instrumentation, and a lyrical direction that chased Genesis's occasional interest in history and mythology to its utmost limit. It was a lovely album, with Collins' performance on "Which Way the Wind Blows" seriously ranking among his finest-ever vocal excursions.

Sadly, Phillips quickly came to regret the drummer's involvement, through no fault of either player. "I don't think you'll find I will be using Phil Collins again, because I really think it is time to push myself away—and the Genesis comparisons are irritating. It is something I have to live with because Mike and I share a very similar 12-string style, but having Phil singing is asking for it. I mean, the fact that we did that before Genesis did *A Trick of the Tail*, and before Phil became lead vocalist, is quite incidental. People don't care about that. The fact that it has come out in this order makes them probably think that I used Phil because Phil was on the crest of a wave. Far from it; it was when Genesis was right in the throes of Gabriel leaving, but anyway there you are!"

The Geese and the Ghost did not chart—indeed, much of its British impact was dulled by the album's appearance as an American import (via the Passport label) some time ahead of its U.K. debut. But reviews were kind, coverage was generous, and the response was sufficient to ensure Phillips has remained active...even hyperactive...ever since, remarkably without even once setting foot on stage. Though he acknowledged, during a short American promotional tour in 1977, that he would "love to take this album on the road." He admitted, "I don't think it will happen for a while because it is going to need a lot of resources, a lot of backup, a lot of musicians. There would be no audience [either]. I mean, there would be a small audience, but the largest part of the audience would be made up of people that weren't really coming to listen to me in 1977 but the guy who left Genesis, and I think it would die."

Certainly he sold himself short—the vast corpus of both new and retrospective albums that Phillips has released since that time have proven his audience to be one of the most dedicated, not to mention single-minded, of the age. But Phillips has also proven so prolific in the studio that the stage would surely prove an unnecessary distraction. Neither, at this point, would he have had the time. Barely had he and Rutherford completed work on *The Geese and the Ghost* than it was time for the latter to rejoin his bandmates and continue confirming Genesis's rebirth.

Genesis relocated to the Netherlands in fall 1976, settled upon the Relight Studios in Hilvarenbeek. It was the first time this so-English of concerns had ever chosen to record outside England. But far from the distractions of London, far from the helpful suggestions of any studio visitors, *Wind and Wuthering* took shape.

The album abstracted its title from Emily Bronte's novel *Wuthering Heights*; and within, the "Unquiet Slumbers for the Sleepers…" and "In That Quiet Earth" coupling was named for the final line of that same novel, a literary mood that was maintained elsewhere across the album's highlights. The epic opener "The Eleventh Earl of Mar" stepped straight out of some lost Sir Walter Scott novel, and "One for the Vine" drifted through the same classical leanings that shaped "The Fountain of Salmacis," back in the *Nursery Cryme* days.

Equally excitingly, Mike Rutherford contributed the shimmering "Your Own Special Way," one of the loveliest love songs in Genesis's entire canon—and a song that was destined, three long years after "I Know What I Like," to bring Genesis its second hit single, albeit a lowly No. 43. (It reached No. 62 in America, Genesis's first-ever Top 100 entry.) The album itself, meanwhile, would climb to No. 7 in Britain, a distinct step backward from *A Trick of the Tail* but an easily explicable falter.

Throughout the previous year, Britain's London-based music press had been championing a new musical movement, punk rock, spearheaded by four ferocious young iconoclasts called the Sex Pistols. Building their musical appeal on the twin foundations of adrenalined garage rock and a ferocious dislike of rock's monumental past, these punk rockers remained reasonably inconsequential in mainstream terms, even after the Pistols landed a record deal with EMI. It was December 1976 before punk rock finally broke out of the underground, catapulted into daylight by the Pistols' tastily profane appearance on a London television magazine show; by the end of the month, punk and its precepts were adopted by kids up and down the country—and, amid those precepts, there came an echoing loathing for bands whose latest word had once been regarded as a sermon from the mount.

Overnight—as Santa began filling that year's Christmas orders—the face of British rock was transformed. Albums that had seemed sure-fire stocking stuffers in late November were all but remaindered by early December, and the new year's release schedules—once bloated with the promise of new albums by Yes, Emerson Lake and Palmer, Jethro Tull, and Elton John—now creaked beneath the threat of the same. An entire generation of record buyers had changed musical horses in midstream, and Genesis, the first of the so-called heavyweights to wade into the ensuing turmoil, would also be the first to feel the sting.

The drop in temperature was apparent from the outset. Reviews of *Wind and Wuthering*, where they would once have applauded Genesis's ability to maintain its proven course, now condemned its refusal to move with the times…regardless of the fact that those times had themselves started moving only a couple of weeks earlier. Then, with the album still reeling from the critical barbs that porcupined its flesh, the group's once much-anticipated return to live action, with three sold-out nights at the London Rainbow, were attended not with excitement but with impatience…get out of there early enough, and you'd still have time to hop the tube into central London to catch the opening night of the new punk nightclub, the Roxy.

Of course, there were still a lot of people who didn't care about anarchy, anger, and one chord thuggery, and Phil Collins remembered, "You could go to our provincial dates and see people with AC/DC badges, Megadeth, or whatever…Nazareth…." And they remained loyal. Similarly, if Genesis was even aware of the conundrum that punk apparently dealt it, its live show did not let on. It was just as grand, just as bombastic, just as technically brilliant as ever. And, if you looked carefully, just as adventurous.

Bill Bruford had moved on, to link with Roxy Music's Eddie Jobson and Uriah Heep's John Wetton as a new rock supergroup, UK. Looking to plug a hole at the back of the stage, Genesis could probably have had its pick of rock's percussive leviathans. Instead, they looked toward the jazzy pastures opened by Brand X and echoed by the last album's "Los Endos" and the new set's "Wot Gorilla?" and they drew in former Frank Zappa/Weather Report drummer Chester Thompson.

It was another Weather Reporter, bassist Alfonso Johnson, who made the intro-duction. A close friend of Collins's, Johnson "really liked *A Trick of the Tail*," Thompson explained. "We were traveling through Europe, and he would always play that album." When the call from Collins came, then, Thompson could already guess what would be required of him, and he jumped at the opportunity.

Yet it was not necessarily a blessed decision. While Thompson was undeniably a great drummer, he was also a considerably less immediate one than either Bruford or Collins himself. What he lacked in power and spontaneity, he amply replaced with a precision that, as *Melody Maker*'s Chris Welch pointed out, occasionally touched perfection. Unfortunately, it did so at the expense of feeling. "This became all the more marked," Welch wrote of the first night at the Rainbow, "when Phil Collins finally ceased singing and returned to his [own] drum kit." Only then could the band truly "take off."

Peter Gabriel, too, was disappointed by Genesis's first show of 1977. He'd at-tended the Hammersmith show on the last tour and professed himself im-pressed. "But I was disappointed at the Rainbow...Chester was like a fish out of water. The feel wasn't coming through at all." Thompson would quickly find his place in the setup (Gabriel caught the show again in Bristol, three weeks later, and declared it "much better"), and he ultimately remained alongside them for the next 15 years. In the immediacy of 1977, however, even a hint of that future was still to unfold for Thompson and for his new bandmates.

> If he couldn't even bring himself to be diplomatically noncommittal when expressing a negative opinion...

The drummer detailed a rehearsal, very early on in his incumbency, when his colleagues played him a piece of music and asked what he thought of it. It was, Thompson enthused, "really bad..." meaning, of course, really good. But Collins, Banks, and Rutherford weren't even vaguely acquainted with the slang that Thompson took for granted and spent the next weeks convinced that the drummer was going to walk out on them any moment, so great was his hatred of their music. After all, if he couldn't even bring himself to be diplomatically noncommittal when expressing a negative opinion....

Neither was the miscommunication all one way. Thompson revealed, "The first time I toured with them made me realize just how different the English are. I'd be sitting in a room full of people speaking English, and I wouldn't understand a word of what was going on."

Revised only to allow the new album to shine, the live set retained all the favorites from last time, again including "Supper's Ready," a grandiose grind through "Lilywhite Lilith," and even a reprise for "The Musical Box." But journalist Welch's review condemned "Cold Genesis" regardless; and, though the remainder of the tour saw the first night's gremlins dispatched with more efficiency than past versions of the band might have managed, still there was a sudden sense of pointlessness hanging over…not only the tour, but the group's British aspirations as a whole.

Punk had come to destroy the Old Farts, or, at least, to pack them off to the United States, where the new music was never truly to find a firm footing and the dinosaurs could continue to graze supreme. With *Wind and Wuthering* already bound for a Top 30 berth, Genesis opened its own latest American tour in Boulder, Colorado, on Feb. 2, 1977, and having returned to London in July, to headline three nights at London's cavernous, 18,000-capacity Earl's Court Arena, the next close to three years would see the group play just one further British concert.

In purely iconographical terms, Genesis may well have been able to accept the change in temperature as a sign of the musical times—British rock changes its heroes like some people change wives. Punk rock, however, had one further cruel trick up its sleeve. For, even as its denizens rejected Genesis as another epitome of pompous, stodgy irrelevance, the returning Peter Gabriel was welcomed back as virtual royalty.

The past year had seen Gabriel stir only briefly. He had launched a writing partnership with songsmith Martin Hall—a contributor to the Colin Scot album way back when—and had already offered one of their compositions, "No More Mickey," to Charisma as a single. It was turned down flat, and Chris Adams remembers, going into Charisma one day to find Gabriel "sitting in the listening booth by himself, with his new stuff playing. He smiled that sheepish smile, as though to acknowledge that his place on the Charisma wheel had turned full circle. Later I found that Strat had walked out midsong to answer a phone call, a very obvious slight, at the center of what was a busy office."

A second Gabriel-Hall composition, "Get the Guns," would be recorded by singer Alan Ross in 1977; and a third, "You'll Never Know," became the subject of one of Gabriel's most unusual ventures.

Acting upon one of Tony Stratton Smith's more bizarre notions, May 1975 found Gabriel in the studio with veteran English comedian Charlie Drake, transforming "You'll Never Know" into a frantic novelty sing-along tailored to each of Drake's vocal strengths. Neither was Gabriel the only major name involved in the session. Recorded at George Martin's AIR Studios at London's Oxford Circus, the supporting cast included Fairport Convention's Sandy Denny, Phil Collins, and Percy Jones, jazz organist Keith Tippett, and Robert Fripp, who looked back on the venture a few years later and quipped, "This was arguably the strangest session of the entire era."

> "This was arguably the strangest session of the entire era."

Hall and Gabriel, meanwhile, talked wistfully of launching their own writers' collective, very much along the lines of Genesis's original intentions. "Some of my new stuff is very emotional," Gabriel told the *New Musical Express* late in 1975. "Genesis wasn't a platform for personal songs; you couldn't have a good dose of self-pity." He was also adamant, although he would "probably" record an album soon, "There won't be any heavy sell solo career, and I'm not going on the road yet, because that would defeat a lot of the objects I left the band for."

For a year, he stuck to those principles. The following spring, Gabriel contributed a magnificently distinctive version of the Beatles' "Strawberry Fields Forever" to the soundtrack of Lou Reizner's *All This and World War Two* movie—a somewhat audacious (but brilliantly realized) montage of stock war footage married to a wealth of specially commissioned Beatles covers. Rod Stewart, Roy Wood, Elton John, and some of the biggest names in rock threw their all into the project and emerged with some fine performances—Stewart's soundtrack version of "Get Back" even proved a major U.K. hit in late 1976. But Gabriel was not to allow the album's success to overshadow his own intentions.

"After I left Genesis, I wanted to spend a while completely away from the music business," he explained. "I needed time to look at things, to get into situations where I was something other than a focal point. So I followed up various interests—made babies, worked in the garden...."

Another line of thought found Gabriel interesting himself in psychic research, in particular the brand of new age investigation being undertaken in the United States by counterculture activist and mystic Ira "Unicorn" Einhorn and so-called mind doctor Andrija Puharich, a leading member of the mystic cult the Nine and one of the men responsible for bringing Uri Geller to the attention of the western world.

Master of ceremonies at the first Earth Day in Philadelphia in 1970, Einhorn was very much a pioneer of the cultural potpourri that is today labeled *new age*, and in 1973, he wrote a fascinating introduction to a new edition of Puharich's best-known book, *Beyond Telepathy—An Exploration of the Personal World of Your Own Mind.*

Gabriel was fascinated by the book—so much so that, in 1976, his then sister-in-law extended an invitation for Einhorn and girlfriend Holly Maddux to visit the singer and stay at his home. Gabriel and Einhorn then remained in contact for what Gabriel summed up as "a while after," but slowly, Einhorn faded from Gabriel's mind—only to dramatically re-emerge in 2002, when he named Gabriel among a litany of celebrity character witnesses in his upcoming murder trial.

In late 1977, Holly Maddux was reported missing. Eighteen months later, in March 1979, police discovered her decomposed body beneath the floorboards of Einhorn's apartment. He was arrested and charged with murder but, remanded on bail, fled the country in January 1981, shortly before the trial commenced.

Over the next close to two decades, his trail led investigators as far afield as Ireland and France, where Einhorn was allegedly then living under the names Ben Moore and Eugene Mallon; he was finally discovered in France in 1997, and following five years of extradition proceedings, the so-called Unicorn Killer at last returned to the United States.

Turning down an approach to help fund Einhorn's defense, Gabriel also refused to take the stand once the trial commenced in late 2002. Instead, an official statement from the singer angrily declared, "I resent the allegations or implications that I have been asked or have agreed to appear as a character witness in this trial, that

I funded Mr. Einhorn on the run, or that somehow I endorse violence against women." The following day, Einhorn was found guilty of first-degree murder.

卍卍卍

Around so many distractions, Gabriel continued songwriting, and summer 1976 saw him book into Trident Studios to begin demoing. The first sessions drew in the musicians with whom he was most comfortable—Anthony Phillips on piano, Mike Rutherford on bass, and Phil Collins on drums. But, from the outset, it was clear that the end result would never satisfy Gabriel. "It sounded terribly, terribly like Genesis," Phillips reflected, "and I thought…'hell, what's he gonna do?'"

What he was going to do was take the demos and flee to Canada with them, heading out to Toronto that fall, to begin recording with producer Bob Ezrin. There, with Ezrin pulling out every one of the stops he employed earlier in the decade, when the Baron of Bombast oversaw gargantuan albums by Lou Reed, Alice Cooper, and KISS, eight songs were forged into *Peter Gabriel*, an electrifying mélange of crunchy riffs, mordant moods, and mutant funk, shot through with everything from a barbershop quartet to the London Symphony Orchestra.

> "It sounded terribly, terribly like Genesis, and I thought…'hell, what's he gonna do?'"

It was Ezrin who picked the accompanying musicians, too—Gabriel acknowledged there were just three players he insisted on recruiting: Robert Fripp, synth player Larry Fast, "and Bruce Springsteen's piano player [Roy Bittan], who I'd rehearsed with in the past. However, he couldn't manage to play on the album because of Bruce's managerial problems, and needing to tour to make money, so I chose…Josef Chiowski."

Of this trio, Fripp was inevitably the name to attract the most attention. Close to three years had passed since the guitarist shattered King Crimson for what then seemed to be the final time, three years during which he had melted completely from view. His appearance on the Charlie Drake single was still a secret among all but his closest admirers; to the rest of the planet, he was already cloaked in the same kind of mythology as consumes other of rock's greatest recluses…Syd Barrett, Scott

146

Walker, Brian Wilson. But, if the news that he was stirring once more came as a shock, at least the person he was stirring for was not so great a surprise.

Ezrin's choices, meanwhile, included guitarists Steve Hunter and Dick Wagner, veterans of many of his past sessions, bassist Tony Levin, and drummer Allan Schwartzberg, a heavy-duty quartet that itself drove in directions that Genesis may never have conceived, which was the idea. "I've tried to get right away from Genesis and establish a separate identity," Gabriel acknowledged as he awaited the February 1977 release of his first, self-titled album. "I think...I hope...I've succeeded."

Even the record's title proved a touchstone—taking a listener phone-in on London's Capital Radio during the lead-up to the LP's release, Gabriel was asked why he chose nothing more gripping than *Peter Gabriel*. "I saw it on my birth certificate and liked the way it sounded," he deadpanned—and he was apparently telling the truth. *Peter Gabriel* became, incredibly, the first of four consecutive U.K. albums to share that title, a nightmare for record company publicists and fans who like making lists of their favorite records ("Whaddyamean, *Peter Gabriel*'s the best one? *Peter Gabriel*'s far better") but a rare sign of consistency in a career that would otherwise skew across the musical firmament.

Charisma scheduled the release of *Peter Gabriel* for Feb. 25, 1977, little more than six weeks after the fruits of Genesis's latest studio labors would be unveiled. And comparisons were inevitable. It swiftly proved, however, that they were also futile. In all but the most literal sense, Peter Gabriel was now no more the former singer of Genesis than Genesis was Peter Gabriel's former band. The musicians knew it, the music press knew it, the fans knew it. Few separations have ever been so skillfully enacted.

Nor have their end results ever been so diametrically opposed, as Peter Gabriel was afforded nothing but apparent goodwill as he stepped out of the shadows. Without necessarily conforming to the distinction that many fans have drawn between "good" (as in Gabriel-era) and "bad" (as in all subsequent lineups) Genesis, it was plain that the singer's departure had itself etched an indelible line through the group's career,

> "Gabriel went onstage with a cabbage on his head—and you didn't see that very often on *Top of the Pops*."

allowing the earlier material to somehow rise above its peers and attain a value that, queerly, escaped the wrath of the punk crowd altogether.

Singer-songwriter T.V. Smith, whose own band, the Adverts, was among the most prominent of all punk's sonic standard-bearers—its "One Chord Wonders" anthem said it all—explained, "Gabriel-era Genesis was accepted by the punks, because it was obvious that Gabriel was pursuing his own unique vision, that was nothing to do with the mainstream music industry—which was exactly what punks were trying to do.

"There was no formula to the stuff Gabriel was writing. You never knew where the songs were going, and they were full of bizarre, twisted lyrics far away from the traditional pop song. He went onstage with a cabbage on his head—and you didn't see that very often on *Top of the Pops*. But after Gabriel left, Genesis soon slipped into middle-of-the-road mainstream dross, just a bunch of musicians showing how well they could play, which is of course the total antithesis of punk." And, besides, "Phil Collins never appeared with a cabbage on his head, although it would have been an improvement."

Across the musical spectrum, Gabriel's "comeback" was viewed with appreciation, with the arrival of the album and accompanying single, "Solsbury Hill," afforded both extravagant reviews and grand sales. While *Peter Gabriel* effortlessly breached the Top Ten, "Solsbury Hill" lost no time in rushing to No. 13 on the U.K. chart, establishing itself in the process as the highest-charting 45 yet from the Genesis camp, as well as offering rock psychologists their own glimpse into Gabriel's departure from the group. "It's strange," Gabriel said of the song's success, "because at one point it wasn't going to be on the album." It gave away just a little too much.

Though the lyric itself is oftentimes mired in the oblique imagery that permeated the remainder of *Peter Gabriel*, still it was easy to isolate the key lines that culminated in an triumphant, and certainly self-exorcising, cry of "You can keep my things, they've come to take me home"—surely a reference to Gabriel's removal not only from Genesis but also from the theatrical strictures that had become so much of his persona over the past four years. Certainly there were none to be seen as Gabriel made his live debut in Passaic, New Jersey, on March 3, 1977, nor, a two-month tour of America behind him, as he made his U.K. return at the Hammersmith Odeon, over three nights at the end of April.

With Robert Fripp (or Dusty Roads as he preferred to be introduced) still on board, the spirit of Genesis itself was only fleetingly invoked, in a violent rendition of *Lamb*'s "Back in New York City." Although Gabriel also considered performing "The Carpet Crawlers" (and even, fleetingly, "Supper's Ready"—or so he told *Sounds*), he ultimately opted to fill in around the new material with one even newer song, the endearingly Chipmunk-like "Song with No Words," and a brace of covers: Marvin Gaye's "Ain't That Peculiar," rushing him back to his formative days as a soul freak, and the Kinks' "All Day and All of the Night." And, in front of a long sold-out Hammersmith Odeon, he could do nothing wrong.

A period fanzine, hammered out on a typewriter the day after the first show, captures the mood of the event—triumphant, light-hearted, and ever so slightly wry. "Backstage following his first solo London concert, at the Hammersmith Odeon on April 24, 1977, Peter Gabriel is signing autographs. One young man asks him to write something about goats—Gabriel obliges with a flourished 'Goats to you.' Another proffers a pound note: Gabriel returns it with the notation, 'This pound note is now officially worthless.' A third, a roughshod little man who looks remarkably like Phil Collins, steps forward—'Peter, will you sign my breasts?'; then, while a look of total surprise scoots across the singer's face, he produces a pair of novelty knockers from a plastic bag. Gabriel laughs and signs.

"Watching from the other side of the room, Mike Rutherford, Steve Hackett, and Tony Banks (but no Phil Collins…hmmm, maybe that *was* him?) smile to one another. 'What's the most outrageous thing you've ever been asked to autograph?' a lurking fan asks. 'Slide rules,' replies Rutherford. 'We sign a lot of slide rules.'

"He's joking (probably), but there's a certain truth to the jest regardless. Throughout the six years that they were together, Peter Gabriel and Genesis were a very far cry from the average rock 'n' roll animal. No rampant plaster-casting backstage shenanigans for these boys. Quiet, studious, intense…divorce their music from the increasingly absurd spectacle of Gabriel's on-stage costuming, and Genesis could readily have been the college band that earnestly rehearsed in the room next to yours', quietly filling the air with their classically inclined noodling and only really impacting on anyone when the Moog fed-back, a bass-pedal backfired, or, indeed, a slide-rule rattled.

"Photographs of the quintet only confirmed that impression. Beards and spectacles, cardigans and flairs, a towering beanpole at one end of the lineup, a diminutive shorty at the other. A lot of receding hairlines. True, one of the five would occasionally turn up disguised as a flower or a fox, or hover with gigantic bat-wings spouting from the sides of his head. But, if you looked closely, there'd be at least one pair of eyes directed quizzically towards him, as if to ask 'What's *that* doing here?'"

"They weren't even proper rock 'n' rollers, not by the standards of 70s excess, at any rate. Rock legend still chortles over reports of Genesis setting out on tour with their prepacked picnic lunches and never squabbling over anything more pertinent than who'd get the front seat in the bus. Tonight, however, Genesis are very much taking a backseat. Two years have passed since Peter Gabriel quit the band at what most critics assumed was the height of their success; two years during which his once anonymous bandmates have taken center stage while the frontman has sunk into total anonymity.

"We sign a lot of slide rules."

"But he resurfaced last summer with that odd 'Strawberry Fields (Forever)' and, as he said at Hammersmith, 'Actually, it all fell into place rather nicely. I thought. I've done the soundtrack, so I might as well do an album.' Then, 'I've done an album, so I might as well get a band.' Then 'I've got a band, so I might as well tour.'" It really was as simple as that, and that's how Gabriel intends keeping it. No fuss, no bother, no wardrobes full of outlandish costumes to drag from trench to toilet.

"But, when a fan asks Gabriel why he doesn't dress up for concerts anymore, the singer looks shocked, hurt, and, finally, indignant. He spent most of the show in a hooded tracksuit, the kind of thing you'd wear while jogging round a soggy park. The encores, however, were a real blast from the past, as he reached back to the peak of his old band's best play acting, and performed *Lamb Lies Down*'s 'Back in New York City' in full Rael drag…jeans, T-shirt, leather jacket. 'I was dressed up!' he protests, then turns in protest towards the Phil Collins character. 'You tell him.'

"'Phil,' however, is still trying to fathom out the straps on the back of his false breasts and merely grunts—a response that Gabriel politely echoes when, as he prepares to leave (a few steps behind Steve Hunter, who races from dressing room to bus without even a second glance at the fans who await him), he is asked whether there's any chance that the 'classic' Genesis would get back together again. 'I can't answer that,' the singer replied. 'I don't even know what time I'm going to get to bed tonight.'"

CHAPTER TWELVE

MURDER AT THE VICARAGE

The sessions for *Wind and Wuthering* were some of the most productive Genesis had ever undertaken, resulting in far more material than could comfortably have been fit onto the album—the lessons of *Selling England by the Pound* were not forgotten. To allow the excess material to simply rot on the archive was not an option, however. Instead, the band compiled three of the finest outtakes for release as a stand-alone EP. Stung, one may say, into action by its dismissal by the punks, May 1977's *Spot the Pigeon* EP saw the group eschewing many of the values that had hitherto been its trademarks and drive deliberately into the heart of the sharp, concise, and, most of all, electrifyingly energetic, pop song.

Forget the somewhat drab prison ballad "Inside and Out" and the Everyman documentary "Match of the Day" (named for a popular British soccer highlights digest), *Spot the Pigeon* was dominated by the frenetically quirky "Pigeons," a scientific discussion of the personal habits of, indeed, pigeons. And it is ironic that, in a year when the younger generation was professedly taking control of rock from the foul-mouthed grassroots up, it was Genesis that triumphantly carried a four-letter word the furthest up the British chart, as "Pigeons" pointedly asked who dumped so much "shit" on the home office roof.

Shocked, British radio preferred to treat "Match of the Day" as the record's lead track. But the very title of the EP left nobody in doubt how Genesis felt the tracks should be arranged. *Spot the Pigeon* climbed to No. 14 and, once its Rutherford-penned lyrics had been heard, only the Sex Pistols' patriot-baiting

"God Save the Queen," a dozen places higher up the chart, generated more controversy among those who would keep the airwaves as clean as our underwear ought to be.

" 'Pigeons' is fun," Tony Banks enthused. He seriously disliked "Match of the Day," he later admitted—"The lyric is just embarrassing." But "Pigeons" "…is interesting. It was really a little experiment to try and do a song around one note really. It's a good little song from that period. I like it."

Tony Stratton Smith was especially delighted with the single's success, pointing out to *Trouser Press* that it finally vindicated one of his most firmly held (but frequently disproved) theories that nonalbum singles and B-sides were vital to every artist's success. "The use of B-sides that weren't otherwise available was really a ploy in the early days, especially with Genesis. Genesis never had any real acceptance as a singles band, so the use of an unreleased or live track on the B-side was simply to get the Genesis following to support the single in its early days. And it worked…with 'I Know What I Like' and [it certainly worked with] the *Spot the Pigeon* EP. *Spot the Pigeon* made the Top 20…and we weren't even on the bloody BBC playlist."

> Genesis triumphantly carried a four-letter word the furthest up the British chart.

Following trips across the United States and down to Brazil, Genesis was back in Europe as *Spot the Pigeon* did its business, for shows across Germany, Belgium, France, and the Netherlands and that apparently valedictory return to London across June 23, 24, and 25. Supporting was Richie Havens, as Genesis repaid the old boy for his generosity to them, back in 1973, and Tony Stratton Smith smilingly remembered, "Richie was the only person who wasn't scared of having them support him. It was nice to be able to say thank you like that." (Havens would return to the group's orbit two years later, among the guest vocalists on Steve Hackett's sophomore solo album *Please Don't Touch*.)

Close to 60,000 seats were sold for the three London shows—proof that you can't always believe what you read in the fashion pages—with demand for tickets so great that Genesis took the unheard-of step of inviting Capital Radio to air a live broadcast of the last of the three. And why not? Although the bootleggers' tapes were certainly rolling all across the English south that evening, even the most hi-fidelity recording could not capture the true magnificence of the performance, as the light show rose to become an even vaster visual tonic than Peter Gabriel's most brobdingagian costume and the hitherto regimented Chester Thompson proved that six months of near-constant touring had done more than simply loosen him up. It also brought him a near-telepathic understanding with Collins, unleashed to absolutely stunning effect every time the pair lined up together at their respective kits.

Again, the critics compared the entire performance to gargling with a particularly anodyne antiseptic mouthwash. But in terms of sheer stagecraft, there was not a hair out of place, and, besides, not every industry observer felt so uncharitable. "At the same time as I was playing Peter Gabriel's first solo album on air," Boston new wave DJ Tony V enthused, "I was going to Genesis concerts. It was a band at the height of their musical powers, and the drummer, some guy who has also chased down a solo career, deftly moved from kit to front as needed. And his voice was quite good and emotional."

Having wrapped up the *Wind and Wuthering* tour with one final show in Munich on July 3, 1977, Genesis returned to Britain first to attend the premier of the *Genesis in Concert* movie, as shot the previous summer, and then to begin the marathon task of selecting material for the group's next release, the two-LP live album they had been stockpiling tapes toward for the past 18 months. Virtually every gig of both the Bruford and Thompson eras was recorded, and after all the gnashing of teeth and wringing of hands that had accompanied the gestation of Genesis's first live album, in 1973, this time the quartet was desperate for it to materialize.

For it was neither a document of the stirring rebirth that Genesis had undergone over the past 18 months nor a staggering indictment of every critic who predicted that Chester Thompson's time with the band would necessarily be short...of all the songs selected for the final album, only one number, "The Cinema Show," dated from Bill Bruford's sojourn. It was also—cue soap operatic cliffhanging pause—Steve Hackett's final album with Genesis.

Leaving the group was not a decision that the guitarist took lightly, either at the time or in later years. He reflected, "I found I [was] writing more and more things, particularly after *Voyage of the Acolyte*, and I felt, 'Now I've switched the tap on, I must not switch it off.' So, by the time we'd done *Wind and Wuthering*, I'd probably written as much material for that as I would for any solo album. And then I'd put things to one side and think, 'Well, the band aren't going to do this, but basically this idea is strong, and I'm going to use it.'

"Please Don't Touch," the unconscionably heavyweight title track to Hackett's second solo album, he explained, "was something we worked up as a band during that album [*Wind and Wuthering*], which became sidelined, even though I felt there were weaker things on the record." ("Wot Gorilla?" was one effort that he regularly singled out for condemnation.) Other new numbers, including the superbly bizarre Agatha Christie tribute "Carry On up the Vicarage," may have been less suited to the group but deserved an airing regardless. "Finally I felt, 'Well, this band is heading in a different direction; it's no longer embracing the spirit of fusion…real fusion, not jazz…and I don't think I want to go there.'

"I was writing more and more, but the band incorporated less and less. I had an abundance of ideas, but it didn't affect the overall ratio of Hackett songs to, let's face it, Tony Banks song." In fact, if one really wanted to start getting conspiratorial, there was even a sense abroad that some of Hackett's personal finest moments, *Voyage of the Acolyte* included, were already being subsumed into the Genesis Body Politik, as "In That Quiet Earth," one of the instrumental highpoints of *Wind and Wuthering*, pointedly lifted one of that album's most distinctive passages for its own.

> "This band is heading in a different direction; it's no longer embracing the spirit of fusion."

Hackett objected, he admitted, to his colleagues' growing interest in love songs, acknowledged that it clashed horribly with the fascination he expressed at one of his first-ever meetings with the group, eight years earlier, for "songs that had less to do with the mating ritual and more romances of other kinds—times, places, situations, stories." Indeed, of all that Genesis would lose once Hackett departed; it was the sheer romanticism of their music and lyric that was the most apparent, although Collins is adamant that it was replaced by honesty. "The guys were starting to come out and say 'I love you,' having had this repressed public school upbringing, when you didn't say things like that."

Even more crippling, however, was Hackett's belief that he was journeying backward in his career. "After having done a solo album, [returning to Genesis] was a bit like going back to school. Once you start to gain a certain amount of confidence, it's very hard to go back to being 'the new boy' and deferring to the other experts. " Still, his initial intention was simply to step out of the band on an occasional basis to record and release the material for which Genesis itself had no use. It should not have been a big deal—*Voyage of the Acolyte* proved that. But the success of that album, it seems, proved something else as well, that his fellows faced sufficient competition from their former members, without the current lineup adding to the barrage.

Phil Collins alone had no problem with his plan, Hackett found, "probably because he'd already got Brand X running, and maybe if I'd been willing to form a band like that, nobody would have minded." But he was already in one band. Why would he want to form another? He stuck doggedly to the notion of launching a solo career under his own name; Tony Banks and Mike Rutherford were cemented equally adamantly to their insistence that he shouldn't.

"I think there was a lot to be learned, then," Hackett admitted. "It's just that sometimes, the lessons that you learn tend not so much to come out of heated debate and argument, as much as periods of subconscious incubation that you have to go through in order to live with a potential idea for a while and let it develop. When you're young and fiery and you're doing a lot of gigs and you're tired all the time, it's 'For God's sake, can't we get a move on and do this?' Rather than…now, what happens is, my ideas don't come to me in a flash of inspiration, I get an idea for a time and I live with it for six months, or six years, then I realize what the next part of it is." In 1978, he was still young and fiery. There may have been a resolution to the stalemate of Genesis. But he neither cared to wait nor, more than two decades later, does he regret his decision.

The new Genesis live album, soon to be titled *Seconds Out*, was still in the selection phase when Hackett announced he was quitting, phoning the studio while the others were awaiting his arrival to announce that he wouldn't be in. And, though all three professed themselves utterly blindsided by his decision, it also freed them up to continue moving in the direction that Hackett apparently hated so much and abandoning all that they no longer had use for. Across four sides of vinyl, *Seconds*

Out marked the last hurrah for any quantity of old favorites. Only five tracks—a beautiful rendering of "Afterglow" and a brutal "Dance on a Volcano" among them—represented the group's recent endeavors. Of the remainder, it was farewell (or, at least, *adieu*) to "Supper's Ready," "Carpet Crawl," "Cinema Show," and *The Lamb Lies Down on Broadway*....

The split itself was as amicable as such things can be, but an interview Hackett gave with an American newspaper, in which he laid out his reasons for departing with a little more venom than may have been politic, would do much to sour both his own relations with the musicians he left behind, and—even after the personal misunderstandings were sorted out—the fans' comprehension of those relations.

"I have a tremendous amount of affection for them all," Hackett insisted in 2003. "I'm very proud to have worked with them. I don't think there ever has been a band that had such a strong collection of committed indi-

> "I came out sounding like I hated their guts."

viduals, who continued to work together for so long." But an interview in which "I came out sounding like I hated their guts" is a difficult obstacle to surmount, and there was a period, as many fans may testify, when remaining a Genesis enthusiast was transformed from a mere matter of musical tastes to one of literally taking sides.

If you followed Steve Hackett, you wanted nothing more to do with those other swine. And, if you followed Genesis, then the turncoat guitarist was *persona non grata*. It would be several years more before *Please Don't Touch*, Hackett's first post-Genesis album, and the wryly titled *...And Then There Were Three*, Genesis's first post-Hackett effort, could nestle together in the same record collection. And the fact that the former included at least a handful of tracks, and many more ideas and passages, that may well have dignified any recent band LP only compounded the schism.

Within the musicians' personal circles, meanwhile, Hackett's departure did more than further simplify the group's writing and decision-making process. It also allowed the surviving trio to sit back and take a long, hard look at what Genesis represented to themselves, to their fans, and to the world outside. And the first lesson that they grasped was delivered via Peter Gabriel's latest activities.

His second album, naturally titled *Peter Gabriel*, was already in the works, and, once again, it displayed the singer moving off on a fresh tangent, reuniting with the now-seemingly ubiquitous Robert Fripp to record an album of icicle angularity, alive with the tenets and notions of the new wave movement that was driving out of punk's once single-minded determination, and willing to take chances not only with musical formulae but with Gabriel's reputation as well.

Stark indications of the album's intent had already been laid out on the road. Gabriel toured Britain through fall 1977 with an almost wholly new troupe—with only bassist Tony Levin remaining from the last outing, former Leonard Cohen and Barry Manilow guitarist Sid McGinnis, drummer Jerry Marotta, and Automatic Man's singularly named keyboardist Bayette now accompanied him. The outfit may have been even larger—there was talk of bringing in an extra percussionist while Gabriel also spent three weeks rehearsing with former David Bowie guitarist Mick Ronson, before—as Ronson put it—realizing that "the material was great, but it didn't really need an extra guitarist."

This lineup would remain intact as Gabriel returned to the studio and, with the fall tour still ringing in their ears, few people lured into view by Gabriel's first album would have been overly shocked by what they encountered within his second. They would, however, be hard-pressed to recognize it. Where Bob Ezrin opened the songs wide to the skies and then filled the void with choirs, guitars and effects, Fripp screwed even the most expansive notion into a tight little ball and then dipped it into the most stygian textures.

Ultimately, it was not an especially successful partnership, as Gabriel conceded. "Fripp is probably still my favorite guitar player. But, as a producer, I don't think it worked too well; neither he nor I ended up that satisfied with the second album." They would try again, uniting for a couple of tracks on Fripp's solo debut, *Exposure*—titled for, and featuring a rerun of, one of the lesser tracks on the Gabriel album itself. But still that second *Peter Gabriel* cast a shadow of its own over the time and the place into which it was unleashed.

Even on paper, an album that opens with the ruminations of a hermit ham radio operator, closes with a high-rise suicide, and is sliced amidships by a paean to the "Mother of Violence" is scarcely guaranteed to be a bundle of giggles, and *Peter Gabriel* ultimately emerged so dark that its maker's former bandmates would have had difficulty identifying their old singer in there. The challenge for Genesis was to reinvent itself as thoroughly and, though it was never going to be easy, as courageously.

Leaving *Seconds Out* to hold the fort in its absence—it climbed to No. 4 in Britain, a remarkable feat for a double live album packed with familiar material—Genesis returned to the Netherlands.

The first business was to ponder how to replace the departed Hackett and draw up a short list of ideal substitutes. At the top of that list was Robert Fripp.

In every history, there is a moment where one can only begin to wonder precisely what may have transpired had the actors taken one course instead of another—if the Beatles had not sacked Pete Best, if Roxy Music never shed Eno, if Frank Zappa never destructed the original Mothers of Invention. Or if Robert Fripp had accepted Tony Smith's invitation to join Genesis.

Talking of a different Robert Fripp and a different Genesis altogether—the scientist author's *The Becoming: Notes on the Evolution of a Small Planet*—novelist John Fowles wrote, ""Robert Fripp's ingenious idea—to resurrect Genesis in the light of our present knowledge of evolutionary process—must, I suppose, count as a literary curiosity." Those words ring true here as well. Fripp, after all, is more than a guitarist, more than a songwriter, more than a musician. He is, in many ways, a life force of his own making—as Peter Gabriel mused, around the time of his second solo album, "He has a menace, and he's a 'coloring agent' that you can drop into all sorts of corners. He'll suddenly cast his little shadow over what he's doing and give it an edge that I like very much."

What kind of shadow would he have cast over Genesis, what sort of an edge would he have brought to the band? And what possible vision would his three fellows have been able to maintain (and, more crucially, come to represent), had he accepted?

Ironically, the King Crimson webzine *Frakctured.net* once ran its own "Alternate Futures" poll, positing a universe in which Crimson broke up in 1970, and Fripp found himself being offered three different gigs: with Genesis (as a replacement for Anthony Phillips), with Yes (stepping in for Peter Banks), and with Van der Graaf Generator (which had never bothered recruiting a guitarist in the first place). The winner, by some five to one, was Van der Graaf…. Genesis received just two votes.

And so it was in 1978. Fripp may still have been uncertain how he saw his immediate musical future unfolding. But he had no doubt that it did not involve joining an already established rock band.

Other names on Genesis's shortlist were equally optimistic. The great Jeff Beck was apparently spoken of as a possible replacement, the pioneering love of fusion that dictated his most recent releases clearly a deciding factor—Beck's latest album, a union with Dutch percussionist Jan Hammer, was among Genesis's own personal favorite recent releases. But the mercurial Beck had already turned down the Rolling Stones in recent years and was on the verge of changing his mind about fusion as well. Genesis could offer him nothing his own career was incapable of providing him.

Consideration was also given to the notion of switching Mike Rutherford to lead guitar and bringing in Weather Report's Alphonso Johnson as bassist, and, once again, one can visualize a very different Genesis arising from the combination, the legendary rhythm section of Johnson and Thompson reconnecting again to draw and drive the group into pastures that even Brand X's most fervent imaginings could never have achieved.

With lashings of hindsight, however, one can safely say that whatever may have happened with any of these projections, it would not have followed the course that Genesis did embark upon, and, for that reason, perhaps it is as well that the unions never occurred. By the time Collins, Banks, and Rutherford arrived back at Relight Studios to begin work on their next album, they were already confirmed as a trio. And they were already aware of what they needed, and wanted, to do.

In interviews of the period, all three acknowledged that the experiences of *Wind and Wuthering*, of running out of vinyl before they ran out of songs, had left them determined that the storming epic performances of old needed to be dispensed with, that numbers that may once have spread over eight or nine minutes should now be reigned in at half that length, and that the watchword now would be variety, not vastness.

Of course, if Genesis was to be measured by the sum of its songs, as opposed to the prowess of its passages, the group was only reacting, at long last, to the absolute rupture that punk and its associated offspring had forced upon the entire veteran community. It can scarcely be considered any kind of coincidence that no sooner had the full ramifications of punk been felt in the upper echelons of power...that is, in the months *after* Genesis released *Wind and Wuthering*...an entire army of artists that once believed bigger is better had cut back on their peregrinations.

Emerson, Lake, and Palmer, nailed by the media for the sprawling *Works Vol. One*, released just a few weeks after *Wind and Wuthering*, followed through with *Vol. Two*, concocted with indecent haste and devoted in its near entirety to three-or-four minute vignettes. Now that group was in Nassau, working toward a *Love Beach* album that would eschew the pomp and circumstance of old for all time.

Yes delivered the scratchy aggression of *Going for the One* and was now on course for *Tormato*. Jethro Tull rejected the sprawling concept epics of the past and drove into the short, sharp, belligerent folk of *Songs from the Wood* and *Heavy Horses*. Everywhere, acts that could once have been relied upon to plug at least one side of vinyl with an operatic behemoth, were pulling out the pinking shears and snipping away anything that didn't revolve around a verse-chorus-verse.

But Tony Stratton Smith insisted it was misleading ("and particularly Euro-centric") to wholly credit punk and its aftershocks for engendering this new discipline; 1977 was also the year in which the idea of scoring hit singles in Britain finally lost the elitist stigma that had clung to it earlier in the decade. Emerson, Lake, and Palmer, which had hitherto released just one U.K. 45 (1973's "Jerusalem"), sliced a catchy three minutes out of its marathon rendering of Aaron Copeland's "Fanfare for the Common Man" and made it to No. 2 with one of the most dramatic-sounding records of its entire career.

> And the girlfriends just kept on buying it.

Yes hit with both "Wondrous Stories" and "Going for the One." French synthesizer whiz Jean Michel Jarre, former Vinegar Joe vocalist Elkie Brooks, and multi-instrumentalist Mike Oldfield all threatened to become chart regulars. Genesis breached the Top 20 for the first time. Punk may have divided the overall audience for bands that did not fall within its catchment area, but it also polarized those who remained loyal to the old guard, sending them out in ever vaster numbers to prove their allegiance by buying anything that was offered to them.

Further indication of these shifting moods was delivered when, as Genesis prepared to stir for the first time since Hackett's departure, it chose to do so with a single, released a full month ahead of the LP itself. "Follow You, Follow Me" was a romantic ballad cast in much the same vein as "Your Own Special Way" but buoyant with effects-laden guitar, a hook-laden melody, a squeaky-clean synth solo and a once-heard, never-forgotten chorus that would, in short order, become an all-but inescapable mantra in the pubs, clubs, and last-dance discothèques of the land. And that, perhaps, was its crowning glory—a Genesis record that even girlfriends could like.

Producer David Hentschel, on the other hand, seriously disliked the song—so much so that, right up until the last minute, Genesis was unsure whether to include it on the album. Of course they did include it, and the song immediately repaid their faith as the single entered the U.K. chart on March 11, 1978; three weeks later, as "Follow You, Follow Me" hung at No. 18, Genesis broke the habit of a lifetime and made its first-ever appearance on television's *Top of the Pops*. The group was promptly rewarded with a ten-place leap up the chart. A promotional film (the term *video* was still a few years way from popular usage) was shot, a more-or-less straightforward live performance that remarkably utilized two Phil Collins's—one drumming while the other sang. And the girlfriends just kept on buying it.

"Follow You, Follow Me" ultimately peaked at No. 7, rubbing shoulders in those hallowed quarters with the Bee Gees, Showaddywaddy, Suzi Quatro, and the long-forgotten delights of Brian and Michael. It was an utterly unexpected triumph, and one that was only compounded as ...*And Then There Were Three* marched to No. 3, equaling the career best set by *Selling England by the Pound*. The American portents were equally hopeful...continuing Genesis's slow, patient, but apparently inexorable, rise through local affections, ...*And Then There Were Three* reached No. 14, its first-ever Top 20 album while "Follow You, Follow Me" made it to No. 23.

The (comparative) brevity of the songs notwithstanding,...*And Then There Were Three* did not wholly represent a leap in the dark for Genesis. Musicians so instrumentally distinctive as Rutherford, Banks, and Collins

"Ballad of Big" is almost punk in its punch.

were never going to throw away all that was tried and trusted—and that included their audience. It was what they added to the table, rather than what they took away from it, that was instructive, as Banks's banks of keyboards rose to acknowledge the latest synth technologies; as Rutherford, now handling both lead guitar and bass, unleashed some desperately fierce chords and riffs ("Ballad of Big" is almost punk in its punch), and Collins continued growing into his voice's possibilities. The song "Scenes from a Night's Dream" even boasted the first complete Phil Collins lyric since the unrecorded "The Light" back in 1971.

For many long-time fans, however, ...*And Then There Were Three* remains the point at which they and Genesis parted company for the final time. But their grumblings of betrayal, and the band's subsequent, hindsight-flavored acknowledgment that the album had little of the spontaneity and magic that hallmarked Genesis's best efforts, were effortlessly swamped by an entire new generation of fans, one that knew nothing of Hogweeds and Harolds but that knew every nuance of "Many Too Many."

CHAPTER THIRTEEN

THE CAVALCADE MOVES ON

Launching in mid-1978, Genesis's latest world tour was a marathon eight-month outing that cunningly crossed the Atlantic six times in all, as stretches of American gigs were alternated with European shows to reduce the amount of time the band members spent away from their families. Neither was that a mere whim—in financial terms alone, the logistics of transporting the lighting rig, widely touted as the most impressive ever seen in rock, were as immense as the setup itself. Six computerized mirrors, a shipload of lasers, and a set of Boeing 747 landing lights were only the most headline-worthy effects in the package.

Once again, a new face was on the road, as American guitarist Daryl Stuermer stepped out of Jean Luc Ponty's band to fill the Hackett-shaped void that now yawned there. Like Chester Thompson, Stuermer was recommended to Genesis by Alphonso Johnson; like Thompson, his background was in jazz fusion. And the first time they played together, the trio knew they had found their man.

Away from the flights of fancy that once lurked at the top of the group's wish list, American guitarists Pat Thrall and Elliott Randall were both auditioned for the vacancy. But though they impressed, they never intrigued. Stuermer, on the other hand, did both; he was just two songs ("Squonk" and "Down and Out") into his audition when Rutherford called a halt to the proceedings and offered him the job. And the ensuing tour proved the wisdom of Rutherford's intuition. No official recordings from Genesis's 1978 tour have ever been released, but the wealth of

Seconds out...Hackett takes center stage while his bandmates politely rage around him.

bootleg recordings floating around confirm the memory of the most seamless transition in Genesis's entire recent history.

Like Chester Thompson, Stuermer was a recent convert to Genesis. Although he acknowledged, "I used to listen to a lot of English bands like Procol Harum and King Crimson…I had just become a [Genesis] fan after hearing *A Trick of the Tail* and *Wind and Wuthering*," he explained. "Jean Luc Ponty played them to me, and when I heard Chester was in the band, it intrigued me."

Despite his flawed grounding in the group's back catalog, Stuermer readily absorbed all that he needed. Both across the

"You're a permanent part-time member"

Gabriel era material and the more recent cuts, Stuermer first replicated Hackett's trademark parts and then advanced his own personality across them—his performance during "Ripples" alone was sufficiently breathtaking to win a standing ovation every night, and the nostalgia-jerking medley of "Dancing with the Moonlit Knight" and "The Musical Box" that crept into the set during the third American tour in September/October 1978 was positively incandescent.

"At the first gig [I played], I saw a sign which read, simply, 'Steve Hackett,' " Stuermer recalled. "But after I was introduced, the sign came down. I was never given a hard time [by the fans], although I had expected it." By the time the tour was over, both Thompson and Stuermer were assured by Collins, "You're a permanent part-time member"—meaning, though they would never be called upon to contribute to the group's music in the studio, both would remain an integral part of the live Genesis experience for the next 15 years.

Other moments as the year unfolded confirmed Genesis's upward momentum. In June 1978, the band rekindled memories of those days out at the Reading Festival by headlining the massive Knebworth Fayre festival outside of London, and, a month later, as it wrapped up its first-ever visit to Madison Square Garden, it introduced the customary encore, "I Know What I Like," with a most unexpected special guest—Peter Gabriel.

If the truth be told, the rekindling itself was just a little anticlimactic. Clad in the same casual clothes that hallmarked his solo shows (as if he was going to drag out the old wardrobe just for one spontaneous encore!) and clearly less accustomed to

The man in the bulletproof vest—Gabriel onstage, flanked by Tony Levin and Sid McGinnis, 1978.

singing the song than he had once been, Gabriel looked delighted to be there…and just as delighted when it was over. If there was to be, as the press continued to murmur, a "Genesis reunion," clearly this was not a portent that could be taken too much to heart.

Set to launch in early fall, Gabriel's own latest tour would wind itself around much of the same territory as the concluding months of Genesis's outing, although never so close that the two entourages found themselves in the same city…or even the same state…on the same night. Neither, it was apparent, would either act's fans have especially welcomed any further intertwining of their respective careers. In keeping with the *Peter Gabriel* album that preceded it, Gabriel's live show now was a dark, uncomfortable affair, with even the opening voice-and-piano lilt through an unexpected "Me and My Teddy Bear" a discomforting experience.

> "I actually asked Townshend if I could join the Who."

Gone were the brightly lit broad strokes of opulent pomp and circumstance that characterized the 1977 tour dates, the near-orchestral cuts and thrusts that raised each song to anthemic status and filled the stage with brilliant glow. Now the musicians labored in near darkness while Gabriel was most frequently seated behind his keyboard, a stark contrast to the animated being who, just a year before, took his radio microphone on walkabout through the crowd.

There were moments of palpable excitement—the string-driven overture that led into "On the Air" created a genuine sense of expectation, and highlights from the first *Peter Gabriel* album were craftily staggered to ensure that the claustrophobia never grew too intense. But, even with the gloriously thrusting presence of saxophonist Timmy Capello honking through the proceedings, still the solitary introspection of "Flotsam and Jetsam," "White Shadow," and "Home Sweet Home" hung awkwardly over the crowds who arrived to witness the proceedings. And when the evening's highlights were discussed on the journey home, it was the genuine surprise of "The Lamb Lies Down on Broadway," a disrespectfully punkoid rampage through "A Whiter Shade of Pale," and that so-sweet but somehow sinister "Me and My Teddy Bear" that clung most favorably to the memory banks.

While Gabriel continued touring, Genesis finally came off the road in December, following its first-ever concerts in Japan, half a dozen gigs that were among the most hysterically oversubscribed the band had played. Some nine months stretched ahead of them before they needed reconvene, time that Phil Collins, at least, desperately needed as he tried to repair a marriage that, after just four years, seemed finally to have buckled beneath the weight of his career's demands. His wife, Andrea, had fled home to Vancouver, Canada, with the couple's children, Joelly and Simon, and Collins now relocated to that same city, in the hope of rebuilding so many shattered bridges.

For a time, while that hope remained alive, Collins seriously considered leaving Genesis. In 1992, he reflected, "I always wonder whether, if I had known that tour of 77/78 was going to break my first marriage up, [if] I would still have gone ahead with it." He was not to know at that time, after all, all that would subsequently emerge from that most shattering period—"I wouldn't have started writing songs, [for a start]"; rather, as he came off the road and confronted the void that now yawned where he'd left a family life, he could think only of attempting to repair all the damage. And, if that meant finding a new job, he would.

On Sept. 7, 1978, Keith Moon, the madcap drummer with the Who, died; now Collins, already undertaking some session work for Pete Townshend, was wondering whether he could replace the irreplaceable. The Who, after all, had long since settled into a schedule that thought nothing of punctuating albums with two-or-three-year gaps—a far cry from the all but annual cycle that still enveloped Genesis. Collins admitted, "I actually asked Townshend if I could join the Who. I said, 'If you need a drummer, I'll make myself available,' and we got on very well." Unfortunately (for Collins, at least), Townshend had already recruited a replacement, fellow mod icon Kenny Jones, and that was the end of it. But Collins remained convinced that his future may well lay apart from Genesis.

"I remember having dinner with the others and saying, 'If you don't mind coming to Vancouver to record, then we've still got a group. But if you can't, then this is the end.'" Two months later, however, he knew that no amount of relocation could save the marriage. It was over, but songs he wrote during that long, torturous period would not only bring a fresh perspective to Genesis, once the members reconvened in September 1979, they would also give Collins the impetus to launch his so-long delayed solo career. For he was suddenly the only member of the band who hadn't.

Collins, Thompson (obscured), Rutherford, Stuemer, and Banks take a show-closing bow.

Just two years after their fears for unity helped push Steve Hackett out of the door, both Tony Banks and Mike Rutherford had taken advantage of Genesis's longest-ever layoff, each recording a more or less homespun solo album that, in directing their energies into pastures that would never have succeeded in Genesis, furthered the individual players' insistence that when (or *if*, as the gossips were beginning to whisper) they got back together with Collins, it would be to fashion an even wilder variation on the old pattern than even *...And Then There Were Three* had managed.

Overseen by Genesis's now-regular producer, David Hentschel, Rutherford's *Smallcreep's Day* was first off the blocks, a semiconcept album based around the Peter Currell-Brown novel of the same name...a day in the life of, indeed, a character named Smallcreep. It joined, too, with Hackett's *Voyage of the Acolyte* and Phillips's *The Geese and the Ghost* in resuscitating musical themes and ideas that Genesis had passed over long before—the song "Compression" was lifted bodily from one of the band's own ancient outtakes while the presence of Phillips among the supporting cast confirmed the close bond of friendship that the pair had maintained in spite of the demands of Genesis.

Banks, meanwhile, set about writing and recording what he came close to describing as the logical successor to *Wind and Wuthering* and, in particular, his dramatic showcase "One for the Vine." Whereas that album gave him just those ten minutes to truly explore the textures and directions he was pursuing, *A Curious Feeling* was riven with grandiose drama. It was a Cecil B. DeMille–style production set to stirring rhythms and movements and, like Rutherford's effort, initially inspired by a novel, the 1966 opus *Flowers for Algernon* by science fiction author Daniel Keyes. (Algernon is a mouse that science has transformed into a genius.)

Banks originally hoped to record the album wholly around that tale, only to discover that the book had already been optioned for a musical—Charles Strouse and David Rogers' *Charlie and Algernon* premiered at the Edmonton, Canada, Citadel Theater on Dec. 21, 1978. Thus thwarted, Banks concentrated instead on formulating his own tale around Keyes's themes, a harrowing saga of burgeoning madness, seen through the horrified awareness of the madman himself.

Again, music originally composed with Genesis in mind played a part in the album. The majestically moving opening cut, "From the Undertow," was originally written as a short (less than three minutes) overture to *...And Then There Were Three*'s "Undertow"; other songs dated back to that prolific summer three years earlier, when Banks was writing toward *A Trick of the Tail* but keeping a solo album in mind as well. Elements of Genesis, then, lurk everywhere, but the album's own innate originality is never compromised. Rather, as manager Tony Smith rarely tired of pointing out, *A Curious Feeling* simply reminded us that, no matter what else the band did, it would be nothing without Banks.

For accompanying musicians, too, he remained firmly within familiar territory. Although Banks played most of the instruments on the album himself, Chester Thompson was brought in on drums while vocals were delivered by Kim Beacon, once of String Driven Thing and, more recently, one of the unsuccessful audition-ers when Gabriel left Genesis. His throatily emotive tones were one of the album's most delightful surprises, and the result was a No. 21 British hit in October 1979; Rutherford's *Smallcreep's Day*, meanwhile, would climb to No. 13.

The year 1979 also found Peter Gabriel working toward his next, third, album, unsurprisingly titled *Peter Gabriel*. He had recently leased a manor farm close to his home in Bath, wherein he built the studio he had been aching for throughout his solo career so far. Very early on in the new sessions, for example, he celebrated, "There were certain things I was trying to do on the second album, in terms of sound, that I didn't get a chance to try…experimentation…fiddling around using a five-quid amp…." Now, without a studio clock ticking away the dollars, he was free to play to his heart's content.

Gabriel would break out of the studio for a couple of summertime festival appearances; both the Glastonbury and Reading events allowed him to debut the new material he was working on, although anybody expecting the versions aired those afternoons to have any-

> "I didn't get a chance to try fiddling around using a five-quid amp."

thing in common with the "finished" thing reckoned without Gabriel's restless search for new ground—a search that journeyed from "I Don't Remember," a some-what formless percussive number aired throughout the 1978 tour, to a songwriting collaboration with new wave hero Tom Robinson. "Bully for You," the unimpeach-able highlight of the Tom Robinson Band's second album, was a pulsating, elec-tronics-riven anthem whose strident rhythm would, though nobody could have known it at the time, drop at least a few hints toward Gabriel's next move.

Having already worked with two diametrically opposed producers in Bob Ezrin and Robert Fripp, Gabriel now turned to a third. Steve Lilywhite was widely regarded as one of *the* rising new stars of the British studio scene, a sometime protégé of Brian Eno who had since crystallized his own ideas across groundbreaking albums by Ultravox, XTC, and Siouxsie and the Banshees (and who was soon to find even greater acclaim alongside U2). He also reunited with Phil Collins to experiment with a new percus-sive effect that the drummer had devised, in which individual drum beats are fed through a gate compressor to be both condensed and harshly muted. It was a dramatic and, at that time, wholly unheard-of process, and Gabriel used it to maximum effect.

"Peter's album was interesting to do in that he specifically requested that I not use any cymbals," Collins explained. "I know Peter quite well, and I respect him as a man of principle, yet I told him that there are times when using cymbals is good. Yet he remained steadfast in wanting no metal on the album whatsoever, so I said, 'All right,' and got along with it.

"His ideas inspired me to create, on 'No Self Control,' a very interesting drum part. A lot of that was due to [engineer] Hugh Padgham, who set up noise gates and limiters on the drums. I was in the live room just playing some simple patterns on the drums, yet through the headphones [I] was hearing these incredible sounds. The noise gates would clip in and give an added tonal dimension to the sounds coming off the drums. So Hugh's changing the drum sounds on the board and I'm playing off those sounds, each time waiting for the gate to clip in and the noise to stop before playing something else. After a while I began to string some of those sounds into patterns and phrases."

Outside its human components, however, the star of the show was an instrument that very few people had ever even heard of at the time, the Fairlight Sampler. The brainchild of electronic music enthusiasts and designers Peter Vogel, Tony Furse, and Kim Ryrie, founder of *Electronics Today International* Magazine, the Fairlight was born in the mid-'70s, when the trio "set out to develop real-time pure syntheses technology that allowed us to control every parameter of the sound." Ryrie explained, "We wanted to digitally create sounds that were very similar to acoustic musical instruments and that had the same amount of control as a player of an acoustic instrument has over his or her instrument."

That project failed, and, at first, the notion of utilizing real-life sounds struck the team as somehow cheating. Although it gave them "the complexity of sound that we had failed to create digitally," it did not permit the amount of control that they sought. "We could only control things like attack, sustain, vibrato, and decay of a sample, and this was a very, very severe limitation of the original goal that we had set ourselves."

Still, they continued to develop the system, wearily acknowledging that it was better than nothing, and by 1979 they were ready to begin marketing it—uncertain whether anybody would even want such a thing. The sound quality was poor, the equipment was barely portable, and even the lowest-frequency samples lasted no more than a couple of seconds. But having packaged it up with a collection of eight-inch 500-kilobyte floppy discs, each containing 22 stored sounds, the team found widespread industry interest in their "orchestra in a box." Now they had to find a musician to put its potential into practice.

Peter Gabriel strayed into the Fairlight's orbit, he later explained, having first become fascinated with a far simpler slice of technology, "a $60 [drum machine] made by a company called Paia and introduced to me by Larry Fast. For me, as a failed drummer, it was a joy, suddenly, to be able to get grooves that would continue after I lifted my hands off the keyboard."

Two of the songs scheduled for the new album, "No Self Control" and "Biko," mourning the state-sponsored murder of South African activist and journalist Steven Biko, were the immediate fruits of this new musical marriage, with the latter's blend of rock sensibility and indigenous chant and rhythm setting the scene for the world music explosion that was about to descend—Paul Simon's *Graceland* is just one of many albums that conceivably took its lead from the six or so minutes that closed Peter Gabriel's new album with such chilling finality.

But far greater steps were still to come, musically and technologically, after Peter Vogel offered Gabriel an in-house demonstration of the Fairlight. Stunned by the machine's capabilities, Gabriel promptly employed Vogel to operate what the ensuing album's liner notes call a "Computer Musical Instrument." The Fairlight's future was assured—with Gabriel overseeing the U.K. importation and distribution of the Fairlight, the instrument exploded into prominence.

Former Led Zeppelin bassist John Paul Jones purchased the first one; producer Trevor Horn and partner Geoff Downes, Thomas Dolby, Stevie Wonder, Todd Rundgren, and Pink Floyd's Rick Wright all followed—so did Kate Bush, the still-prodigal vocalist who had burst onto the scene just two years earlier with the eerily phrased "Wuthering Heights" and had since established herself among rock's most courageous pioneers. Gabriel was one of her most fervent admirers; Bush's initial exposure to the Fairlight came when she dropped by the studio to graft guest vocals onto another of Gabriel's new songs, "Games without Frontiers."

The pair quickly became keen collaborators. On May 12, 1979, with the album still underway, Gabriel joined Bush and singer Steve Harley at a memorial concert for lighting engineer Bill Duffield—having worked in the past with both Gabriel and Harley, he was overseeing effects on Bush's first (and, as it transpired, only) tour when he fell to his death from the lighting gantry at Poole Arts Centre on April 2.

Later in the year, the two were united once again, when Gabriel appeared as a guest on Bush's BBC TV special *Kate*; first performing his own "Here Comes the Flood," he then joined Bush for a version of Roy Harper's "Another Day." (The couple went on to record versions of both "Another Day" and a new song called "Ibiza," although both remain unreleased.)

Released as a single early in 1980, "Games without Frontiers" itself was destined to become one of Gabriel's most instantly recognizable numbers and certainly one of his most commercial. The song took its inspiration from a long-running Anglo-French television challenge show, *It's a Knock-Out*—a title referenced in the song's chorus; "Games without Frontiers" was an English translation of the show's French title, *Jeux Sans Frontier*, the line that Bush warbles so exquisitely behind Gabriel's lead vocal.

Elsewhere, the deliberate clashing of childish sexual innuendo ("Jane plays with Willy, Willy's happy again" indeed) and adult war games ("Adolf builds a bonfire") in "Games without Frontiers" ensured that the happy-go-lucky nature of the TV show, with its parade of grinning hosts and absurdly ambitious contestants, was never to be more than a thin façade, but that, perhaps, was part of its appeal. Without appearing any more or less obtuse than any past Gabriel lyric, "Games without Frontiers" was playfully peppered with so many familiar references that it was an obvious hit single even before Charisma finally released it as one. It rewarded them by dashing to No. 4 in Britain, behind Fern Kinney, Marti Webb, and Blondie. For one week in early 1980, Peter Gabriel was officially the best-selling man in Britain.

> "Jane plays with Willy, Willy's happy again" indeed.

The album, inevitably titled *Peter Gabriel*, followed that spring and readily established itself as a monster, topping the British chart (the first Genesis-related solo album ever to do so) and proving equally successful in Germany, after Gabriel took the then highly unusual step of rerecording his entire vocal in the German language, specifically for release in that country. David Bowie had made a similar gesture back in 1977, when he recorded the title track to his *Heroes* album in French and German for single release. Undertaking to revoice an entire LP, however, was a remarkable venture, all the more so since Gabriel also took the opportunity to remix the album and emerge with the self-explanatorily titled *Ein Deutsches Album*, a set that many fans considered an even more powerful vision of an already breath-taking achievement.

Only one country seemed unimpressed by Gabriel's activities—or, at least, so Atlantic Records, his American record label, would have him believe. They refused to even consider releasing the album. "I gather Ahmet Ertegun, the chairman, thought it was quite arty," Gabriel reported. "But the A&R department told him it was undesirable, too esoteric. An Atlantic guy who came over to hear us in the studio asked me to make one song ['And Through the Wire'] sound more like the Doobie Brothers."

Gabriel not only refused, he then called up Jam guitarist Paul Weller to send some garage band–shaped chords crashing through the mix. No matter how much Atlantic hated the album before that, now they hated it even more. Only when "Games without Frontiers" began to take off around the world did somebody at the label have second thoughts—Gabriel laughed, "[It] started to get radio play in the States [as an import, so] they tried to buy the LP back. But Charisma wouldn't let them get their hands on it, which gave me considerable satisfaction." Mercury would ultimately release the album in America, and an unde-

"That third album…was knock-out. It set the musical tone for the rest of the century."

sirable slab of esotericism quickly rocketed to No. 22—its predecessors had moved no higher than No. 38 and 45, respectively.

Even vaster than *Peter Gabriel's* commercial success, however, was its musical impact. Opening the album with malevolent resonance, the drum pattern that stalks "The Intruder" would be so widely imitated that it was nigh-on endemic…so much so that when Phil Collins employed it on his first solo album, the following year, many people assumed he'd simply pinched it from everybody else. But that song was merely one of many on an album that remains impossible to play favorites with. Yes, one's interest may fade in places…"No Self Control" and "Not

One of Us" are both better sounds than songs…but a still-admiring Steve Hackett spoke for many when he reflected, in 2003, "That third album…was knock-out. It set the musical tone for the rest of the century."

Yet it was not only its musical tones that appeared to have hit the proverbial nail on the ever-suffering head. For, in the months between "Games without Frontiers" and *Peter Gabriel*, Genesis too had stirred once more, and it, too, was hitting peaks that, hitherto, only its most devoted fans had dreamed of the band attaining.

CHAPTER FOURTEEN

TURNING IT ON AGAIN

In March 1980, a new single, "Turn It On Again," launched a very convincing assault on the British Top Ten with a pulsating riff, a sharp keyboard motif, drums the size of Connecticut, and an unnaturally slippery time signature…most pop songs are in 4/4. Genesis had occasionally strayed into 9/8. "Turn It On Again" lurched along in 13/8—a rhythmic pattern that sounds more or less conventional until you try to tap your toes to it. Neither was its chartbusting success a fluke. In May, "Duchess" at least took a bite out of the Top 50. And, in April, *Duke* went straight to the top.

Once again, Genesis chose to record on the continent, taking over Abba's Polar Studios in Sweden. There, a dozen tracks followed much the same formula as *…And Then There Were Three* had blueprinted, spanning a gulf that stretched from the show-stopping instrumental medley "Duke's Travels"/"Duke's End"—"Los Endos" for a new beginning—to the pure and absolutely irresistible pop of "Misunderstanding," a rolling, harmony- and hook-laden song that grew out of Collins's own tortured domestic life but buried its despair beneath a gorgeous sing-song melody and a lyric of such puppy-dog devotion that it rapidly became a national anthem of sorts for rowing couples the western world over. It was also one of the first Genesis songs to which Collins could lay full claim as composer, and its success, he smiled, "was great for me as a songwriter."

The first Genesis single to breach the American Top 20 (it eventually peaked at No. 14), "Misunderstanding" hangs in the memory as even bigger than that. One of *the* summertime hits of the year, it provided an inescapable soundtrack to everything that summer entails, haunting the airwaves all season long, and, with every fresh airing, drawing more listeners into the album that spawned it and damning Genesis's detractors with an incandescent freshness.

For all the individual activities that preceded it, the *Duke* sessions were fast and painless, the only true stumbling block arriving when the band tried to sequence the songs. The group's initial intention was to take the five full-team compositions ("Behind the Lines," "Duchess," "Turn It On Again," and the "Duke" couplet) and string them together as one side-long suite as "shades of 'Supper's Ready'," as Tony Stratton Smith put it, but that, unfortunately, was one comparison that Genesis did not want to resurrect. The songs were separated out, and while Mike Rutherford did hint at some form of conceptual string binding many of them together, namely a certain bewilderment at the nature of life in this strange new decade, that itself was a constant thread throughout rock 'n' roll during 1980.

> A national anthem of sorts for rowing couples the western world over.

World events were taking one of their periodic ugly turns, as the Soviet invasion of poor, defenseless little Afghanistan saw the United States adopt the role of the beleaguered nation's big brother and push half the planet into nuclear neurosis as the two superpowers' presidents tried out-mouthing one another with threats and retribution. The Iranian hostage crisis was over, but the newly established Islamic Republic remained a violently twisting thorn in the sides of sundry western democracies.

Domestically, too, things were approaching crisis point. With the new British prime minister, Margaret Thatcher, threatening to rain all manner of brutal solutions onto the country's twin flashpoints of unemployment and racism, unrest was already giving way to rioting while she made her own contribution to the threat of nuclear obliteration by opening British bases to American missiles. Everywhere was confusion, fear, and a sense of impending doom, and if *Duke* reflected that (which it unquestionably did), then Genesis was simply responding to the same external pressures as a lot of other people—and doing so with a lot more skill and sensitivity than many of their peers.

Reinforcing this apparent support for the poor, tormented Everyman...Smallcreep magnified by manifold degree...and conscious that its recent absence from the British tour circuit had upset a lot of loyal supporters, Genesis kicked off its 1980 tour schedule with a six-week U.K. tour that completely eschewed the yawning stadium and arena routine in favor of a return to the same intimate theater and cinema shows the band hadn't truly embraced since 1973—Paignton, Guildford, Great Yarmouth, Peterborough, Stoke on Trent, towns that may not have been gifted with a truly major rock show in half a decade but that turned out all but *en masse* to catch this one.

There was even a return to Aylesbury Friars, the so-loyal club that had supported Genesis through the first half of the 1970s but that the band was simply too popular to play since that night in September 1972, when it asked the audience to boo their approval for a set of new songs. This time, the show was staged in semi-secrecy, the night before Genesis's March 23 appearance at London's Hammersmith Odeon, and still the queue for the 1,250 available tickets began forming a full 48 hours before the box office opened.

Several halts on the tour found the promoter forced to add second shows, simply to deal with the ticket demand (more than half a million requests were received for just 80,000 tickets), and Genesis wound up playing some 40 shows in 30 towns, completing its plunge into its history with glorious returns to the Theatre Royal Drury Lane, the London Lyceum, and a nightly encore of "The Knife," back in the set for the first time in seven years.

Genesis's return to the halls that bred it was not wholly inspired by altruism, just as its recent failure to pay more than the most cursory attention to it homeland was not, the group insisted, a deliberate snub. It was just the way things worked out. But though fans will make allowances for a lot of their heroes' failings, desertion—deliberate or logistical—is one crime that is very difficult to forgive.

As a mainstream attraction, Genesis's fame was only ever going to increase. As an object of cultish delight, however, the group had slipped out of time, and the bitterest observers found new obsessions to occupy their ears. One can argue the rights and wrongs of the conclusion until the cows come home, but it was scarcely any coincidence that, as soon as it became apparent that Genesis was turning its back on Britain, Britain found a new face to gaze upon, as the town of Aylesbury—home of the Friars and buried so deep in the heartland of Englishness—disgorged a new band, Silmarillion…a new band but an old approach.

By the time Derek "Fish" Dick, Mark Kelly, Mick Pointer, Steve Rothery, and Peter Trewavas became known to most of their future audience, the group had already abbreviated its name, from the Tolkien-inspired Silmarillion to Marillion alone. But Fish's penchant for mask, masque, and costumery was already firmly in place, and the group's penchant for lengthy, wordy epics of abstruse mythology, anecdote, and incident was already drawing attention from an audience that had spent close to five long years awaiting some kind of rebirth for the progressive spirits of old.

Marillion were not the only young hopefuls pursuing the same overall visions, of course—elsewhere, the Enid was building its own remarkable head of steam, and an entire new genre of reborn hard rock, cunningly christened the New Wave of British Heavy Metal, was arising from the underground to breathe new life not only into sundry old musical genres but into a lot of older talents as well. Distinctly nonmetallic though they were, Atomic Rooster, Wishbone Ash, UFO, and Uriah Heep were just the most noteworthy of the early-'70s veterans who were prompted to reform (or, at least, resurface) as they discovered an entire new audience growing up around their music, and the new blades that sprung up around them—exotically handled outfits such as the Tygers of Pan Tang, Def Leppard, Iron Maiden, and Ethyl the Frog—all professed their devotion to the heroes of their teenaged youth.

> "I wasn't too keen on Marillion or what I'd heard of them."

Stylistically setting themselves aside from this morass but embracing its precepts regardless, Marillion gigged constantly, and though, it cannot be stressed too often, their audience would have brindled furiously at any suggestion that the group was simply reiterating "old" Genesis, still the bare-bones comparisons did the still-unsigned Marillion's drawing power a lot more good than harm. And the fact that this latest Genesis tour was taking the originators at least into spitting range of the tiny clubs that were Marillion's personal fiefdom suggested that they were as aware of that fact as any impartial observer.

Tony Banks would later strike up a remarkably enjoyable partnership with Fish but readily confessed, "I wasn't too keen on Marillion or what I'd heard of them...everyone said that they were like Genesis and all the rest of it. After working with him I went and listened to some of the early Marillion stuff, and I was amazed at how some of the things were so close. What was so amazing about it was that they had a No. 1 album out of it, taking ideas that we'd used on *Foxtrot*, when *Foxtrot* was not a big seller at all. It was more the keyboard player than anyone and the fact that Fish's voice obviously sounds a bit like Peter's."

Genesis's British adventure ended with a satisfied smile of "mission accomplished"—brand loyalty was restored, the fan club was hopping, and sales of the back catalog were bubbling once more. A more conventional tour of North American arenas followed, pursuing the band through May and June 1980. Fans' hopes that the group would then return to Europe were dashed, however, as Genesis came off the road—and Phil Collins entered the studio alone to confront the mass of material he had written over the past year, most of which was aimed at exorcizing the emotions that grew out of the end of his marriage.

"The record's definitely autobiographical," Collins mused, "but [it's] not focusing on the sadness, that's the misconception. It's triggered by an event, [but] it chronicles a life in motion. By the time it was being recorded, I was [already] in another relationship." But still he admitted, its inspiration was traumatic. "I had a wife, two children, and two dogs, and the next day I didn't have anything. So a lot of these songs were written because I was going through these emotional changes."

"In the Air Tonight," the first single from the forthcoming *Face Value*, epitomized each of them—"anger, hurt, bitterness, menace, and, finally, losing your temper at the end, where the drums come in." The track reached the airwaves in early January 1981, a stark, atmospheric, and heart-stoppingly percussive number that purposefully clashed a bare-bones demo-style approach with the high-tech bombast of the drum sound Collins had gifted to Peter Gabriel's "The Intruder."

The result, at more than five minutes in length, was a remarkable piece of work, one that not only made it clear that the artist was not simply chasing the same souls that followed his every move with Genesis but had set his targets on an even vaster audience than that. It reached it as well. In American chart terms, "In the Air

Tonight" rose no higher than No. 19. But, like "Misunderstanding" before it, it dominated the airwaves for months to come.

Collins's home studio had seen little action so far…demo sessions for his third Brand X album, *Product* notwithstanding, he employed it primarily for messing around with equipment, coming to grips with—and learning to love!—drum machines, for example. And that was basically what he was doing as "In the Air Tonight" came together. "I wasn't…intending on writing a song," Collins confessed of the song's genesis. "I was just fooling around. I got these chords that I liked, so I turned the mike on and I started singing. The lyrics you hear are what I wrote spontaneously. That frightens me a bit, but I'm quite proud of the fact that I sing 99.9 percent of those lyrics spontaneously, and when someone said, 'Tell me Phil, what's that song about?' I go, 'I don't know. I've no idea. I just made it up as I went along.'"

Destined to scoop the Ivor Novello award's International Hit of the Year gong the following April, "In the Air Tonight" was originally intended for Genesis. Collins explained, "I played them 'In the Air Tonight' and 'If Leaving Me Is Easy,' but it was kind of too simple for the band. Tony, bless his heart, is a classically trained pianist, and if you ask him to play like 'that,' not 'that' or play the wrong inversions or something, instinct will tell him not to do that. Instinct will tell him to play the 'right' inversions, and sometimes, the 'right' inversions just don't sound right." And so it was with these songs.

In the past, Collins acknowledged, he may have left it at that. But it suddenly occurred to him that he now had "an awful lot of songs that were not really Genesisy and songs that, if I brought [them] into Genesis, would not end up sounding like I wanted them to. 'Misunderstanding' was one of my songs; it was a song that everybody liked, and we didn't change it. But had they wanted to change it, I probably would've said 'hang on a minute.'"

In contrast to its American showing, "In the Air Tonight" rose to No. 2 in the United Kingdom, with only the continued deification of the recently slain John Lennon keeping Collins off the top spot, but there was to be no such restraint for *Face Value*. The album *replaced* Lennon at No. 1 in the United Kingdom, and though *Face Value* raised no higher than number seven in America, still four million sales established it among the most successful debut albums of the age—and

Phil Collins in his '80s phase.

Collins among the handful of artists who, as the 1980s faded into the realm of nostalgia and oldies radio, came to epitomize the decade.

American journalist Amy Hanson wrote, "Phil Collins was everywhere; more than anybody else of that time, he somehow appealed to every audience there was—the hip college kids liked him because of the Genesis connection, older people liked him for the easy-listening angle, teenyboppers liked the pop, MTV loved the videos, and everybody's grandmother adored his smile." More than Bruce Springsteen, REM, U2, or any of the 80s' other icons, Phil Collins straddled the decade like a colossus, and it didn't even matter that, as time passed (and the hits mounted up), the core audience of Genesis fans did tire of his eternal heartbreak and romanticism. He remained the most unlikely superstar of the entire age.

> "At the demo stage, you'd hear clicks where the fridge was going on and off."

For all its success, *Face Value* nevertheless packed an almost homespun feel, a raw edge that prompted at least one reviewer to compare it to Paul McCartney's first solo album, recorded with open microphones in his kitchen while his family and animals went about their lives around him.

It was an innovative approach that, possibly surprising many of his detractors, Collins credited to Brian Eno. "Working with Eno on *Another Green World*, we became quite friendly, and partly from him, I got my demo approach. He'd come into the studio with a Revox tape he'd done the night before, and he wouldn't be worried about hisses or clicks. If it had spirit, he'd use it, and that's what I did.

"At the demo stage, you'd hear clicks where the fridge was going on and off. The phone would ring. And I didn't mind because, at the time, I didn't know there would be an outlet for these tapes. I hadn't set out to make a record, I just did some songs in my room." The actual recording sessions took place in somewhat more professional surroundings—London's Townhouse and Los Angeles's Village Recorders were both employed for the purpose—but that rough-hewn feel was never to be glossed over, as Collins plowed through a remarkable assemblage of songs and notions.

Interviewed by *Melody Maker*, he confessed, "I thought that anybody who would see an album by me out after I've been with Genesis for ten years and Brand X for five would think, 'Oh, another Genesis album, thank you,' whereas I think my album has great potential to appeal to more people than those who like Genesis." It was for that reason, he insisted, that *Face Value* eschewed the anticipated Charisma release and was handled instead by Virgin Records. "I thought for the casual buyer it would certainly help if it was on a different label." (Ironically, Virgin would become Charisma's own distributor in 1983, thus reuniting this slightly fractured family.)

Although the heart of *Face Value* was locked firmly within a doomed romantic pop sphere, still the album packed its share of darker musical atmospheres, as "In the Air Tonight" was joined by the tribally inclined "Droned" ("a rhythm on the black notes," as Collins called it), the percussion-heavy instrumental "Hand in Hand," and a riotously effects-laden and backward tape–heavy trip through the Beatles' "Tomorrow Never Knows." Play *it* backward, and themes from half the rest of the album can be distinguished squirming within the mix.

Most surprising of all, however, was Collins's decision to actually rerecord one of Genesis's most recent highlights, *Duke*'s "Behind the Lines." In the band's hands, the number was a stately, keyboard-driven beauty. One day in the studio, however, as the trio was playing through tapes and fast-forwarding the backing tracks as they did so, each of them was struck by what became of "Behind the Lines" when it flew past at double speed.

"It sounded like a Michael Jackson funky thing," marveled Mike Rutherford, and that was all the encouragement Collins required. Completely recasting the song as a tight R&B number, he recruited the American funketeers Earth Wind and Fire's horn section and introduced a whole new musical angle to the proceedings. Elevated to producer after engineering Peter Gabriel's third album, Hugh Padgham remembered some U.S. rock radio stations actually ignoring Collins's records once they got wind of this collaboration, convinced that he'd gone R&B on them. He no longer "fit the format." Collins continued, "The radio people at Atlantic [his U.S. label] are going to put out a 'black EP' with four of the tracks on it to black radio stations, because there's an awful lot of connotations with Genesis that people will not give it a second chance."

Elsewhere, too, Collins's musical accompanists stepped far beyond Genesis's traditional confines. While Daryl Stuermer provided guitar throughout, the likes of

Stephen Bishop, Eric Clapton, and Joe Partridge made for far higher-profile guests, and there was also a role for veteran English trumpeter Ronnie Scott, fabled owner of the London club where the assembled cast of Charisma Records first caught sight of Genesis. Weather Report's Alfonso Johnson offered further funk basics while the singularly named Indian violinist Shankar, another of the stars of Peter Gabriel's recent recordings, brought his own special magic to the proceedings.

It was Shankar, too, who delivered one of the most surprising of all the accolades Collins would receive, when he compared the drummer's improvisational skills to none other than Frank Zappa. Collins reveled in the comparison, all the more so as his solo career advanced and he developed what he considered an unfounded reputation for musical perfectionism. "I thrive on spontaneous music," he explained. "I used to sit with Brand X and play for days. With Genesis, everything we write comes out of days of playing." His solo albums may have sounded impossibly clean and well crafted, but that was rarely how they started life.

Hopes that Collins might tour in the wake of *Face Value* were not to come to pass (the videos for "In the Air Tonight" and the follow-up "I Missed Again" did the job for him). He played just one concert, appearing at the then-annual *Secret Policeman's Ball* charity comedy event, at the end of 1981, for a sparse performance of "In the Air Tonight." But still the media could not allow the monstrous success of *Face Value* to pass by unremarked upon—barely had the first million copies shipped than rumors of Genesis's impending demise were circulating. In fact, the band was able to reconvene immediately, not only to start work on a new album but also to familiarize itself with the most tangible proceeds of its recent success: its own newly purchased studio, the Farm, in Chiddingfold, Surrey.

The facility was little more than a half-converted cow shed.

Destined, ultimately, to flow over a veritable complex of buildings, the Farm (which, in a previous lifetime, was indeed a working farm) would go on to provide luxurious surroundings for any number of other acts to record in, ranging from the Cure to Brit-pop staples Mansun. When Genesis bought it in November 1980, however, the facility was little more than a half-converted cow shed—as they settled down to begin work, the concrete was still wet, the walls had still to be treated for acoustics, and the monitors were still resting on flight cases. The facility's former occupants, too, were still in evidence—one day as the trio worked, a horse broke out of its own field and was seen staring in through the window behind Tony Banks.

Still, the Farm offered Genesis a luxury the band had never previously experienced, a well-equipped studio in which the members could spend as long as they needed writing and rehearsing.

Even *Duke*, Mike Rutherford once grimaced, was largely worked out in Phil Collins's bedroom, whereas past attempts to fully utilize a studio were waylaid by the musicians' awareness of just how much money they were spending, every hour they devoted to tweaking a guitar riff. "If we took a long break and then couldn't think of anything to play for the next hour, we'd feel pretty miserable. Whereas being able to go in and write in your own time was perfect."

The Farm did not simply save money. It also gave Genesis the opportunity to try out something else they had been considering for some time, attempting to produce for the first time. Although Hugh Padgham was brought in from the *Face Value* sessions, it was Genesis that arranged—or, rather, rearranged—the components of the group's sound, who fashioned the frontal assault that would dominate the album, who set about rebuilding the group's universe from the ground up.

"We tried to change our appeal slightly by altering the arrangements," Tony Banks later explained. "We were trying to avoid the things that had become almost second nature to us." Such adventure can be applauded. However, it was a sad side effect that this also included many of the trademark musical sounds that the band members had developed over the years. Over the next few years and albums, many of Genesis's most recognizable traits—the delicate 12-string guitars, the Yamaha CP 70 electric piano, the Mellotron—would be pushed away as Banks, in particular, replenished his arsenal with the new technology, sadly, at exactly the same time as every other keyboard player made the same transitions. Right now, the process was still in its infancy. But it would reach adulthood very soon.

Face Value itself could not be allowed to pass by unnoticed, of course. At Collins's suggestion, the Earth Wind and Fire horn section was again utilized for two songs ("No Reply At All" and the future single "Paperlate"), although fears that Collins's solo success might transform Genesis into a side project by proxy were undone when it became apparent that the singer had just one new song with which to gift the proceedings, the strangely understated "Man on the Corner"—a total throw-back to the days of "For Absent Friends."

It was indicative of the strength of these particular interludes that many observers assumed that the changes evinced across *Abacab* were wholly down to Collins's influence, an attempt to realign Genesis along the same lines as his solo career—as if there would have been any sense whatsoever in such a maneuver. It was an accusation that the band seem to have predicted—as Collins sings during the horn-laden "No Reply At All," "the buck stops here." In fact, as with every other decision made by Genesis, *Abacab* was wholly a joint creation, built around group decisions and, though all three musicians professed themselves shocked by the sheer weight of wrath ladled onto their heads by long-time fans (the admittedly ghastly "Who Dunnit?" was routinely booed when they played it live), there was plenty to celebrate nevertheless.

The bulk of the songs, too, were full, true group compositions, as the three threw themselves into a period of reinventive experimentation that, more than any past Genesis effort, would leave fans utterly polarized. In the past, even the most ruth-less reshaping of the group had involved merely tinkering with tones, shifting emphasis, and, of course, cutting down on the epics. This time, however, the very sound of the band was being altered, streamlined through computers and whatever other high-tech gadgetry the trio turned their hands to, scythed and sliced into modules of momentum that were, without exception, unrecognizable as the Genesis we once knew and loved.

"People expect certain things from 'Genesis'; when they get something different, they're surprised by it."

"The response to the *Abacab* album infuriated me," Tony Stratton Smith snarled once the reviews were in. "Everywhere, people were screaming betrayal, that Genesis had changed…and they were exactly the same people that were buying Pete [Gabriel]'s albums and celebrating the fact that every one was so different from the one before."

Collins, too, was prone to seethe at the memory. "People expect certain things from 'Genesis'; when they get something different, they're surprised by it. But really, it's just a name we happened to be lumbered with as a group of writers."

The corollary to that argument is the fans' belief that a band name is also a brand name, one that people come to trust to deliver a certain sound, a certain style, a certain type of song. To change any of those commodities is an artist's prerogative. But is it right to continue trading under the old name, when the new sound is so totally removed from any that the audience may expect? If you bought a Picasso and it looked like a Turner, you'd be right to complain. If you bought some cornflakes and found washing-up powder, you'd be right to return them. Even the most forgiving fan was forced to admit that, Collins' vocals notwithstanding, the new Genesis album was Genesis in name alone.

Confined as they were to the fan club, such controversies did nothing to derail the album. *Abacab* crashed into the U.K. charts at No. 1 in September 1981 while the title track—named for the chord sequence around which it was constituted—leaped straight into the Top Ten and deserved to do even better. A punching, throbbing, behemoth of a number, "Abacab" also packed a brutal electro enthusiasm that was absolutely in keeping with the harsher aspects of the so-called synthipop/New Romantic movement then holding Britain and, across the ocean, the fledgling MTV in its thrall.

Synthesizer-fired groups such as Soft Cell, the Human League, Ultravox, and Orchestral Manoeuvres in the Dark were all approaching their musical peak in late 1981, each forging bold new directions for pop that pledged little, if any, allegiance to the traditions of the past. Thus far, however, few of these brave pioneers had racked up more than a hit or two apiece—their audience, the learned sages of the music press determined, was still acclimatizing itself to the possibilities that lay within this new musical force.

But it wasn't Soft Cell's "Tainted Love," OMD's "Joan Of Arc," or the Human League's "Sound of the Crowd" that broke down those last vestiges of resistance. It was "Abacab," squeaking, squealing, and burping its insanely compulsive way into every ear in the land…and inviting everyone into the album, where the necessarily brief hit-single version was stretched out across a dynamic seven minutes…that put the new music through paces that its younger adherents had scarcely even dreamed of.

They'd get round to it next year, of course, although by that time, Genesis had upped the ante even further, with the release of the *Three by Three* EP, a collection once again of outtakes that were too good to be taken out. The lead track was "Paperlate," the latest in the growing line of Genesis songs that somehow referenced the past without actually looking back at it—"paper late" was originally heard as a lyric within "Dancing with the Moonlit Knight" (just as "I Know What I Like" managed to mention the pre-Genesis concern the Garden Wall and, a decade later, *The Way We Walk* live albums turned full circle and pulled their titles from "I Know What We Like"). "You Might Recall" and "Virgil" completed the EP, and Genesis celebrated the antiquated nature of an Extended Play release by packing the record in a brilliant facsimile of a 20-year-old Beatles' EP.

Collins explained, "We did a Beatles parody, with a nice glossy cover photograph of us all jumping off a wall. If you put the *Twist and Shout* EP next to it, there's no difference apart from our faces. We got Tony Barrow [the author of the liners on the Beatles' original] to write the sleeve notes, and he wrote it in the same way he used to for the Beatles, 'These cheeky chappies from Guildford…treasure these three audio-visual representations….'" Collins could only smile when he read the *New Musical Express'* disparaging review of the release. "The guy wasn't alive when the Beatles were going, so he reviewed it totally straight, as though we were serious."

As compensation for omitting mainland Europe from its last touring itinerary, Genesis kicked off its next round of gigs in Spain in September 1981, traveling on throughout the continent for the next month before departing for another American tour. There would then be a break while Collins prepared his next solo album, *Hello, I Must Be Going*. Summer, 1982, however, would see the band back on the road for another two months, revamping the live show to include, for the first time in five years, a spectacular "Supper's Ready." Neither did any negative response to *Abacab* affect the group's pulling power—rather, the 1981–82 tour would go down in the annals of fan lore as one of Genesis's most spectacular displays yet, as the tour unveiled its new light show, a monster extravaganza that gave the world its first glimpse of Vari-Lights, a computer-powered display that would soon become *de rigueur* among so many touring parties.

The light show would become a star, too, of Genesis's next release, a concert film shot at the final shows of 1981, at the massive New Exhibition Centre in Birmingham, England; a double live album, the soundtrack to the film, was released simultaneously, and *Three Sides Live* (so named because the fourth comprised studio material, leftovers from the *Abacab* sessions) shook off any remaining doubts by establishing itself a worthy, even superior, successor to *Seconds Out* and (dare it be said) *Genesis Live*. Close to nine minutes of "Abacab" alone are worth the price of admission. Yet even *Three Sides Live*, the Vari-Lights, and "Supper's Ready" were to pale in the face of Genesis's next move. For, no sooner had the world finally stopped asking whether the "classic" lineup would ever get back together again than…it did.

CHAPTER FIFTEEN

FOUR MINUTES I'D FORGOTTEN

Anybody absorbing the Australian airwaves back in 1981 will have encountered any number of strange and wonderful things. Few, however, have so brilliantly withstood the test of time and remained so supremely strange and wonderful as Johnny Warman's "Screaming Jets."

A compulsive and, if sound effects be our guide, superbly titled glimpse into a postapocalyptic future, "Screaming Jets" racked up sales in excess of 75,000 copies and looked set to transform its English-born performer into one of the biggest stars of the age, as audiences reacted not only to the power of the song but also to the so-distinctive backing vocals that contradicted Warman's calming vocal with maniacal passion.

Duetting with Warman on "Screaming Jets" and loaning his backing band for the rest of the accompanying album, Peter Gabriel was making one of the mere handful of cameo appearances that have pocked his career, contributing a backing vocal line that is as powerful as any he unleashed on his own records and playing a role in the arrangement of the finished record as well. Warman recalled, "We were laying down the track, [and] I kept changing the arrangement, so…I kept shouting out the chord changes so that everyone knew exactly what was going on. Peter…was intrigued and asked if I intended to keep the commands in or else, with a glint in his eye, he said he might try something similar on his next album. I decided to leave it as it was."

Gabriel and company arrived at the sessions by accident. In the weeks before recording began on Dec. 9, 1980 (the day after John Lennon was murdered), Warman initially intended working only with producer Hugh Padgham, himself fresh from Phil Collins's *Face Value* sessions. There was hope that Collins would be available to play on the sessions.

It turned out that he wasn't, but in recommending Warman contact Jerry Marotta instead, he did set a crucial chain of events in motion. Marotta recruited bassist Tony Levin, and then they both recommended Warman bring in Larry Fast. And, before Warman knew where he was, he found himself answering the phone to Gabriel, as he called to talk with one or other of the musicians. "So, cheekily, one day I asked if he'd like to come and sing…." Gabriel agreed, and "Screaming Jets," a song Warman wrote after watching *Apocalypse Now* ("about 25 minutes after…"), was the outcome.

> "Peter…was intrigued and asked if I intended to keep the commands in."

"Screaming Jets," as with the rest of the *Walking Into Mirrors* album, was very much a child of its time, another brittle, vital reminder of the fears that were part and parcel of the early Reagan/Thatcher years, built around a monochromatic sonic landscape that is as electrifying as it is evocative. Awash with electronics, punchy and danceable but dark and foreboding as well, it looked around at the war games that the superpowers were then enacting and then traced them to their then-seemingly inevitable conclusion. "The threat of nuclear war was always there," Warman remembered, "and is reflected in a few of the songs. I have always been fascinated by science fiction and this, too, is very evident…."

The sessions traveled from London to New York's Electric Lady and the House of Music in West Orange before finally returning to London in time to record Peter Gabriel's contributions; Gabriel, meanwhile, was about to begin work on his own next solo album, his fourth, and though he abandoned his sly intention to borrow Warman's key change cries, still *Peter Gabriel* (retitled *Security* in the United States, where the old joke was finally wearing a little thin) posited its creator on a similarly frenetic edge.

Two years had passed since his last album, a period during which Gabriel had again toured exhaustively and become a father for a second time—daughter Isis was born in 1982.

Musically, too, Gabriel was active, training himself to becoming less dependent upon technology, while making technology dependent upon him. "I decided to wipe all the presets from my drum machine and start trying to find 40 or 50 [new] interesting drum patterns," he explained. "That took a while—listening to non-European bits, Tamla bits, and invented rhythms." But the end result placed a universe of rhythmic invention at his fingertips, at a time when other Fairlight fans were still trying to work out which button to push to get the funniest noises.

Gabriel also set to work building an extension onto the Fairlight's already impressive library of sounds and sound effects; the actual recording process itself was complicated as Gabriel spent as much time stripping down his "finished" tracks as he did building them up in the first place.

Released in September 1982, the result was an album of dense rhythms and patterns that traveled as far from the bright pastures of its predecessor as the second *Peter Gabriel* album had from the first.

Unfortunately, the sonic breakthroughs that this latest album represented did much to disguise many of the musical peaks that it also contained. Reviews were tough, sales were patchy, and even hardcore fans confessed their disappointment. If Gabriel's all-conquering third album had any faults, after all, it was in the sheer adventurousness that characterized its finest moments—so much that nothing Gabriel could do thereafter would ever be seen as more than a minor modification of that earlier set's precedents.

So it proved. Even the album's most dramatic timbre, its thoughtful absorption of the ethnic musical forms that would, in later years, be so patronizingly termed *world music*, was seen as little more than an advance on the third album's showcase, the South African township chants of "Biko."

Gabriel's intentions were amplified in his response to the generally lackluster nature of the album's reviews, at least among white journalists and DJs. Echoing one of Phil Collins's proudest boasts, "One of the real satisfactions for me with this record is that I'm played on black stations in America, and even though in the white press I had some fair slagging…I had some very good reviews in black magazines."

Indeed, any failings that the album may labor beneath were effortlessly balanced by the sheer strength of the songs, the commitment of the performance, and Gabriel's innate understanding that the weight of expectation can never be truly satisfied. "Shock the Monkey," a song so powerful that, two decades later, *nu-metal* sweethearts Coal Chamber would need to pull out all its own musical stops (and guest star Ozzy Osbourne) simply to match the intensity of the original; "I Have the Touch," its claustrophobic atmosphere and rhythm seamlessly melding with the rush hour crush of its subject matter; "The Rhythm of the Heat," a Burundi *piece de resistance* as evocative as any "authentic" sampling of tribal percussives—these are the songs that became *Peter Gabriel*'s best-loved moments, yet to single them out is to disrupt the exquisite flow of the entire suite, eight songs, and almost as many shifting moods that may not amount to the *best* Peter Gabriel album but certainly represent the quintessential one.

In and around the recording of *Peter Gabriel*, the singer had spent much of the past year formulating WOMAD—the World of Music Arts and Dance, an organization that targeted the groundswell of interest in, again, "world music" that flourished around his own albums by spotlighting the work of artists and performers who truly exemplified the manifold musics of the world.

It was a vastly ambitious enterprise and a costly one as well. Gabriel's intentions to stage a WOMAD festival during the summer of 1981 were scuppered by his inability to secure a major financial backer. It was July 1982 before the event could take place in Shepton Mallet, England, close to Gabriel's home.

Spread across four days, the festival was intended to be the largest event of its kind ever staged—an ambition that it may well have attained, had the local authorities not weighed in with a series of costly prohibitions, the most unreasonable of which demanded that no more than 4,000 fans could witness any one performer. Thus, both Gabriel, as he premiered his entire new album, and the weekend's other headliners, the Liverpool new wavers Echo and the Bunnymen, were confined to the Showering Pavilion, when they ought to have been headlining the rolling fields outside.

For those fans who did make it in, both acts played extraordinary sets, with the Bunnymen's set hitting a staggering high when it unrolled a version of the group's own "Zimbo," darkly rearranged around the propulsive energies of the Royal Burundi Drummers. "That was the whole point of [the festival]," guitarist Will Sergeant later mused. "All sorts of bands from different cultures hanging out and playing together. [Unfortunately], nobody else did it except for us."

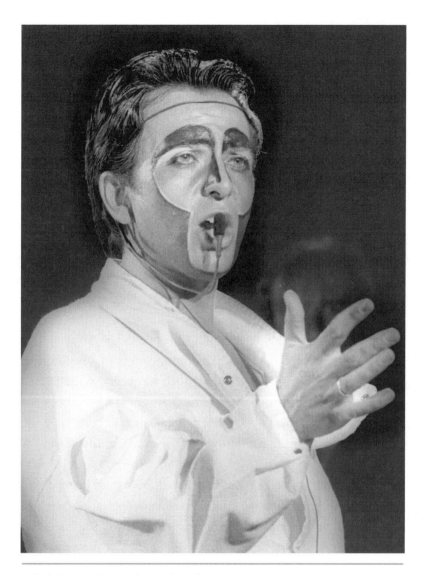

A lightly masked Gabriel plays live, 1983.

Vocalist Ian McCulloch agreed—"That was the only point where all the WOMAD stuff about cultures meeting really happened. 'Twas like being on another planet." In fact, Gabriel also shared his stage with another musical discipline, as he was joined first by Ekome, a Ghanaian drum troupe that was now based just up the road in Bristol, and then by Indian violinist Shankar, who accompanied Gabriel and a passing Peter Hammill for a lengthy, and quite astonishing, set of improvisation. As much as the Bunnymen's achievement, that performance established the vast parameters within which WOMAD intended to work.

A British television special, broadcast in Melvyn Bragg's *South Bank Show* series of documentaries that Halloween, only enhanced the ambition with which Gabriel was approaching the organization. There, he voiced his belief that the hybrid nature of *Peter Gabriel* was only the dawn not only of his intended explorations, but of other players' as well. "I think a lot more musicians are now working in this area, and there will be a [corresponding] style of music to emerge in the 1980s, which I think will be very important and influential."

> "There Goes a Tenner" echoed the narrative form of so many early Genesis numbers.

The rudiments of that fusion were already poking their heads above the parapet. Adam and the Ants and Bow Wow Wow, two of the hottest pop bands of the hour, were both operating within a tribal framework that the Burundi drummers would certainly have recognized—indeed, Gabriel cursed that "most people who haven't seen the Drummers of Burundi are still a bit cynical about them because of all the hipness of Adam and the Ants and Bow Wow Wow." But delve deeper into the rock underground of the age, and matters were somewhat less frivolous. *The Return of the Giant Slits*, the second album by the Slits, one of the most powerful graduates of the British punk scene, had seamlessly woven reggae and African beat influences into its soul, a mood that vocalist Ari Up continued when she linked with dub producer Adrian Sherwood in his New Age Steppers combine.

Kate Bush, too, was working on the fringe of any incipient new style. Powered by ferocious didgeridoo and wobble-board, the title track to her latest LP, 1982's *The Dreaming*, was a resourceful recapitulation of indigenous Australian sounds. The remainder of the album, too, fearlessly pursued *Peter Gabriel* into what the mainstream rock market regarded as uncharted musical territories (the landmark "There Goes a Tenner" even echoed the narrative form of so many early Genesis numbers).

Police drummer Stewart Copeland, too, was looking abroad for inspiration and would soon be off to Africa, where he conceived the startling *The Rhythmatist* solo album. In the meantime, he linked with Gabriel, Shankar, and David Rhodes to create "Across the River," a dynamic percussive soundscape that would highlight Gabriel's next project, the double album world music sampler *Music and Rhythm*.

Released to coincide with the WOMAD Festival itself, a panoply of artists ranged from the pop-ska of the Beat to the bright calypso of Mighty Sparrow, from arch-experimentalists Peter Hammill, Jon Hassell, and Holger Czukay to Pakistan's Nusrat Fatel Ali Khan and Ghana's Alhaji Ibrahim Abdulai, and on through both modern western explorers…David Byrne, Pete Townshend, and Morris Pert…and long-ago African pioneers—a track by Malawian 12-year-olds Lonesi Chewane and Joni Hetare was taped in 1958 by field recorder Hugh Tracey.

Unfortunately, such gestures did little to pay off the huge debts that WOMAD accumulated over the course of the festival. Neither, though Gabriel was certainly grateful for so much vocal support, did the applause and well wishes of the music industry. "We had been fired up by our own imagination and enthusiasm and thought everybody else would be," he confessed as he surveyed the bills for the workshops, lectures, fairgrounds, art exhibitions, food tents, and performers that had converged for the WOMAD experience.

The liquidators were looming, and the unpleasant realities of business were lurking around every corner. Gabriel did not need kind words now; he needed firm action—which is when his old colleagues in Genesis

> "I just hope they haven't built it up into something it can never be."

stepped in, and with Steve Hackett likewise enthused by the prospect, what had once seemed a fleeting dream quickly began to take on flesh. Taking over the massive outdoor festival bowl at Milton Keynes, England, on Oct. 2, 1982, Genesis …Peter Gabriel, Steve Hackett, Tony Banks, Phil Collins, and Mike Rutherford—who was simultaneously celebrating his 32nd birthday…would reunite for one night only. All proceeds would be donated to WOMAD.

Sets by folk guitarist John Martyn (Collins played on his last two albums, *Grace and Danger* and *Dangerous Fool*), Paul Jones's Blues Band, and new wavers Talk Talk opened the afternoon, but all eyes were on the last attraction of the evening, regardless.

"What's strange," Tony Banks mused, "is that the last tour we did with Pete, playing *The Lamb Lies Down on Broadway*, we were playing town halls and not even filling most of them, but now there's an awful lot of people who want to hear it. I just hope they haven't built it up into something it can never be." Phil Collins continued, "It's actually eight years since Peter left so there are going to be a lot of people at the gig who have never seen him with us. For them it won't be a reunion, it will be a new experience."

"Fifteen years ago I went back to my old school Charterhouse..." compeer Jonathan King's introduction was drowned out by a hail of well-meaning abuse from the audience, but he confessed he expected nothing less. Now firmly established as the doyen of all that was tackiest about British pop, and with *pop* a wholly derogatory term where King's musical tastes were concerned, the old entrepreneur reveled in the cries of "fuck off" that flew from the crowd and pressed on to describe how he named the band and cut their first album, how they underwent sundry lineup changes, and how they wound up with "new, even more talented members...and tonight for the first time in a long while, they're all on stage for you."

A repetitive drum beat and fieldwide handclapping serenaded the group's appearance onstage, as roadies struggled beneath the weight of the coffin that they were inexplicably bearing on their shoulders. Then the beat kicked into a heavyweight "Back in New York City," the coffin flew open, and Gabriel leaped out for the opening lyric.

"This is a reunion with Peter Gabriel...to raise money for WOMAD, which means that it's an excuse for us to play all our old songs again," Mike Rutherford explained. "I don't think I'd want to go out and play most of the old songs if it wasn't for a one-off evening, which should just be a lot of fun for everyone. That's why it's important that it's just one show and not a series. It will have highs and lows, but the best bits should be exhilarating.

"I don't think any of us realized how much work this was going to be. It can take a surprising amount of time to learn a song you haven't played for ten years—when I played a tape of 'The Musical Box' the other day, there were about four minutes in the middle that I'd completely forgotten!" He confessed that much of the rehearsal had taken place on the tour bus but admitted, "I can't compare [the old songs] to what we do now because it's another era. Genesis and Pete have gone in very different directions since we parted." But that was "irrelevant for an event like this. I'm just looking forward to seeing Pete back on stage with us and having Phil back on drums again for one show, just to remember what it used to be like."

With Steve Hackett opting to turn out only for the encores, and Phil Collins determined to maintain Genesis's twin-drum attack, both Chester Thompson and Daryl Stuermer were incorporated into the evening's entertainment, with Stuermer remarking, "Personally, I find it hard to see how [Gabriel and Genesis] were ever in the same band, because the way Genesis is now, it's very hard to see a connection. But then I didn't grow up with it. I actually wish we *were* doing it for several nights so that I can really get into it. I'll be OK on the old songs that we still play, but on the others such as 'Musical Box' and 'The Knife' I'll really have to think about what I'm doing. But that's a challenge. After you've been with a band for a while, it's good to make a change, even if it's only for one show."

Intriguingly, Anthony Phillips later revealed that he came close to breaking his career-long aversion to the concert setting, to appear at the event, no matter that he had not stepped on stage since his last show with Genesis, 12 years earlier, "I was approached by Tony Smith who was managing Genesis as well as myself at the time, to see if I would be interested in taking part and I said 'yes.' However, before things went too far, it was taken out of my hands, and the Genesis management decided that I wouldn't need to take part. I was in the middle of recording *Invisible Men* at the time, and it was probably felt that I should concentrate on that. If I had been involved and had to chose a track to play, I think I would have gone for something like 'Visions of Angels.'"

Journeying home after the show, it was difficult to divide expectation from experience—there were no costumes, and that was a disappointment. But there were no embarrassments, and that was a surprise—how many superstar reunions have fallen flat on their faces, crushed not by the weight of anticipation that surrounded their return but by the suddenly dawning knowledge that there was a reason why the musicians separated in the first place and that the intervening years have done nothing to dismiss it.

Reminiscing on the event, Tony Stratton Smith described Hackett as "the loose horse" for that very reason. But he still acknowledged him among "the last great axe men still working," as Hackett carved out the solid string of inventive albums that ensured that he, like his former bandmates, remained an album chart regular. *Spectral Mornings* reached No. 22 in 1979; the following year's *Defector* went to No. 9, and 1981's oddly commercial *Cured* peaked at No. 15.

But Hackett had never forgotten where his audience came from in the first place, and, though his own supporters demanded nothing more than the music they heard on his own records, he was—and remains—prone to dropping a few oldies into the show as well; "mainly," he explained in 2003, "ones that I had a large part in composing, that I consider to be if not entirely, then in a large part mine."

Tonight he made an exception to that rule, surging through both "I Know What I Like" and "The Knife" and reveling in the experience. "At the end of the day, you play what [the audience] want you to play. If the Who ever managed to reform and survive, I'd sincerely hope the remaining members manage to get together 'My Generation,' as opposed to, 'Here's another number from our new album.'"

There would be just "one number from our new album" on display tonight. With Gabriel moving behind the drum kit to rekindle memories of his earliest days as a musician, Collins took the microphone for a pleasing "Turn It On Again"— Genesis's response to the airing, a little earlier, of Gabriel's "Solsbury Hill." Elsewhere, however, it was nostalgia a-go-go…"Dancing with the Moonlit Knight," a wild sing-along through "The Carpet Crawlers," "Firth of Fifth," "The Musical Box," a massive *Lamb Lies Down on Broadway* medley, a super-effective "Supper's Ready," and finally, those two triumphant encores.

The purposes of the evening were never allowed to slip out of sight, however. "Some of you might be wondering what we're doing here," Gabriel remarked to the audience. "This is a sequel to a previous event…a group of people I was working with in Bristol, 600 artists, school kids, mask making, all sorts of performances…the end result was that it was a great event and we lost a pile of money, but I'm very lucky to have a group of people [here] who are prepared to support these ideals—

and in return for your cash, we will try and give what we think you'd like to hear from this combination."

They succeeded with room to spare, and if history has any regrets about the occasion, it is that the only available recordings of the show were the variable-quality bootlegs that began appearing on the streets within weeks of the concert (just in time for Christmas) and that captured the fission, if not the actual feel, of a genuinely special evening. Neither have the members of Genesis shown any sign of needing to relive the evening—Steve Hackett, contrarily, remains the only player to have immortalized the occasion, with the in-concert staple "Time Lapse at Milton Keynes."

Milton Keynes was the final night of Genesis's tour. Little more than a month later, however, both Peter Gabriel and, stepping out alone for the first time, Phil Collins were on the road in their own right, undertaking tours that would stretch into the new year and catapult their personal popularity to fresh heights.

For Gabriel, it was a period capped by the release of his first in-concert album, the double *Peter Gabriel Plays Live*. Demand for such a disc had been rising since the first tour—there was already a thriving market in bootlegs, but Gabriel's sole concessions to the market were the mere handful of cuts that crept out on a promotional flexidisc (a great "Solsbury Hill," from 1977) and the *Bristol Recorder* "talking LP" in 1981.

Conceived as a local music magazine for that corner of western England, the *Recorder* invited contributions from local musicians only—Gabriel was joined by the lesser-known Fish Food, Radicals, X Certs, and Welders, but his offerings were nothing to turn your nose up at, as three tracks, from three separate tours, peaked with the *only* official airing of "Ain't That Peculiar." The double album *Peter Gabriel Plays Live* offered a somewhat longer-lasting experience—when CDs finally arrived on the scene, the albums' 16 tracks overflowed even that format, prompting all digital releases to trim off three full tracks.

An even more visceral peak was conquered when Gabriel undertook a handful of August 1983 shows around Canada, opening for David Bowie, as he undertook his *Serious Moonlight* tour in the shadow of the *Let's Dance* rebirth. (The Tubes completed the bill.)

From a connoisseur's point of view, it was an intriguing pairing, albeit one that perhaps fell a few years too late to be truly meaningful. A decade earlier, though

Bowie and Genesis's musical approaches had lain in stark opposition, the common ground of theater that the pair shared had justified at least whispering their names in the same breath. Shift forward to the late '70s and, with Bowie joining Gabriel in the rarified ranks of "old farts" who appealed to the new wave (and sharing with him the services of Robert Fripp—the guitarist appeared on Bowie's 1977 *Heroes* album), the pair can claim equal credit for the new musical ideas they brought to the post-punk diaspora.

Since that time, however, Bowie's impact had lessened. By 1983, three years had passed since the epochal *Scary Monsters* album, and first impressions of the funk-fired *Let's Dance* were never going to match it with the avant-pop triumphs of old. Gabriel, on the other hand, was still pushing his—and rock's—frontiers forward. Had Bowie only been interested in matching him, the billing at the shows they played together could have ascended to legend. As it was…well, it remained intriguing.

Collins's outing, meanwhile, fascinated as much for the whimsicality of its billing as for the expectations of its audience. In keeping with the irreverent humor that saw him title his new album, *Hello, I Must Be Going*, from a line in the Groucho Marx song "Captain Spaulding" (from the *Animal Crackers* movie), the tour promised "Phil Collins in Concert with the Fabulous Jacuzzis and the One Neat Guy"—the guy in question being a reference to the host of different guests Collins had lined up for each show in turn.

Assuming a Phil Collins audience was actually prone to rioting.

Reconvening many of the musicians who starred on *Face Value*, retaining, too, the occasionally homespun nature of that album's highest points, *Hello, I Must Be Going* was, in many ways, a direct continuation of its predecessor—both "I Don't Care Anymore" and "Through These Walls" all but Xeroxed "In the Air Tonight," as they crept through a spectral landscape of paranoid lyric, echoing drums, and haunted keys. There was little to match that earlier set's strong points, but still it made very few false moves. "Don't Let Him Steal Your Heart Away" is a pretty, piano-powered ballad, and the instrumental "The West Side" kicks off like a Brand X outtake, before soaking into a sultry sax ballad.

A buoyant cover of the Supremes' "You Can't Hurry Love" was endemic on radio and TV that season and topped the U.K. chart before Christmas; the album itself shipped more than three million copies in the United States, and the tour, which saw Chester Thompson join Daryl Stuermer in Collins' backing group, was a riotous success. Assuming a Phil Collins audience was actually prone to rioting.

The tour wrapped up in Washington, DC, on Feb. 20, 1983; apparently infused with more energy than any mere human should be allowed to possess, Collins swept immediately from stage to studio to oversee the latest solo album by Abba songstress Anni-Frid "Frida" Lyngstad-Fredriksson. Her first since Abba fell apart amid a torrent of acrimony and severed relationships, *There's Something Going On* would spawn its own monster hit in the form of the title track, and Collins's all-but untried reputation as a record producer was confirmed overnight.

Frida selected Collins, unsurprisingly, on the strength of *Face Value*. She, too, was experiencing the collapse of her marriage, to Abba bandmate Benny Andersson, as she explained to Collins at their first meeting: "I love what you do, and I think you'd be sympathetic to what I want to do, because I'm just in the process of going through a divorce." In fact, the sessions proved somewhat more fractious than either party might have expected, as Frida fell prey to a colossal attack of nerves and insecurities. Although she had worked as a solo artist in the past, never before had she actually overseen her own project without one watchful eye or another keeping a close watch on the sessions.

Here, only the studio itself—Abba's own Polar setup, of course—was familiar. Collins selected both the musicians and his engineer, all of them English, while the musical freedoms that he extended toward the singer were also a shock. In the past, Abba's Bjorn and Benny had taken full control of the proceedings, and she had learned to keep her opinions to herself. When Collins asked Frida what she thought of something they'd just completed, he was stunned when she shot back, "I don't know—what do *you* think?"

It was "two or three weeks," Collins reported, before "she really started to come through," and still there were problems, as Frida rejected many of the songs Collins recommended to her. Covers of such latter-day songsmiths as Elvis Costello, Squeeze, Joe Jackson, and Phil Lynott were all thrown aside in favor—among other things—of "Here We Stay," a maudlin little ballad that Frida discovered among the unsuccessful also-rans in the U.K. heat of the 1980 Eurovision Song Contest. Given the utter scorn with which the British public regard even

Eurovision's most successful offerings (Abba's "Waterloo" among them!), the producer's mortification can only be imagined. But he had scarcely even begun to tremble. Before the sessions began, he promised to duet with Frida on one song of her choosing. She selected "Here We Stay."

Collins was horrified. "That was a complete lapse of taste on my part," he admitted to *Sounds*. "I think it's hideous. When we chose the song I was singing it to her to try and get her to loosen up, because it's different if you're foreign to sing English lyrics, and I didn't think Frida sounded convincing on that track. So she said, 'Maybe you could sing this with me,' and at the time I didn't think of it as a duet, as we were both going to sing all of it. But because of the different key registers, it ended up sounding like Rita 'n' Kris or Elton 'n' Kiki—but I was committed to it by then. It is hideous!"

For all its growing pains, however, *Something's Going On* was a major success—a chart-topper in Sweden naturally, but Top 20 in the United Kingdom and Top 40 (actually, 41) in the United States. The so-vigorous title track, too, proved enormous, a No. 13 hit in America, and it was only Collins's refusal to sanction its release as a single that prevented "Here We Stay" from following "Something's Going On" to similar (possibly even greater) heights. "I said, 'No way am I going to be associated with this as a single,' and we used the record company excuse to stop it, by saying that Virgin, Charisma, and Atlantic would cause a fuss."

Pausing to reunite with Banks and Rutherford at the 28th Ivor Novello Awards ceremony in May 1983, where Genesis received the gong for "Outstanding Contribution to British Music," the Frida sessions were no sooner at an end than Collins was hastening to pick up his next gig, taking a backseat role in former Led Zeppelin frontman Robert Plant's band, as he recorded his *Principle of Moments* album at Rockfield Studios in Monmouth, Wales.

"Fucking hell, what if he's a bit of an arsehole?"

He had filled the role once before, as one of several guest musicians on Plant's *Pictures at Eleven* debut album in 1982, as the singer stretched his solo legs for the first time since the demise of Led Zeppelin. It was an awkward period for Plant, who subsequently confessed that he was expecting to be crucified in the music press—Led Zeppelin, after all, was a hard act for anybody to follow. Neither was his insecurity confined to the response to his new music—the very making of it filled him with nerves, as he found himself working with a whole new contingent of musicians, including some he had never met before they arrived at the studio.

Phil Collins fit into that category, and Plant reminisced of their first-ever meeting, "He was a great surprise. I love his drumming, his use of dynamics on things like 'In the Air Tonight.' His phrasing on the kit is great; he works around the beat, rather than on top of it. We did six tracks in three days [Cozy Powell played on the remainder of the LP], which was phenomenal, really, and it was quite a relief because, before he arrived, we were all going, 'Fucking hell, what if he's a bit of an arsehole?' We'd never met him before he came up to do the session."

Clearly Plant had not been following the English music press's already-burgeoning obsession with Collins as "the nicest guy in rock"—an only halfway complimentary reflection on his cheerful demeanor, smiling chops, and sensitive muse, but still he had nothing to worry about. Collins and Plant became fast friends, and having reprised his drumming role across *Principle of Moments*, Collins stunned onlookers by joining Plant's live group as well, for a six-week North American jaunt through August/September 1983.

It was an exhausting itinerary, but Collins was indefatigable. "It's not like work," he reasoned. "People say to me, 'How can you keep doing it?' [but] it's not like work, doing things that I've been doing. I've never done anything else, and it's just fun to do. It's great. I'm very lucky to be paid for doing this."

CHAPTER SIXTEEN

DO YOU STILL WEAR BELL-BOTTOMS?

Like Phil Collins, both Tony Banks and Mike Rutherford were busy during Genesis's latest hiatus. Rutherford was constructing the oddly titled *Acting Very Strange* solo album, and Banks was throwing himself into scoring Michael Winner's remake of *The Wicked Lady*. The director had recently completed a successful pairing with Jimmy Page and was keen to continue working in a rock vein—Banks was recommended to him by a mutual acquaintance at Atlantic Records and, though he was not initially enthused by the project, agreed because it afforded him the opportunity to work with an orchestra. The end result, Banks later admitted, saw him operating more as an arranger than a performer, and far more of his attention was targeted toward the solo album he was recording at the same time, *The Fugitive*.

Recording with Daryl Stuermer and session men Mo Foster, Tony Beard, and Steve Gadd, Banks admitted that the most significant element of the album was his decision to take the lead vocals himself. "Once I'd done that, then I had to work out what I was capable of singing because my voice is limited. I'd tried singing some slightly more elaborate things such as I'd written for Peter or Phil to sing, and I realized that I couldn't handle that—it didn't really work, especially with certain kinds of words that I made them sing!"

Nevertheless, *The Fugitive* emerged a tremendous album, a collection of tight, uncluttered numbers, with the opening "This Is Love" a powerhouse that spotlighted a voice that had no problems adapting itself to its punchy surroundings, as

Banks himself later agreed. "I was surprised with my voice as well; I could take how I sounded. It's often difficult when you hear your own voice, to hear yourself as a singer, but I thought to myself that I sounded as good as a lot of people who like to call themselves singers."

With so many other outlets for their songs at their disposal, then, it was small wonder that, as they reunited at the Farm Studios in early 1983 to begin work on a new Genesis album, the three suddenly discovered that, though they weren't exactly bereft of new material, they were nevertheless in shorter supply than they may normally have been.

The eventual title of this new opus, too, suggested a certain paucity of fresh ideas. Peter Gabriel may have spent his career so far naming all his albums after himself, but for Genesis to come up with nothing more imaginative than *Genesis* was not what the fans wanted to hear. The explanation, that the group needed to reaffirm its own identity after all the excitement surrounding the solo releases, was itself reasonable enough. But still, it made little impression on a core audience raised on such sleights of linguistic hand as *Selling England by the Pound*, *A Trick of the Tail*, and *...And Then There Were Three*. Neither, to judge from the album's placings in subsequent "fan's favorite"-type polls, were the record's contents to make any greater impression.

> "I sounded as good as a lot of people who like to call themselves singers."

Behind the scenes, much had changed since the release of *Three Sides Live*, as Genesis transferred its contractual affections to Charisma's distributor, Virgin—the first step toward the final demise of Charisma Records in 1985. It was not a painful death—rather, as Tony Stratton Smith put it, it was simply time to let go and move on. The label, like the music industry in general, had lost a lot of its life force in recent years; it had become more concerned with numbers and returns than with the simple art of making music.

With the departure of Genesis, not one of the label's founding fathers remained on board, although the careers of most—Peter Hammill and the latest configuration of Lindisfarne included—continued unabated. Peter Gabriel, too, had moved to Virgin, and Steve Hackett departed after one row too many...he wanted to release a live album, but the label demanded a straightforward follow-up to *Cured*, and that, too, rankled with Stratton Smith. He still made decisions at the label, but increasingly he felt that he made only *some* of them. Other interests decided other matters.

But Stratton Smith, too, had other interests, and these began to consume his attention more and more. He was a governor of the Sports Aid Foundation and the owner of a number of successful racehorses...Chukeroo, Baronial, Fighting Chance, Gylippus, and Beggars Bridge. Charisma even sponsored its own race, the Charisma Gold Cup at Kempton Park. (The race retains that name to this day.) He had dabbled in publishing—Charisma was responsible for some of the first serious rock books ever published in Britain, including a compendium of early writings from *Zig Zag* magazine and the legendary *No-one Waved Goodbye*, a series of essays mourning rock's fallen heroes. And he had thrown himself into movies, raising the financing for *Monty Python and the Holy Grail* and producing efforts ranging from *The Eye of a Dictator* to former Bonzo Viv Stanshall's *Sir Henry at Rawlinson End*.

That was the direction in which he now intended moving. His first television screenplay, *The Last Enemy*, was already in production, with Anthony Andrews and Patrick McGoohan in the starring roles, and there was more, much more, in the pipeline. On June 27, 1985, Stratton Smith signed his name to a piece of Charisma Records stationery for the final time. Pointing out, first, "that I am not getting any younger" (he was now 54), he informed recipients of this final letter, "I have decided...to reduce my day-to-day involvement in music, and, towards that end, I am selling my shares in Charisma records to Richard Branson of the Virgin Group." After four years as distributor, Virgin was now the label's sole owner—and Charisma, as an identifiable imprint in its own right, vanished soon after. Fittingly, the label's final release was a single by Tony Banks.

Sadly, Stratton Smith—now living in Las Palmas—would not have long in which to pursue his latest interests. Visiting a friend on the island of Jersey, Stratton Smith's heart gave out on him on March 19, 1987.

Of course, such matters, the iconography of a record label, the passing of its visionary founder, and a switch in corporate branding make little difference to the general public. It was, for some fans, strange to pick up a new Genesis album and not see the familiar old Mad Hatter logo raising a salutary teacup somewhere on the sleeve; it was odd, too, to imagine that the entire project was pieced together without "Strat" maintaining a fatherly ear on the proceedings. But it was no stranger than picking up a new Genesis album and discovering everything else that the band had in store.

The most successful numbers were those that retained the most readily identifiable elements of Genesis's past—the two-part "Home by the Sea"/"Second Home by the Sea," for instance, was an almost-traditional epic, awash with dynamic instrumental passages and built around melodies that came to light during one of the trio's trademark jam sessions. "That's All," meanwhile, was a sublimely plaintive number that lifted its melody near wholesale from an old Procol Harum song and, in so doing, doffed a very reverential cap in the direction of a group whose career, through the late '60s and early '70s, had mirrored many of the defiant shifts and shudders that Genesis itself was now taking as a matter of course.

Whether such subtlety was either intended by the band or registered by their listeners matters not. Although Collins was prone to introducing "That's All" as "a little country-and-western number," it remained a joyfully jaunty little piece, undemanding, perhaps, but preciously precocious all the same.

A U.K. Top Five hit, "Mama" was even more astonishing, compensating in atmosphere and feeling for what it lacked in terms of tradition. Stealthily riding a full-frontal "Intruder"/"In the Air Tonight" drum beat, this six-and-a-half-minute ode to a prostitute was constructed around a drum pattern devised by Mike Rutherford, fed back through a reverb unit. "A lot of the lyrics came from the sound of the voice," Phil Collins explained. "You play with the sound." The song was, he said, "slightly simple, sustained chords and dramatic." But it was also remarkably effective, not least of all that moment when Collins unleashed a deep-throated, sinister chortle—which, he subsequently confessed, was inspired by a rap record. Producer Hugh Padgham was playing Grandmaster Flash's so-seminal "The Message" in the studio; the idea of the laughter was lifted from that.

Elsewhere, however, there was the frenetic near-funk of "Taking It All Too Hard"; there was the frame-shaking gibberish of "Illegal Alien"; and over it all, there was the sense that too much of *Genesis* knowingly sacrificed the humor, hubris, and humility that had once laid at the heart of the group's music. Even at its most rewarding, past commercial success itself appeared as nothing more than a by-product of the music. This time, for the first time, a Genesis album felt purposefully crafted with

Rutherford and Collins spot a carpet crawler.

more than one eye on the marketplace and more than one ear turned to the requirements of Top 40 radio.

The shift was very deliberate. Collins confessed, "We tried to stick to one tempo for each song. In the past we used to employ a lot of tempo slowdowns and speedups, in which the tempos would vary from verse to chorus, along with signature changes from four to seven to nine, a solo in thirteen, that sort of thing. We did so almost just to prove that we could, and because, at the time, during the early 70s, bands were doing that sort of thing." But, he continued, "once you've learned how to use odd times in your music you no longer need to prove to yourself that you can. Of course one never really masters that avenue of playing, and you can always learn more, yet as our songwriting—which is the main thrust of the band—changed, we moved away from that school of playing."

Hugh Padgham's production itself forced nothing dynamically new and/or offensive into the sound. But, where the drums were once as loud as they needed to be, now they deliberately shook the speakers and rattled the guts. Where the keyboards once played symphonies, now every riff was draped in the drama of overtures. And, where Collins's voice once clung tenuously to whichever melodies were closest to hand, now it bellowed across them all. In the cold light of subsequent decades, we can describe *Genesis* as '80s arena rock *in excelsis*. In the less subjective light of 1983, the album was simply one more in a growing litany of hyperactive overproduced jobs, and if you listened close and hard enough, you could hear the kitchen sink rattle. Yes, they'd even thrown that into the mix.

Despite all the evidence piling up against them, the group battled hard against the perception that they had somehow "changed." Collins complained once more, "We think of ourselves as songwriters who can do a bit of this, a bit of that...whereas other people think of us as *Genesis*, this sacred cow which mustn't do anything else, like a brand name. But really, it's whatever we do."

Such overstated musical bombast had its place in the market, of course—at least, in America. Although "That's All" alone delivered a major hit single ("Mama" reached No. 73, "Taking It All Too Hard" hit No. 50, "Illegal Alien" No. 44), the parent album soared to No. 9, selling more than four million copies in the process.

In Britain and Europe, where ears have always been better attuned to darker thoughts, deeper melodies, dryer humor, and tiny theaters, *Genesis* was always going to be too richly egged for most local tastes. America, however, has little time for subtlety, little patience with poignancy. In a land where most fans' first gig finds them playing humanoid-a-go-go with 40,000 other arena-goers, and the view from the cheapest seats is half a mile or more from the stage, bigger is better, biggest is best, and, having already delivered a record of such gargantuan proportions, some of the venues where Genesis played during that winter of 1983/84 were among the vastest the United States had to offer, from the small city-sized Hollywood Sportatorium to Madison Square Gardens, from the Atlanta Omni to the Tampa Expo Hall, and onto the outsized concrete hubcap that is the Tacoma Dome.

There was room, however, for just one stop in Europe, a five-night stint at the Birmingham NEC, at the end of February, an omission that seemed to speak volumes for where Genesis's priorities now lay.

Cynics could take solace from the fact that each of the Birmingham shows passed its profits onto charity, but the pre-advertised presence of the Prince and Princess of Wales at the final night added to the hubris of the "ordinary" fan, as the event was transformed

> "People think of us as *Genesis*, this sacred cow which mustn't do anything else."

from a mere rock concert to one of those "Events" that draw its audience not from the people who want to see the star attraction but who needed to be seen themselves. Flashbulbs that once were reserved for the musicians spent the entire evening scouring the crowd for tabloid headlines, and if the entire affair could be condemned as another indication of the royal family's decline in decorum and distance, it also served up another symptom of the establishment's increasing co-opting of rock 'n' roll for its own self-aggrandizing purposes.

But Genesis was not making records for resentful locals and traditionalist stick-in-the-muds. One could (and many did) spite the group for turning its back on the European preferences and prejudices wherein it had once flourished so brightly, but rock 'n' roll is a business as much as an art form, and if you're not in business to do the best you can, why bother going into it at all? America was the biggest market in the world, and as the 1980s picked up speed, America needed bands such as

Genesis—not to intrigue them with tales of pedophile ghosts and somnambulant sheep, but to help them escape the real-life nightmares that made characters such as that seem infantile by comparison.

The Afghan crisis was over now; so were those other hideous humps that haunted the national psyche during the early '80s: the Iranian hostage crisis, the ever-churning revelations over just what a mess was made of the Vietnam War (barely half-a-decade gone and still a festering wound), the increasingly right-wing rhetoric of the incumbent Reagan presidency. But the Cold War's frigid fingers were still poised above the little red button that would unleash a nuclear holocaust upon Everyday America; American troops were still fighting and dying in the name of other nations' petty wars. The economy was tanking, and memories of the 70s oil crisis were growing stronger every day.

Unemployment was soaring, and hope was plunging. If society had anything to cling onto, it was music that didn't simply take one out of oneself; it transported the body as readily as the spirit, on waves of rhythm that elevated the adrenalin, on swollen hooks that turned mundanity to magic. They may not all have been the *biggest* albums of 1983, but the most memorable ones were undoubtedly those that kicked introspection in the teeth and bathed the entire world in the sound of soaring hope—Bowie's *Let's Dance*, U2's *War*, Michael Jackson's *Thriller*, of course…and Genesis's *Genesis*, an album of such unrelenting optimism that, when Phil Collins pledged on the final track, "It's Gonna Get Better," an entire nation could believe he was singing straight at them. And, if the truth be told, he was.

Hardly surprisingly, Collins was the first of the three musicians to make a major splash in the aftermath of the tour, as he took an unremarkable outtake from the *Face Value* sessions, "How Can You Sit There?" and transformed it into the instantly irresistible theme for the forthcoming Taylor Hackford movie, *Against All Odds*, "Against All Odds (Take a Look at Me Now)." Both Mike Rutherford and Peter Gabriel also contributed music to the soundtrack, but it was Collins's effort that hit the heights, as three weeks at the top of the U.S. chart in April saw the record become Collins's first-ever American million-selling single.

"I was a bit peeved, but that's life."

Unfortunately, the experience would be soured when Oscar time rolled around and "Against All Odds" emerged a hot favorite among the nominees for Song of the Year. Excitedly, Collins contacted the Academy and offered to perform the song live, only to have his offer declined via a letter addressed to "Mr. Phil Cooper." Dancer Ann Reinking had already been lined up to perform the song. Collins vented his spleen in the press, but the snub itself still rankled.

"I was a bit peeved, but that's life," Collins told *Playboy* later. "That night, I was sitting in my seat, and poor old Ann Reinking, who was singing the song, came in. She knew I was there and knew about all the fuss that had gone on about it. And…well, she may be a dancer, but she can't sing. She was awful. I felt sorry for her. Kenny Loggins was sitting behind me. and he said, 'I can't believe what they did to your song.' He wasn't performing his, either, so all I could say was, 'You've got yours to come, mate.' There was politics behind it. But after the whole thing, they sent me an application for membership. I thought it was a joke. So now I'm a fully paid-up member of the Academy." (The Oscar itself was ultimately awarded to Stevie Wonder's "I Just Called to Say I Love You.")

There were no such problems with Collins's next performance, as he confirmed his status (alongside Duran Duran!) among Princess Diana's favorite performers, by appearing at the third-annual Prince's Trust Rock Gala at London's Royal Albert Hall. Launched by Prince Charles in 1976, the Trust was geared toward providing training, mentoring, and financial support for 14–30 year olds attempting to overcome troubled backgrounds and make their way in the world. As a nervous solo debutante in 1982, Collins appeared at the charity's first-ever Rock Gala, drumming behind Ian Anderson and Robert Plant. Now, having played a major part in persuading the charity to launch the event as an annual affair, he was headlining alongside the returning Plant and Kate Bush.

"Diana was first a fan of my music because of the romantic side, you know, the ballads," Collins told *Playboy*. "When I saw her one of the first times, she said, 'I love "Separate Lives",' and I told her I'd send her a copy. She told me she already had one. Once I actually gave [her] a complete set of the *Genesis* albums and the next concert I played, she came up afterward and asked, 'Why didn't you play more from *A Trick of the Tail*?' I mean, she actually had listened to the things and remembered the songs we hadn't played."

There would be no further new music as the year passed along, but still Collins seemed ubiquitous. In October, he made his television acting debut when he appeared as a smarmy English game show host, Phil the Shill, in an episode of the cop show *Miami Vice*; in November, he made it onto the big screen with a role in Tom Cruise's *Risky Business.*

"*Miami Vice* was great fun. The script was written for me after the writers saw this bit I did on stage, introducing the members of the band. I was a game show host…this tasteless cad who had terrible clothes. They tried to write all the English expressions I might say, and at one point, they wanted me to say, 'You must take me for a right wanker.' They had heard British people use the word *wanker*, but they didn't know it was a word for masturbator. In another place in the script, they wanted me to hang up the phone and say, 'I hope he dies impotent.' I thought it wasn't the kind of thing I would say, so I told them I should hang up and say, 'I hope his ghoulies fall off.' Meaning his balls. When some producer came in from L.A., he heard that and told me I couldn't say that. [But] wanker was OK."

> "I hope his ghoulies fall off."

December 1984 saw Collins take his place among the cast of dozens who filed into a London recording studio at the behest of Boomtown Rats frontman Bob Geldof, to line up as Band Aid. The cream of early 80s British rock was there—Bananarama, Duran Duran, Paul Young, Culture Club…and an awful lot of faces and names that mean nothing today. But still, "Do They Know It's Christmas," a benefit single for victims of the then-ongoing famine in Ethiopia, would become the fastest- and biggest-selling single ever in British history, and if Collins's role in that success was simply that of playing the drums, as the Band Aid organization picked up steam, he was destined to become one of its most memorable participants.

According to Collins, Geldof rang him the day after watching the first BBC TV report on the famine. "He said, 'It's disgusting. We have to do something. I want to make a record, and we need a famous drummer.' Two weeks later, I went to the studio for the session. It was phenomenal. There were about 60 bands there. I think I was the oldest one there. Youch…."

A new Phil Collins album finally descended in the new year. *No Jacket Required* was titled after the jobsworth *maitre'd* who refused him entry to a plush restaurant because the drummer's own jacket didn't match the dress code. The fact that Collins's dining partner, a distinctly jacketless (but, infinitely more recognizable) Robert Plant, had already been obsequiously ushered to his seat did not impress the drummer one iota.

The album was, Collins warned, very hurriedly written and recorded, but that was not about to dampen enthusiasm for it, as Hugh Padgham and Collins conspired to create a giddily vivacious album, alive with the keyboard and drum sounds that now dominate our memories of mid-80s music…the moment the needle hits the punchy, riff-driven "Only You and I Know," the mind is transported back to an absolutely unmistakable time and place.

To pigeonhole the entire album on the strength of its most familiar moments, however, is to overlook Collins's own attempts to break out of the easy-listening straitjacket into which the media was already wrapping him. Even he admitted it was entertaining to find himself compared with Barry Manilow; and he agreed that great swathes of his audience may have filed their albums together beneath the cocktail cabinet.

But "Long Long Way to Go," so hauntingly hypnotic, offered up a downbeat cousin of "In the Air Tonight" in its emphasis on atmospheric claustrophobia; the hyperactive "Who Said I Would" punched a squealing Gary Barnacle sax solo into orbit, and the rousing finale "Take Me Home" not only brought guest appearances from Sting and sometime Culture Club backing singer Helen Terry, it also numbered Peter Gabriel among its vocal cast. As reunions go, it did not necessarily sound like the answer to three years worth of older fans' prayers, but the percolating tribal percussives, a savage Stuermer solo, and a Collins vocal that bordered on affecting frailty closed *No Jacket Required* as effectively as "Tomorrow Never Knows" concluded his debut.

With the first single from the set, the funky "Sussudio," slamming into overdrive in January 1985, *No Jacket Required* was an inevitable chart-topper. The accompanying world tour was as all-encompassing as any Genesis had ever attempted, and an apparently unlikely duet with former Earth Wind and Fire vocalist Philip Bailey (Collins produced his latest album, *Chinese Wall*) proved there was no limit to the possibilities open to Collins, when the softly languid "Easy Lover" shot to No. 1 in Britain, No. 2 in America, in March.

Phil Collins onstage in 1985.

The record was enormous, but Collins nevertheless recalled it as "a real struggle. Bailey got a lot of flak for being produced by someone who is white. There was this paranoia that [it] would not be played by black stations. They didn't want to know about me, because I'm white. We did it, though, and broke down some of those walls. 'Easy Lover' was a black hit and a pop hit, and my song 'Sussudio' was a No. 3 record on the black charts, as a result of the thing being opened up by 'Easy Lover.' And the reason I was on the video for 'Easy Lover' was that I knew it would-n't be shown [by MTV] if it was just Phil Bailey." At the time, Collins condemned, "If you're Prince or Lionel Richie, you [could] get played on MTV, but not many other black artists [could]."

The *No Jacket Required* tour wound down in New York City at the beginning of July 1985; just days later, on July 13, Collins was back in the headlines as Bob Geldof crowned six months of planning with Live Aid, two massive benefit concerts staged simultaneously in London and Philadelphia and drawing in performances from virtually every major-league performer of the age. Collins (but not, strangely, Genesis) was inevitably among them.

Across a day of stellar triumphs, broadcast live around the globe, any number of artists emerged with career-best or, at least, career-defining performances—Bryan Ferry, David Bowie, and U2 included. But it was Collins who left the most indelible mark, as he conspired (via the supersonic jet Concorde) to appear at both the British and American events, at 3:30 p.m. in London and again at 6 p.m. in Philly. He was on stage, too, for both Eric Clapton and the near-reformed Led Zeppelin's performances, the latter renewing his acquaintance with Robert Plant, the former previewing his blossoming relationship with Clapton—the guitar legend's just-released *Behind the Sun* album was the latest Phil Collins production; soon, the pair would be touring together. ("The first time I put my finger on the control button and said, 'Do you want to do that guitar solo again?' was a big moment," Collins later laughed.)

"You could get the Concorde and actually be in Philadelphia in time to play."

"I was on tour for *No Jacket Required* when Sting rang up," Collins reflected of his recruitment to Live Aid. "He found me somewhere in America and rang up and asked if we should do something together…. I said 'yes,' and he came down to my place, and we rehearsed a couple of his songs, then rehearsed a couple of my songs, just me and him. [But] during the course of the tour, a conversation had come up about whether I could play drums with anybody. And all my friends were playing at the American portion of the event in Philadelphia.

"So someone, I think it was Harvey Goldsmith, who was organizing the British side of the event, said to me, 'You could get the Concorde and actually be in Philadelphia in time to play.' So I said "OK, I don't mind doing that," not knowing it was going to be *such* an event, and that people would *still* be talking about me doing two concerts in one day [a decade later]. Really, at the time, it was just a logistical exercise…the whole day was crazy, and, to be honest, it wasn't until the next day that I realized just how big the event was. I mean, to me, it was just a concert. I'd been doing concerts like that for the past nine months, so I wasn't aware of the size and the stature of the event until afterwards."

Nor was Collins to allow the event to simply slip into the past, as did many of his fellow performers. "Colours," the eight-minute epic that would distinguish his next album, *No Jacket Required*, followed through his feelings as he strove "to get across a simple point—that each of those kids you saw on the famous famine footage has a name. They have a mum, dad, brothers, and sisters. And there's anger in the second half of the song—how much longer do we have to be told it's getting better, when nothing changes?"

While Collins continued to occupy the eyes of the world, both of his bandmates were equally busy, albeit with somewhat less satisfactory results. For Banks, a great part of the latest layoff was spent (or "wasted," as he put it) working toward a soundtrack for the then-embryonic follow-up to Stanley Kubrick's landmark *2001: A Space Odyssey* movie, *2010*. No matter what he submitted, however, the studio demanded something else, and when Banks finally despaired of the entire project, it was in the knowledge that he had been forced to turn down a crop of other projects in the meantime—a soundtrack to Arnold Schwarzenegger's first *Terminator* movie included.

Instead, the only complete scores he completed during this period were for the blink-and-you'll-miss-it cult classic *Quicksilver*, wherein one track, "Short Cut to Nowhere," paired Banks with Marillion's Fish, and for the super-low-budget sci-fi exploitation turkey *Lorca and the Outlaws,* a project best dignified for Banks by the caliber of artist with whom he found himself working—singers Jim Diamond, riding the success of his 1984 U.K. chart-topper "I Should Have Known Better," and Toyah Wilcox (Mrs. Robert Fripp) both voiced tracks for the project. Shelved for releases in their own right, it would be left to Banks's 1986 solo album *Soundtracks* to bring both of these into the light of day.

Mike Rutherford, meanwhile, had apparently dispensed with any notion of a solo career *per se* and devoted himself instead to forming a new band, titled with majestic mundanity, Mike and the Mechanics. Compiled around the contributions of one-time Ace vocalist Paul Carrack and former Sad Café mainstay Paul Young, songwriter B.A. Robertson (famed both for his own short-lived solo career and a successful spell writing for Cliff Richard), and producer Chris Neil, Mike and the Mechanics got off to a flying start as its self-titled debut album rose into the American Top 30, and the single, "Silent Running," soared to No. 6 in late 1985.

Rutherford explained, "The idea for Mike and the Mechanics came because I wanted to write shorter songs, songs that would fit easier on the radio. I called two of my favorite singers [Carrack and Young], and when both of them said 'yes,' it was full-steam ahead with the project. The idea to write fresh, radio-friendly pop songs would get an extra dimension if I could use two different voices. The synergy between the three of us has resulted in something magic, something which I could only describe as being Mike and the Mechanics."

Early in the new year, the group's next single, "All I Need Is a Miracle" climbed to No. 5, and a tour through the early summer months proved similarly, phenomenally, successful. It was all a staggering development that could, had Rutherford had no other preoccupations, have rendered Mike and the Mechanics among the giants of the age, at least in the United States. (British and European interest was somewhat less pronounced.) That, however, was not likely to happen. Speaking in 1999 but reiterating sentiments he'd been expressing for 13 years before that, Rutherford explained, "It would be very natural and easy for me to fix on the Mechanics and do nothing else, but I think it's quite important at this stage to actually spend a bit of time in other areas, developing other sides of writing as well."

By mid-1986, though the individual members were active, three years had elapsed since *Genesis,* a period marked only by the release of yet another live video,

The Mama Tour, and the resumption of the rumor-go-round concerning the future. In fact, the group was in and out of the studio together since the previous fall, piecing together what would become the *Invisible Touch* album and reveling in the fresh energies and new enthusiasms with which the recent hiatus had imbibed the group.

Again they worked from a whole new template. Although the group's appetite for epics would be granted plenty of scope by the 14-minute "Domino," the heart of *Invisible Touch* was to be dominated by one short, sharp shock after another: "Tonight Tonight Tonight," "Land of Confusion," "In Too Deep," "Throwing It All Away," and "Invisible Touch" itself. Once again, critics would eye Collins's solo career and wonder whether he was maybe exerting more influence upon the band's direction than a three-way democracy should ordinarily allow.

Collins shared their suspicions, if only jocularly. "On a generous day, I'll blame me for the change," he conceded, and it is true that the keyboard sound that powers "Invisible Touch" is all but identical to that driving his own "Only You Know and I Know." More seriously, however, Collins was adamant. "I don't dominate Genesis. It's just that since *Duke*, I've become an equal third. To those that wish I'd go back to being subservient to Mike and Tony, well, we're all changing. I answer those fans by saying, 'Do you still wear bellbottoms, read the same books, like the same kind of girls?' Of course not. Well, we don't like the same kind of music. Allow us to change."

The sound of *Invisible Touch*, he insisted, was the sound of the three band members "growing up, listening to different things. We were always a group of songwriters who would write 3-, 10- and 20-minute songs. We still write 10-minute songs, like 'Domino,' but, unfortunately, the three-minute songs have gotten better and become hits. I don't feel we've bastardized the way we were, as we still work the same way. Diehard fans will say, 'Rubbish. "The Carpet Crawlers," "I Know What I Like"—that was progressive!' But I don't see that. We'd have killed for hit singles back in the early days!"

By the time BBC Television's *Whistle Test* cameras arrived at the Farm that May to document the band's rehearsals on the eve of the album's release, they found the trio in contagiously high spirits, toying with a clutch of songs that—even before they hit radio and TV—appeared destined to dominate the airwaves for the remainder of the year. And so it proved. *Invisible Touch* retained the spirits and inclinations of its most immediate predecessors, of course. But, in absorbing both the pop purity of Collins's solo career and the reflected glories of the vast success that he was now enjoying, it placed Genesis on an altogether different plateau from any it had hitherto scaled, at the top of a commercial tree that would see it establish itself not simply as the biggest draw of the day but one of the biggest of the decade, a vastly successful hit-making machine whose past incarnations weren't even ancient history to the millions who now flocked to buy Genesis music. They were absolutely irrelevant.

It was not all good, of course. With fame of that magnitude, an artist enters an entirely different sphere of media attention, where the music itself is sidelined as merely a by-product of the personalities involved—personality, of course, being what separates a mere star from a superstar. Suddenly it was not the quality of the records that mattered to so many observers, it was the appearance of the musicians who made them, the lifestyles they entertained, the beliefs that they espoused. Half a decade later, when Nirvana's Kurt Cobain complained that he never wanted to be "famous," the cynical response was, "So why did you form a band?"

But there is fame and there is *fame*, and it is a long way indeed from the cover of *Spin* or the *New Musical Express* to the front cover of *Vogue* and a lead fluff-piece on *Entertainment Tonight*—such a long way that precious few of even rock's greatest celebrities have ever traveled the full distance. Cobain did, and it ultimately destroyed him. Genesis did not destruct. But they were just as baffled by the transition as he, even as the members acknowledged their own parts in creating it.

"We had these tracks that really did make us seem like a pop band," Tony Banks later reflected. "It's not necessarily the work I'm proudest of, although it [was] fun to have done it." Other acolytes agree with him—Alan Hewitt, founder of Genesis's official *The Waiting Room* fanzine, later described *Invisible Touch* as the first Genesis album he ever played once and then turned into a frisbee.

He was, however, in the minority. *Invisible Touch* was an instant chart-topper across Europe, Top Three in America, and a veritable monster elsewhere around the world. All-pervading singles spun out like shrapnel: "Invisible Touch" crowned the U.S. chart for a week in July; "Tonight Tonight Tonight" and "In Too Deep" both reached No. 3; "Throwing It All Away" and "Land of Confusion" peaked just one notch lower.

The album even set new (albeit necessarily short-lived) records as the biggest-selling British compact disc of all time. The new format was just a matter of years old in 1986; it was still widely regarded as either the province of fanatical audiophiles or the latest cynical music business attempt to make us buy all the same old records one more time. The notion that it would swiftly rise up to push both vinyl and the cassette—at that time, the only formats in which music was made available—into extinction seemed incredible and incredibly optimistic.

But Virgin sensed the direction in which the technological winds were blowing, and *Invisible Touch* became the first new rock record ever to be released in all three formats simultaneously. Less than a month later, it was being reported that, of the 100,000 or so copies *Invisible Touch* had shifted in the United Kingdom, more than 10 percent of them were CDs, an absolutely unheard of quantity but one that Virgin were swift to take advantage of. Long before many larger record companies ever got around to looking back at their own past releases, Virgin were inaugurating a CD reissue campaign that included a healthy clutch of classic Charisma albums in its earliest batches—Genesis, Van der Graaf Generator, Peter Hammill, and Lindisfarne were all amply represented on the CD shelves before the end of the 1980s.

The world of video, too, opened itself wide to Genesis. The group had been issuing videos (or promotional clips as they were known back then) since 1976, when director Bruce Gowers shot perfunctorily staged visions of "Ripples" and "Robbery, Assault and Battery." The advent of MTV in 1980, however, saw Genesis—like so many others, of course—hurl itself into the process, with often scintillating results.

Teaming with Stuart Orme in 1981, Genesis shot a string of increasingly eye-catching videos that peaked, in 1983, with "Illegal Alien." (Orme would also handle Phil Collins's early shoots, as well as Frida's Collins–produced "There's Something Going On"); at year's end, however, the group teamed up for the first time with Jim Yukich to shoot the charming bum's-eye vistas of "That's All" and inaugurate a partnership that would extend into the next decade.

Just one of the videos would be farmed out elsewhere, and it remains one of the 1980s most pervasive images. "Land of Confusion" was handled by Peter Fluck and

Roger Law, the minds behind British television's then massively successful *Spitting Image*, a political puppet show that itself has been described among the most brilliantly vicious satires ever granted mainstream exposure.

Phil Collins had already been caricatured within the show's vast corpus of cruelly accurate but hideously exaggerated puppet figures—under the guidance of resident songwriter Phillip Pope, Collins "appeared" performing the ruthlessly accurate parody "Oh, You Must Be Leaving" while weeping such copious tears that, once preparations for the Genesis video got under way, the puppeteers found they needed to make a new Collins doll. The existing one's eyes were too teary.

The latex approximations of Collins, Banks, and Rutherford were not the sole stars of the ensuing video. Virtually the entire puppet cast of *Spitting Image* made an appearance, faces that ranged from Madonna and Prince to the Pope and the British royal family, President and Mrs. Reagan, a slew of British politicians... replaying the video today is an experience akin to rewatching the original Band Aid film, where face after face of dimly remembered familiarity files past the lens, and all of them seem to be named "Him (or Her) Out of Thingy."

Deservedly, "Land of Confusion" wound up claiming several of the video industry's most prestigious awards (including a Grammy), even as the single drove into the American Top Five. And the honors it didn't snag were scooped up by Peter Gabriel, whose return to action in 1986 saw him, too, advance to a commercial peak that had never seemed even vaguely plausible in the past. As *Invisible Touch* commenced its assault on the top of the U.K. chart, the greatest obstacle that it had to surmount was Gabriel's own latest chart-topper, *So*.

CHAPTER SEVENTEEN

SLEDGEHAMMERED BY THE WHEELS OF INDUSTRY

The four years that elapsed following the release of the fourth *Peter Gabriel* album were, by the singer's admission, difficult. A trial separation from his wife Jill, and the glaring publicity brought on by his friendship with actress Rosanna Arquette, left him very much cut off from his customary calm. Furthermore, attempts to record a new album with producer David Bascombe, based in part on Gabriel's recent visits to Senegal and Brazil and in part on his studies of indigenous Japanese and Portuguese musics, were doomed to such a protracted gestation that he found it difficult to settle to anything.

Certainly Gabriel's contributions to two movie soundtracks, *Gremlins* and (alongside both Phil Collins and Mike Rutherford) *Against All Odds*, found him struggling—the former film was scarcely dignified by the inclusion of Gabriel's "Out, Out," and *Against All Odds'* "Walk Through the Fire" was little more than a revamp of an outtake from the third *Peter Gabriel* album. Of course, that same approach had worked for Phil Collins, but any further similarities ended there.

There was more recycling in store as Gabriel settled to his first full-length score, but the results, this time, were anything but perfunctory. Alan Parker's *Birdy* was an extraordinary movie whose grim reality—the painful rehabilitation of a Vietnam vet—found a truly lifelike mirror in Gabriel's work. No matter that the soundtrack album's own liner notes cautioned purchasers not to expect any new material, as Gabriel concentrated instead on extrapolating from material released on the last two *Peter Gabriel* albums. As with the movie itself, it is remembrance, not revision, that lingers longest for the listener, as Gabriel and producer Daniel Lanois rendered *Birdy* as fascinating and compulsive an addendum to the original recordings as the two German-language versions (buoyed by the success of the first *Ein Deutsche Album*, Gabriel cut a second to accompany *Peter Gabriel/Security*).

Birdy also marked the end of Gabriel's most overtly experimental musical phase. With the singer's musical intentions constantly shifting, there were times when even the most patient fan began to despair of ever hearing a "new" Peter Gabriel album. The David Bascombe sessions had already been abandoned; but Daniel Lanois, who moved straight from *Birdy* to this next project, was making no greater headway.

French-Canadian Lanois was just 15 when he opened his first studio, in the family basement in Hamilton, Ontario. Mastersound Recording played host to a steady stream of local outfits, including several featuring the young Rick James. Lanois later estimated that he and brother Bob recorded "hundreds" of bands there, although the duo's fame had apparently still to escape their immediate environs when Lanois was contacted by Brian Eno, to whom he had recently sent tapes of his music.

The pair began collaborating on some stylized interpretations of modern classicist Harold Budd to be spread across Eno's albums *On Land, the Pearl, Plateau of Mirror* and *Apollo*. In 1981, Lanois alone worked as engineer on Martha and the Muffins' *This Is the Ice Age* album, but he remained close to Eno. And when, in 1983, Eno was approached to produce U2's *The Unforgettable Fire* album, he introduced Lanois to the setup, igniting a relationship that has survived to this day.

"I'll play you mine if you play me yours."

Birdy was Lanois's next major project, offered up after Gabriel heard one of the Harold Budd records. "Given that I know it's a slow process, it's not really fair to inflict that upon a mere mortal," Gabriel once remarked of Lanois's involvement in his work. "But Dan and I, we did have a sort of, 'I'll play you mine if you play me yours,' type thing [going]"—Lanois also nursed his own recording ambitions at that point, and the competitiveness seemed to suit both men.

Lanois's arrival at the Gabriel sessions initially did much to kick-start the process, if only because he proved such a polar foil for Gabriel to bounce off. "We have incredibly strong and differing opinions," Gabriel said of their relationship. "But opinions that are quite frequently reversed. Something you were prepared to kill for on Tuesday, you're ready to kill on Friday." Still, however, the process was slow; and, as first a July 31, 1985, deadline and then a Dec. 14 crunch passed, Lanois knew it was time to take matters into his own hands.

Back in 1964, Rolling Stones manager Andrew Loog Oldham tired of asking the young Mick Jagger and Keith Richard to try writing a song together and locked them in the kitchen until they finally put pen to paper. The result, as history tells us, was the birth of one of the most successful songwriting partnerships in musical history. Lanois did not expect similar dividends, but he, too, knew that the time had come to resort to dramatic and markedly similar extremes. Dispatching Gabriel to one of the studio's rear rooms, Lanois then slammed the door shut, locked it, and issued Gabriel with the same ultimatum that Oldham gave his reluctant Stones. "And you can stay there until you've written something." Gabriel wrote.

The first single from the ensuing *So* album was released in late April 1986. "Sledgehammer" initially seemed to say little for what the main attraction would hold—a buoyantly upbeat number that Gabriel described as a tribute to his teenage idol Otis Redding. It was a vibrant distillation of Gabriel's customary musical soundtracks, reshaped through an irresistibly catchy pop sheen. Equally distinctive was the video that accompanied it, as director Stephen R Johnson employed the still-novel (and extraordinarily expensive—the video cost around $180,000) effect of frame-by-frame animation to produce a spectacular sequence of effects and images.

Only the Talking Heads had previously employed a similar effect in rock video, again under Johnson's supervision, but whereas the New Yorkers' "Road to Nowhere" had little impact beyond MTV's inevitable fascination with the process, "Sledgehammer" hit the airwaves like, indeed, a sledgehammer. And, just as *Invisible Touch* would have the satisfaction of nudging *So* off the top of the U.K. charts, so Gabriel returned the favor when "Sledgehammer" knocked "Invisible Touch" from the American peak.

How deceptive was "Sledgehammer," however? There is a school of thought that insists that its defiant employment of novelty and style over anything approaching the substance of Gabriel's earlier work was the most honest facet of the entire album experience, as the singer took a pronounced swerve from any but the loosest interpretation of his other recent fascinations and turned in an album that was custom-built for fast-track success.

Certainly, it would be very easy to go through life without ever hearing "Big Time" ("Sledgehammer" part two, only without the exciting bits) again…but not likely. In February 2004, the song turned up in an automobile commercial. Equally, the album's wide-screen ballad numbers…"Don't Give Up," featuring a duet with Kate Bush, and "In Your Eyes" were rendered little more than easy-listening ooze by a production that smoothed down even the bluntest edge. That said, Gabriel himself revealed that "Don't Give Up" remains one of his most heavily analyzed songs and, ultimately, one of his most personally influential. "It was a funny thing, but all sort of people wrote and told me things. In one case, somebody thought it kept them from suicide, someone else drugs. And I started to think about how people use music as emotional tools, and if I was looking at my record collection, what would be my emotional toolkit? And what would I be missing?"

Against these lows were balanced the opening tumult of "Red Rain," a welcome studio airing, at last, for the long-time live workhorse "We Do What We're Told," and the really-rather-pretty "Mercy Street," a revealing number that bared only part of its soul in the on-cover dedication to the late American poet Anne Sexton. Titled for one of Sexton's most controversial books, "Mercy Street" was less concerned with that particular work and investigated instead the poetess herself. Stricken by mental illness, Sexton used her suffering as the basis for almost all her poetry; indeed, she began writing solely for its therapeutic value. The song's references to priests and doctors (namely, psychiatrists), then, reflect some of her most valued imagery, and the final lyric, "…out in the boat, riding the water…," is clearly a reference to one of Sexton's last books, *The Awful Rowing Toward God*.

Gabriel himself explained he had been aware of Sexton's work for only "a couple of year," after he discovered a collection of her poetry in a New York bookstore. "I had been looking through the poetry section, and, as I read through her work, I found myself fascinated, excited, and moved. The images were startlingly light and very vivid…." "Mercy Street" is a dramatic piece of work, a seething slice of claustrophobic loneliness and loathing that comes closer than anything else on the album to what one may have expected from the fifth Peter Gabriel album, had he actually completed the work he'd begun, three years earlier.

Buoyed by a battery of awards—four Grammy nominations, three BPIs, and a unique sweep of three separate categories in the *Rolling Stone* readers poll—Gabriel toured extensively in the wake of *So*, first as a member of the Amnesty International–fired Conspiracy of Hope outing that hit half a dozen American cities alongside U2, the Police, and the then all-powerful Bryan Adams and then in his own right, a gargantuan outing that swung back across the United States through November and December and then crisscrossed both Europe and, again, America during the summer of 1987.

Genesis's latest world-scouring tour, too, was its largest ever. Titled for the album, *Invisible Touch* was a 112-date outing that sold close to two million tickets during its nine-month span, September 1986 through July 1987. Japan received only its second-ever glimpse of the group; Australia and New Zealand were granted their first and were treated to an extra-special treat as Genesis augmented the five-man live lineup with a four-piece string section.

Again, cameras rolled as the band performed, with the *Live at Wembley* concert film emerging a solidly spectacular document of a now-unimpeachable hit machine. Yet, with the tour over, all returned to their own careers without a backward glance, with Collins adding yet another string to his bow by looking once again to the silver screen and taking the title role in the movie *Buster*.

He had intended taking a break, "learning to relax," as he put it. "But it doesn't come naturally. After the…tour, I started building a model railway in my cellar, which was completely different from anything else I've done

> "I started building a model railway in my cellar."

in my life. I had a hobby for the first time. I muck around with it still—I build the models, I make the scenery, and I get satisfaction from it." But he kept his eyes open for fresh challenges all along, and *Buster* certainly offered that.

A dramatization of the life of Ronald "Buster" Edwards, one of the ringleaders of Britain's notorious Great Train Robbers, Edwards's story is one of the incontrovertible legends of British criminology—a daring heist in 1964, robbing a mail train as it sped toward London, was only the beginning of the adventure, as the police manhunt absorbed the entire nation's attention, only for the most notorious of the robbers, Ronnie Biggs, to then escape from prison and flee the country, first to a new life in Australia and then onto Brazil.

Edwards's part in this saga was less picturesque. While Biggs was feted by an admiring media, sought out by the Sex Pistols (with whom, incredibly, he recorded a hit single, "No One Is Innocent") and remained a constant thorn in the side of a British judicial system that was never able to extradite him, Edwards did succeed in fleeing, only to find his chosen bolt-hole in Mexico souring as his wife June tired of the entire experience.

Finally she returned home, leaving Edwards alone and miserable to decide which fate was worse, the continued torment of his foreign exile or the prison cell that inevitably awaited him back in Britain. He chose prison, returning to Britain in September 1966, to serve a nine-year sentence for his part in the robbery. (Buster Edwards committed suicide in November 1994.)

Director David Green selected Collins after catching his *Miami Vice* appearance. "I...was bowled over. He's perfect for the character of Buster, similar in both age and looks. But more than that, he's a genuinely warm family man, happy go lucky and with a great sense of humor." But still Collins acknowledged there were some nervous moments at the beginning of the production. "I overprepared myself so much that I knew everybody else's part as well as my own. But when I got out onto the set with the cameraman saying, 'That's your mark there,' I thought, 'Oh fuck, I forgot about that! I've actually got to talk, move, and hit the mark.' That's when I suddenly realized, maybe I should have stayed a drummer! But after that I did slip very easily into it."

Collins played the part well—it was, after all, a role he had rehearsed for every night that he portrayed the small-time crook of "Robbery, Assault and Battery" while that song remained in Genesis's live set. Now he proved himself eminently capable of embracing both the role of a major criminal and the demands of a major production while, he also managed to wrangle another couple of hits from the production, as his own "Two Hearts" (co-written with Motown legend Lamont Dozier) and a cover of the Mindbenders' oldie "Groovy Kind of Love" tore off the 60s-centric *Buster* soundtrack and into the chart. (The soundtrack subsequently won the Best Film Soundtrack award at the BRIT awards; "Two Hearts" took the Oscar for Best Film Theme.)

A new Collins album followed, and it seemed incredible that 1989's *But Seriously* was his first in five years—as Collins confessed. "It doesn't seem like five years, and I know that most people would probably say 'Oh *Christ*, it doesn't seem like five years,' because so much has gone on in between; there was my tour, sorry, my album and then my tour and then the Genesis album and Genesis tour, Eric Clapton album, and Eric Clapton tour, *Buster*, 'Groovy Kind Of Love,' 'Two Hearts.' Yes, it's been a busy five years really, but if I'd known it was going to be five years, I'd have been very depressed knowing it was going to be that long before I had another crack at doing another album.

"In the long run, I think it's probably a good thing. I have accumulated an awful lot of material. There is a bit on the album that was actually written in 1978, but there's bits that have happened…since I'd finished the last album. I started writing and kept writing. So, there are things that have been around that long. Most of the things, I suppose, have been written in the last couple of years."

Recorded with a string of guests…David Crosby, Steve Winwood, and Eric Clapton all did cameos…*But Seriously* naturally continued both thematically and commercially in the footsteps of its predecessors—topping the British chart for 15 weeks, it became the latest, fastest-selling album in British history. The corresponding tour behaved likewise—indeed, the newly christened Serious Band's *Serious Hits…Live!* album that arrived in 1990 remains one of the most successful in concert recordings of recent years. Its four-million U.S. sales may not be a patch on the 13 and counting that Bruce Springsteen's boxed concert anthology notched up in 1986, but in an industry climate that continues to regard live albums as little more than makeweight space fillers, it was an impressive tally.

Collins remained ubiquitous. He performed at Prince Charles's 40th birthday bash in February 1989 and described the host's mother, the Queen of England, as "a pretty good jiver." He starred at the American Songwriters Hall of Fame 20th anniversary show in New York in May and landed another U.S. chart-topper (his seventh) with the thoughtful "Another Day in Paradise," provocatively highlighting the problems of urban homelessness. Neither was he simply picking up on an emotive subject in order to wring some heartfelt dollars out of society's guilt—Collins

Collins comtemplates yet another day in paradise.

remained committed to the cause as he toured, inviting the Coalition for Temporary Shelter to solicit donations at his shows. The organization ultimately raised in excess of $21,000 and, in August 1990, presented Collins with a Certificate of Appreciation.

"The day I cut the record, I was leaving the cutting room in London, me and Hugh Padgham, and we crossed the street and we were walking towards my car and this lady was sitting on the side of the street, with two kids...she said, 'Lend us some money, Guv' and I froze...you know, I almost pretended I didn't hear it, the same as everyone else does. I mean I do a lot for charity and I'm not saying I look the other way…it's just that, in this particular instance, I froze and I thought 'God…' and as I was carrying on walking, I thought, 'I'm carrying on walking and she's just asked me.'

"She's obviously…she's got two kids, and she hasn't got any money…maybe she hasn't got a home at all, who knows. She must have somewhere to live…she's got two kids. And here I am, and I've just finished cutting the record so I've heard it a dozen times and…it's frightening. People like me, and I think everybody's the same, have got to do something. But I'm not talking about alcoholism or drug abuse. I'm talking about your man on the street who actually just hasn't got a roof over his head, and there's so much of that in Europe, in America, all over the world, it's not just specific places that have always had that problem. It's everywhere."

Neither was "Another Day in Paradise" the album's sole stab at social comment. Equally effective, though American audiences were less likely to feel its sting, was "That's Just the Way It Is," a number Collins wrote in response to the ongoing conflict in Northern Ireland.

It was a topic that had exercised other musical minds in the past—John Lennon and Paul McCartney both commented on the Irish troubles in the early years of their respective solo careers, since when artists as far apart as the ever-conscientious Sting and German disco heroes Boney M (not to mention Irish outfits U2 and Stiff Little Fingers) had addressed the seemingly eternal conflict. "In England, we are used to it all the time," Collins reflected. "Ireland, of course, it's on the doorstep. Everywhere else in the world, it's just another news report, but if you are living in England, and you [are] constantly getting people blown to smithereens because [of] this thing that's been going on for the last 20 [years], a lot longer in Ireland, [but] it's only just come to the front in the last 20 years. You see newsreels of kids throwing petrol bombs because their brothers throw them, and then their dads throw them and their dad's dads, and it's just inbred now, this violence, and I just thought someone somewhere…and it's got to be from both sides…has got to say, 'Hang on, life means more than this. This has got to stop.'"

> "Hang on, life means more than this. This has got to stop."

With Phil Collins's success all but taken for granted, it was Mike Rutherford's next move that was the most sharply watched. The success of *Mike and the Mechanics* took many observers by surprise, but there were just as many who readily suggested that it was little more than a one-off—that the true worth of Mike and the Mechanics lay in what, if anything, happened to its next album.

The band regrouped in spring 1988, with Rutherford introducing one fresh face to the setup, former Sutherland Brothers and Quiver, Al Stewart, and T.V. Smith guitarist Tim Renwick. His so-tasteful leads, those that dignified records as far apart as "The Year of the Cat" and "The Beautiful Bomb" (which had, in addition, been recruited to the onstage backing for the likes of Pink Floyd and Nick Heyward), would prove among the greatest of all the new Mechanics' attributes, and November 1988's *The Living Years* was feted accordingly.

With Britain finally boarding the busload of admirers, both the album and the title track single rose to No. 2; in America, meanwhile, "The Living Years" went even further, knocking pop siren Debbie Gibson off the top of the *Billboard* chart—and then, apparently, proceeded to rap loudly on Tony Banks' door as well. Spurred into action, he acknowledged, by the success of Mike and the Mechanics, Banks also resurfaced in 1989, at the helm of his own new "band," Bankstatement.

Fronted by two vocalists, the Other Ones' Janet Klimek and Alistair Gordon, and with former Gong guitarist Steve Hillage taking the helm as producer, Bankstatement released a delightful, eponymous album that August, albeit one that was all but ignored by fans and record buyers alike. To the former, the CD's emphasis on pop songs and ballads, as opposed to vast orchestral scores and keyboard passages, seemed little more than a brutal rejection of Banks' natural talents; and to the public at large, there simply wasn't anything on the album that truly caught the attention.

It wasn't a bad release; it just wasn't an especially exciting one, with Banks subsequently confessing to *The Waiting Room* that he was less than enamored by the album. "There are two or three tracks that I really love…[but] in some ways I'm least happy with this record." It was difficult for him to isolate any particular faults with the album, but paramount was certainly—if surprisingly—the choice of producer.

"Having decided to have another go [at a solo album], I thought I should do it and get it right. Virgin said that I should use a producer, so I said fine. I had a few conversations with people who I didn't really see eye to eye with. Then I met Steve

Hillage, and I thought, well, he's a musician and he's kind of weird,' and I thought he would be quite fun to work with. But we didn't really see eye to eye on everything, [and] eventually I felt I had to step in and take a few things back and one or two tracks for me suffered as a result of that."

Banks returned to the drawing board, if not to basics, as 1991 saw him unveil *Still*, a new solo album that brought Janet Klimek back from the Bankstatement days, and the now ex–Marillion Fish from *Quicksilver*, and then drew in a clutch of other name vocalists as well, former '80s idol Nik Kershaw among them. Again, however, the end result was less dramatic than it may have been, and it was growing increasingly difficult to shake the suspicion that Banks, unlike colleagues Rutherford and Collins, was holding his best (or, at least, most characteristic) writing back for some other project. And even before it became apparent just what that project may be, a lot of people were already making educated guesses. Genesis was on the move once more.

The group had not remained wholly silent since the end of the *Invisible Touch* tour. A short set at Atlantic Records' 40th anniversary bash on May 15, 1988, had reminded industry insiders of its continued existence, even if the group's repertoire that evening was more concerned with solo material than band compositions; and there was also the now-inevitable stream of video releases…the *Invisible Touch* concert VHS, and a pair of "greatest video hits"–style compilations.

Genesis expressed further proof of its continued existence on June 30, 1990, when the group regrouped for a headlining appearance at Knebworth Park, at a benefit for the Nordoff-Robbins Music Therapy Centre for handicapped children and the BRIT School for Performing Arts and Technology. Widely touted as one of the biggest British charity events since Live Aid, 120,000 people turned out in the driving rain as three successive generations of British rock filed across the stage, a bill that stretched from '60s survivors Paul McCartney, Cliff Richard, and the Shadows, through 70s boogie merchants Status Quo, and onto the '80s Tears for Fears. Mark Knopfler, Eric Clapton, and Elton John brought the afternoon's first supergroup team-up; later in the day, Robert Plant's solo set served up an unexpected jolt when ex–Led Zeppelin bandmate Jimmy Page joined in for a couple of numbers.

Towering, grandiose, and absolutely spellbinding, Pink Floyd closed the show, but, just as at Live Aid, it was Phil Collins who caught the most admiring eye, as he ran first through a set with his Serious Band and then when he augmented that lineup with "my two best friends," for a closing 20 minutes of Genesis that offered no clues *whatsoever* of the group's future.

Not one new song crept into the equation; rather, the band simply relaxed back into a ten-minute medley that opened with a clattering "Turn It On Again" and then imploded through a clutch of songs whose only relevance to Genesis was their presence in Banks's and Rutherford's schoolboy songbook from the days when Chris Stewart still played drums, Peter Gabriel danced on refectory tables, and the best songwriting ideas were swiped from the hymnal…"Everybody Needs Somebody to Love," "In the Midnight Hour," and "Reach Out, I'll Be There." Plus, for some reason, the set included a snatch of "Pinball Wizard."

"If someone told me I had to choose between Genesis and my solo career…."

Though the medley was familiar from the last band tour, it was a peculiar gesture and a disturbing one as well. As always, when Genesis lapsed into silence, the doom mongers had come out in force, claiming that *this* time, the band really was finished. But this time, they may have been correct. Looking at the success that now embraced Rutherford as well as Collins, one really could wonder what possible point there may be in Genesis ever reconvening for anything more than the occasional one-off charity concert. It wasn't like they needed the money after all; and, given the vast palettes upon which their solo recordings were now spreading, there was very little that they could accomplish as members of a band that they couldn't execute equally successfully in their own rights.

To take such a view of the group, however, is to overlook the qualities that make a group a group in the first place. It is not the mechanics of the music, after all, that bind three, four, five players together. It is the chemistry that sparks between them when they are together, and not only is that irreplaceable, it is also the reason why so many bands simply fall apart when they try replacing one member with another.

There is a balance to every relationship, and any disruption to that balance can prove fatal—as Genesis was aware when they neglected to replace either Gabriel or Hackett. It was better to carry on with what the remaining musicians sparked

Peter Gabriel stepping into the 1990s.

between them than to risk extinguishing that spark with some well-meaning stranger. No matter, therefore, what Collins, Banks, and Rutherford may be able to create on their own; still, what they could do with Genesis was something else entirely, and no matter how false a dawn was prophesized by the Knebworth show, once the trio was back in the studio together, the old alchemy readily fell back into place—so readily that Genesis actually commissioned a video documentary, *No Admittance*, of the six months the group would spend recording the next album.

And that, as Phil Collins reminded *Playboy* (among so many others!), was the reason why he maintained his membership of the group, when all around, observers were scratching their heads and wondering why.

"We all find it interesting to sustain this chemistry that we have. It is a completely different experience from writing and performing solo. Genesis fills a specific role. If someone told me I had to choose between Genesis and my solo career, I'd choose my solo career; I'm totally responsible for it. But I don't have to choose. It's good fun to have both. I also feel a loyalty to the band. I certainly wouldn't want to be the one to say I don't want to do this anymore. But that's not the real reason I'm still in Genesis. It's because of the experience of writing with Tony Banks and Mike Rutherford, playing with them."

Work on the latest Genesis album commenced in March 1991, as Mike Rutherford completed the third Mike and the Mechanics album, *Word of Mouth*. It was not an especially powerful record or a joyous experience; by his own admission, Rutherford had lost interest in the concept, or, at least, in the massive commercial expectations that now adhered to it. But his attempt to breathe new life into the project, by recruiting producer Russ Titelman to replace Chris Neil, never truly got off the ground, and neither did the album. With Rutherford already socked away in the Farm with Genesis when *Word of Mouth* was released, the album received minimal promotion and minimal exposure—it was left, indeed, to fend by word of mouth alone. And that was never going to be enough.

The Genesis sessions, too, got off to a rocky start, as Rutherford later confessed. The first week, in particular, was "a bit nerve-wracking…." No new songs had been written, relationships were a little rusty, and Tony Banks admitted, "I was amazed that Phil came back." But, Rutherford continued, "It didn't take long to get going. You just start jamming around, and out of chaos hopefully comes a strong moment." And he reinforced the point, "What it's all about [is] the chemistry of the three of us playing together."

And the chemistry was electrifying. Although many of the reviews that awaited what became *We Can't Dance* were tentative, they were written in the expectation of another *Invisible Touch*. Instead, *We Can't Dance* leaned more toward the *Wind and Wuthering/…And Then There Were Three* era, the sharply defined songs draped in overtures and pomp; there were sufficient long-form songs on board to justify,

Mike Rutherford onstage.

once the inevitable world tour was over, the release of two very separate live albums, one dedicated to the shorter numbers (self-explanatorily titled *The Shorts*), one to the epics (*The Longs*).

That Genesis was able to stretch out in a manner the group had all but eschewed for the past decade was wholly down to the advent and, in the years since *Invisible Touch*, supremacy of the compact disc. No longer beholden to the 45–50 minutes of vinyl that had so undone *Selling England by the Pound*, a "single" disc album (as opposed to the prestigious doubles of old) could now stretch to 70-plus minutes. Of course, that is a luxury that simply begged to be abused, as too many artists confused "value for money" with stuffing the disc with all the filler they could find, but that was never going to be an issue with Genesis—only *Invisible Touch*, of all their albums to date, had not been scarred in the members' minds by the lack of space in which to air all the songs, and *We Can't Dance* reveled in the newfound freedom.

Audiences responded with equal zeal. No matter that the world was about to be convulsed on the one hand by Nirvana, the short-lived godheads of the Seattle-centered grunge scene, and on the other by Brit-pop, the sharp-tongued Anglo response to the Americans' pain, guilt, and suffering. Past musical revolutions had painstakingly abhorred the past, but this one reveled in it, both musically and culturally, acknowledging the vast debt its heroes owed to the past and frequently rubbing shoulders with them, too.

"There was nothing in there that was offensive, other than to those people who *should* have been offended by it!"

Over the next few years, the generations would meet again and again, as Pearl Jam sided with Neil Young, Oasis with Paul Weller, and Blur with the Kinks' Ray Davies. None of these new blades, it is true, singled Genesis out as their own guiding star. But neither did they dismiss them, as past pop upheavals were so prone to do. Released in November 1991, *We Can't Dance* became Genesis's fourth-consecutive U.K. chart-topper, rudely elbowing new age songstress Enya out of the way, and reached No. 4 in America.

Nirvana's *Nevermind*, inevitably, was among the albums that held it that far back, but sales of four million plus kept *We Can't Dance* on the chart for the next year and a half while the accompanying string of singles—the plaintive "No Son of

Mine," the Stonesy grind of the putative title track "I Can't Dance," the sweetly bal-ladic "Hold On My Heart"—each took up residence in the Top 20.

There was even a quick storm of controversy, as the album's *fourth* single, "Jesus, He Knows Me," drew down the self-righteous condemnation of an American reli-gious right whose ability to dictate the country's listening habits was apparently gathering speed every year—and who were decidedly unimpressed by Genesis's attack on the grease and sleaze of TV evangelism. Nor, somewhat surprisingly, was the controversy restricted to the United States alone. Back home, the BBC also took exception, banning the accompanying video while an astonished Collins sputtered, "[They] felt it was offensive. [But] there was nothing in there that was offensive, other than to those people who *should* have been offended by it!"

A monumental success though the album was, hindsight, sadly, has done *We Can't Dance* few favors. In the cold light of a decade later, it is very much a drab lit-tle disc, with too many songs simply simpering along, Genesis by numbers. No matter what one's opinion may be of the albums that preceded it, there is no deny-ing that *Abacab*, *Genesis*, and *Invisible Touch* packed a power and personality (not to mention production) that could overwhelm all but the bitterest cynic. *We Can't Dance*, by comparison, left the studio trickery far behind it and let the songs carry all the weight…and a lot of them, quite frankly, weren't up to it.

Not in the studio, anyway. But the world tour that followed drew entire new dimensions out of almost all of them, as a 60-plus concert itinerary brought out an entire new arsenal of technological bells and whistles, ranging from a herd of mon-ster Sony Jumbotron video screens that projected the action to the back of the arena, to an oversized cardboard television, within which Collins performed "Jesus He Knows Me." The elaborate affair was, Mike Rutherford confessed, the most complex setup Genesis had ever taken out with it and, in some ways, the most mystifying.

"There was a lot of 'who knows?' about [it], having a big roof, all the lights, the screens," he revealed. "Whenever you start something different, the people who are working with you get so caught up in it [that] they don't really tell you quite how guinea-pig-ish you are until you get there." A plastic roof designed to waterproof the outdoor arenas that the band was playing reacted in different ways to different climates—sometimes it would stretch and dip; other times, it would shrink and snap. The giant screens, too, proved temperamental, particularly if they were exposed to even the slightest dampness. In Philadelphia, Phil Collins shrugged, "We actually had someone going out and buying every available hairdryer from all the local shops, to get everybody at the back of the screens drying them out."

The tour was not, however, to travel altogether happily, with the fourth show in Tampa, Florida, setting a worrisome precedent as Collins succumbed to a foul cold and was forced to leave the stage just two songs ("Land of Confusion" and "No Son of Mine") into the show. The remainder of the concert was canceled, and the audience came close to rioting before it finally dispersed.

Although it was the group's decision to begin with, Genesis was not overly cheered to be playing such massive venues. Collins told *Penthouse*, "It came down to this: We can do ten months of arenas or three months of stadiums, and the latter option won. The bigger venues aren't as much fun—they're an event of a different kind—but we don't want to be like Dire Straits and Sting and go out on the road for two or three years."

He was also less appreciative of the crowd response in such places. "As enthusiastic…as an American audience [is], unfortunately, the ambient noise in America is [overwhelming]. If you do a quiet song that's a cue for all the jerks in the audience to shout out how much they love you, which is great, and of course they're not all insensitive, but you only need a thousand out of 15,000 to really stuff it up. If you're doing a 3–4,000 seater the shows are fantastic. But it never ceases to amaze me, when you're playing a place like Dodger Stadium in L.A., how many people have to go to the toilet. It's an incredible distraction because it's like all these little ants walking up and down in the light. The subtlety starts being honed off a show when you take it to America; all those fine moments when you can have a little aside to the audience and suddenly somebody gets the joke and a ripple goes through [the crowd]."

Yet the European dates packed problems of their own, as Genesis's tour ran straight into a continental truckers strike, which forced the scaling back of some shows and, again, the outright cancellation of others. Tragedy struck when a member of the road crew was killed in an accident, and a proposed two-day return to Knebworth Park at the beginning of August was shattered when further "logistical difficulties" forced the cancellation of the first show.

The suggestion that sluggish ticket sales also contributed to the show's downfall was hastily dismissed by the band, but it, too, served to cast a pall over the proceedings—to complement that which continued to complain, with increasing justification, that Genesis was still bent on snubbing their British support. No less than in 1980, the fans were accusingly reckoning up precisely how many shows the band had played on home turf; and, no less than in 1980, the answer was shocking. Since 1983, Genesis had undertaken just 13 concerts in its homeland, confined exclusively to the megastadia and arena of the Birmingham NEC, Wembley Stadium, Glasgow's Hampden Park, Knebworth, and Leeds' Roundhay Park.

What worked before would work again. Barely was the arena tour at an end than Genesis announced a string of further U.K. concerts for later in the year, returning to theatres and cities they had not touched since the early '80s. Of course, the outing required them to scale back the size of the stage show somewhat, but Southampton, Newcastle, Manchester, Torquay, Newport, Wolverhampton, and Nottingham had no problem with that.

Besides, anybody seeking a jolt of the full-size production could always make their way to one of the half-dozen additional shows that were added at London's Earl's Court—to be filmed for yet another home video release and, subsequently, Genesis's first live DVD release, *The Way We Walk Live*. More classically minded listeners, meanwhile, could absorb the group within the confines of the Royal Albert Hall, and anyone who couldn't actually get tickets for any of the performances could simply stay at home and catch the show on the radio.

CHAPTER EIGHTEEN

CAN'T DANCE, WON'T DANCE

Once again, this latest outburst of Genesis activity coincided with Peter Gabriel's own renewal, as he broke his five-year hiatus to finally follow up *So*.

He had not been wholly idle during the intervening period. The *So* tour finally over at the end of 1987, Gabriel promptly signed up for another Amnesty package, 1988's three-month *Human Rights Now* tour. There were appearances, too, at the 1988 Prince's Trust Gala, where a showcase rendition of "Sledgehammer" reunited him for a few minutes with Phil Collins, and the same pair was naturally among the star turns at the Wembley Stadium extravaganza that marked the still-imprisoned Nelson Mandela's 70th birthday. There, Gabriel combined with reggae rhythm section Sly and Robbie for a powerful "Set Them Free," before taking the stage once again with Simple Minds for a deeply impassioned "Biko."

WOMAD was finally up and running, with its annual festival now established as an integral part of the U.K. summer circuit; Gabriel had also created his own Real World recording studios and record label, through which his continued passion for multicultural music could finally find full expression, without any need for mainstream record company involvement. Real World's first full release would fall exquisitely into every niche that the setup made available, as Gabriel wrote and recorded the soundtrack to director Martin Scorcese's so-controversial movie *The Last Temptation of Christ*.

Passion, as Gabriel christened the soundtrack, stands among his most unconventional works yet, a full-blooded blending of ideas and disciplines that even the best of his "regular" albums had only been able to hint toward. The very sessions for the album, Gabriel later revealed, were instructive. "*Passion* taught me a fluidity of sound and instrumentation," he explained. "I was just coming across sounds that were beautiful to work with." He would continue refining those sounds across his work of the next decade and more.

Possibly inspired by his long-ago relationship with the fugitive Unicorn Killer, Gabriel was also planning "an album...[about] Death Row, on capital punishment, and I started reading about convicted murderers, what made them tick." But amid so much activity, there remained a mainstream audience to satisfy, and early 1992 found Gabriel and Daniel Lanois putting the finishing touches to *Us*, an album that was as dangerously dark and violent as its predecessor was superficial and quirk laden; it emerged, as the British *Vox* magazine pointed out, "a cross between *So* and *Passion*."

"I started reading about convicted murderers, what made them tick."

Lyrically, however, *Us* comprised some of Gabriel's most immediately personal writing yet; like Phil Collins's *Face Value* (and Frida's *Something Going On!*), *Us* was at least partially inspired by the final collapse of its maker's marriage, with Gabriel shrugging, "To write a very *me*-type record is, I'm sure, very unfashionable now. But it's sort of what's going on, and I think if you can get that stuff dealt with, you can look outside more." An intense course of therapy, meanwhile, had allowed Gabriel to discover "the bastard in me, if you like, and I was trying to get in touch with that, and put it in some of the songs."

"Digging the Dirt," the first single from *Us* followed that excavation...literally, in the case of the accompanying video, as wildlife filmmaker John Downer filled the screen with rotting vegetables, squirming bugs, the entire process of life, death, and decay below ground. But whereas Collins's treatment of the ensuing themes was clear to all, Gabriel's vision rarely subjects itself to direct scrutiny, a symbolic obscurity that was only exacerbated by the series of illustrations, contributed by ten artists from around the world, that accompanied each of the song titles in the CD booklet.

It was this refusal to kowtow to any predictable imagery that fired Gabriel's next live presentation, as he hired designer Robert LePage to design a stage set built around some implausible collision of the mystic, represented by the imagery of yin and yang, with the mundane—a bright-red British telephone box and a tree. *The Secret World* tour would spend a year traveling the globe, spawning a new live album and in-concert video and reaching a peak of sorts as it brought Gabriel to the 1994 Woodstock Festival—that most apparently misguided but ultimately successful celebration of '60s love and peace amid the contrary materialism of the early '90s.

There, on a bill that seamlessly mismatched the fruits of both the original Woodstock generation and those that had trailed after them, Gabriel delivered a live show of such startling intensity and power that, when the time came to deliver a souvenir live album of the event, there was only one song with which the two CD package could close, a tumultuous, triumphant "Biko."

Gabriel, however, was already moving on. In tandem with Brian Eno and Laurie Anderson, he was working toward the creation of an interactive theme park in Barcelona, Spain—a slice of absolute science fiction in the hills of Basque Country. He was also adapting the technological mechanics of his stage show for a step into another new frontier, the *Xplora 1* CD-ROM.

Described by the technology media of the day as the finest interactive CD yet released…a tag that it still merits, despite the actual format's subsequent fall from grace…*Xplora 1* was nothing less than a multidimensional invitation into Gabriel's universe, a guided tour of the Real World studio wherein humorously hippy-haired staff allowed you to lay your hands on anything you chose, from remixing a Gabriel song to revisiting past career highlights—the BRIT Awards, the Grammys, the WOMAD Festivals, and so forth.

Esoteric musical instruments allowed the user to toy with the sounds that WOMAD itself was dedicated to, and Gabriel's continued devotion to the Human Rights movement brought an introduction to the Witness Project, an organization dedicated to dispatching video cameras to various world trouble spots, to capture the events that the conventional news media either glossed over or ignored completely. In interviews, however, he pointed out that none of these innovations were truly "new"—that their application simply reinforced the very reasons he put forth for leaving Genesis back in 1975, when he insisted, "I believe the use of sound and visual images can be developed much more than we have done. As an artist, I need to absorb a wide range of experiences." Absorb and disseminate.

Walking through fire, Gabriel explores the *Secret World* in 1993.

Peter Gabriel, 1993.

Yet there was also opportunity for less "worthy" activities. In 1992, long-time Gabriel collaborator David Rhodes was approached by Japanese musician Akira Inoue to compose some music for a forth-coming Japanese CD based around the short story *Snowflake* by Paul Gallico. "I was intrigued," Rhodes explained, "[although] I was not familiar with *Snowflake*...when I read it, I was delighted." When he mentioned the project to Gabriel, then, he was aston-

> Humorously hippy-haired staff allowed you to lay your hands on anything you chose.

ished to learn that the singer not only remembered the story from his childhood but he had treasured the memory ever since—"He felt that it had helped to give him a sense of inner strength." While Rhodes and Inoue wrote and recorded the music, Gabriel agreed to narrate the tale, emerging with one of those so-rare but ever-so-delightful storybook records for which the rock *milieu* is distinctly not renowned.

▢▢▢

For Genesis, the end of the *We Can't Dance* tour naturally, and predictably, presaged another protracted period of hibernation, as the trio returned once again to that half life wherein the solo careers gathered speed and the group itself was simply a Sunday suit, to be worn out on special occasions. Interviewed by the U.K. magazine *Vox* toward the end of the year, the group admitted that their next break may well be its longest yet...or even the final one.

"There have been periods for each of us, and also for members who aren't with us anymore, when you wonder if this is really what you still want to do," Phil Collins mused. "In another four or five years, you're talking about it being nearly the turn of the century, and do you want to go out at the age of 46?"

Mike Rutherford acknowledged that he felt the same way. "You go in to write a new album—is it going to work? Will it happen? Are you going to get excited about the writing process?" *We Can't Dance*, he admitted, was easier than he had expected—"The lengthy gap didn't seem to make that much difference." But would the same thing happen next time? "That would be the point when we would most likely knock it on the head," Collins continued.

On Sept. 18, 1993, Genesis resurfaced alongside Pink Floyd among the headliners at the picturesquely named Cowdrey Ruins for a charity gig in aid of Oxford's King Edward VII hospice. It was an entertaining show for observers and players alike—Collins later deadpanned, "The Floyd I've never loved apart from 'Arnold Layne.' But we did this gig...I went to the sound check, and I was listening to the Floyd and a couple of the things they played I thought, 'I quite like that. There's a couple of things in there that, you know. They show promise.'

But the success of its intentions notwithstanding, it was a low-profile show. Few people would ever have believed that it was also Phil Collins's final appearance with the band he'd now fronted for 18 unexpected years.

In an uncanny echo of Peter Gabriel's departure 20 tumultuous years earlier,

254

Genesis was dining with manager Tony Smith when Collins announced his decision. There was, he was adamant, no particular flashpoint that ignited his decision. The rapid development of his solo career, as it galloped away from the rock arena and into the sphere of a fully rounded family entertainment, played a part, even though it was a juggling act he had long since accustomed himself to.

Another factor was his burgeoning acting career, as he prepared to leap back into the spotlight with writer/director Stephen Elliot's *Frauds*, a surreal black comedy about an increasingly crazy insurance investigation.

"The evidence of irritable faxes that he had sent her."

The messy and tabloid-taunted breakup of Collins's second marriage, to schoolteacher Jill Tavelman, was a contributing element, too, as it reinforced the vast gulf that existed between his media persona and that of his bandmates. Amid all the acres of newsprint that the media felt duty-bound to devote to the breakup (and, in particular, to what the *Daily Express* called "the evidence of irritable faxes that he had sent her"), Genesis scarcely merited a mention. Although the rage and frustrations that Collins felt had already found an outlet in his most recent solo album, 1993's frighteningly sparse but so volcanic *Both Sides*, the violation remained raw. If Collins suddenly regarded the continued existence of Genesis as somehow irrelevant to his life, he had plenty of reasons for doing so.

There was also a sense that Genesis had finally run its course—a course that had survived longer than anybody could ever have predicted and that had achieved riches no one would ever have guessed. It was a situation whose roots lay in any of the many decisions that the band members had taken over the past decade, from the first of their longer layoffs, in the wake of *Genesis*, through the five-year wait for *We Can't Dance*, and onto the inevitable sidelining of the group once again, as each returned to his own projects…to his own life.

Bands can, and do, exist in abeyance. The Rolling Stones, for instance, stirred to make an all-new album just three times in the 1980s and thrice more during the 1990s. Other veteran artists adhered to an even sparser schedule while even so-called "new" acts thought nothing of taking two, three, even four years off between albums, pointing to the vast promotional machinery that now creaked into place around each one and the fact that it could take a couple of years for them to even get off the road.

Genesis, however, was not like "other bands"; it did not thrive in silence, and it could not exist wholly in the longings of its audience and the anticipation of the musicians. The back catalog was thriving, it was true—the 1993 release of the *We Can't Dance* live albums and video was followed, during 1994, by the remastered reissue of the group's entire 1970s/early-'80s output, and the group's debut album, *From Genesis to Revelation*, had now been repackaged so often that there seemed to be a fresh revision coming out every year.

Plans were afoot for at least one career-spanning Genesis box set, as band members past and present looked toward the latest marketing obsession...the days when an artist needed to be either very old or very dead (or, preferably, both) before his canon was collated into an impressive stand-alone package had long since passed; now, even the humblest of veteran also-rans were seeing their vaults excavated for flash compendiums, and, already, Genesis rated among the mere handful of truly "name" acts who had yet to take a similar journey.

But, Collins could not help but ask himself, was he truly ready to indulge in such retrospection? And, if the answer to that question was "no," then what did that say for the future of Genesis, a band whose reputation was as firmly locked in the past as its oldest records? The increasingly apparent disappointment of *We Can't Dance* had already alerted the trio to the fact that the group was at least partially cruising along on former glories, but did any of them have the will to try and divert that course? Banks and Rutherford would have said 'yes'—and would go on to at least try and prove that fact. But Collins felt otherwise, and once he had shared that feeling with his bandmates, the only question that remained to be answered was, when should they break it to the rest of the world?

Not yet. Close to two years would elapse before Collins's decision was finally made public, a period during which it appeared to be business as usual.

Tony Banks issued one more in that series of ever-baffling solo albums, the *Strictly Inc.* collaboration with Huang Chung's Jack Hues that not only underplayed Banks' abilities one more time but that also neglected to actually mention his involvement on the cover. It sank like a stone.

Phil Collins, meanwhile, unleashed his fifth solo album, the first on his own newly formed label, Face Value Records, the unutterably breezy *Dance Into the Light*. It was a well-received set, a blending of world themes and instincts that led at least one reviewer to compare it with some of Peter Gabriel's more esoteric adventuring (a lazy comparison, of course, but a nevertheless accurate one); but, while the critics applauded the record, the public stayed away in droves. Collins's poorest selling solo album yet could not even make the American Top 20, earned nothing more spectacular than a gold disc (each of its predecessors went multi-platinum), and spun off just a couple of very minor hit singles (the title track and "It's in Your Eyes").

Neither did Collins appear especially perplexed by the failure. Rather, he marked his return to the live arena by placing his solo pop stardom on hold, to tour instead with his Phil Collins's Big Band jazz ensemble, a vast gathering that rendered both solo and Genesis numbers to a light jazz veneer, and recruited veteran crooner Tony Bennett to handle vocals.

> "We have often been described as 'boring middle-aged rockers' who simply can't compete."

Mike Rutherford's return to action, on the other hand, was to travel in the other direction entirely, as he reconvened the Mechanics for a new album, *Beggar on the Beach of Gold*—and ended up with one of the best extra-Genesis projects yet.

In many ways, it was the relative failure of *Word of Mouth* that made this new set such a marvel. Expectations were low, from both the musicians' point of view and the public's, and that in turn heightened awareness of just what a strong album the team made. Though the United States paid no attention whatsoever, the lead single, "Over My Shoulder," made a glorious adornment to the U.K. chart as it flew to No. 12 in February 1995, while the album itself would go Top Ten the following month, paving the way less than a year later for *Hits*, a Mechanics compilation that went all the way to No. 3, and a corresponding U.K. tour that came close to rivaling some of Genesis's recent outings in terms of audience response.

"We have often been described as 'boring middle-aged rockers' who simply can't compete against the recent flood of new and upcoming 'talent,'" Paul Carrack mused. "I think it's once again a proof that people are fed up by listening to the same crap all day, that people really want to hear music! During our set, I do a long rendition of the Ace classic 'How Long' with lots of attention for the Hammond organ which really brings the roof down. Just before that song Paul Young does his big Sad Café hit 'Everyday Hurts,' and after my song we directly follow with 'I Can't Dance' from Genesis. Middle aged or not, everyone in the audience is up on their feet, dancing, soaking in sweat, singing. Isn't that the essence of a concert: making sure everyone gets a damn good time?"

Rutherford and his Mechanics were, in fact, on the road—and having a damn good time—with the *Hits* package when Collins's decision to leave Genesis was finally made public, and, typically, it was done so with a vivacity that few observers could ever have predicted.

On March 29, 1996, Virgin issued a press release headlined abruptly but so ironically, "Genesis end 20 year experiment: Decide to replace Peter Gabriel as vocalist."

Back in 1992, asked by *Vox* magazine what would happen were one of the trio to leave, Tony Banks initially answered, "I think the chances are, that would be it. We wouldn't try another incarnation." But then he thought for a moment and added, "But…it would really depend on the situation and how bloody-minded you are." One week's worth of looking at the newspaper headlines that instinctively equated Collins's departure with the end of Genesis was sufficient to render him very bloody-minded indeed. The group would continue.

While Genesis deliberated over its future, one past member—Steve Hackett— was very much coming to grips with the group's past. An almost inconceivable amount of time had passed since he left the group—18 years represented more than three times the span he spent with Genesis, and one often marvels at the sheer tenacity of an audience that remains devoted to an artist long after he departed the initial trigger for that devotion.

Hackett had led a willfully individual career over the past two decades, journeying from the blatant pop of *Cured*, through a 1986 union with Yes guitarist Steve Howe, in GTR, an all-out AOR supergroup, and finally, into an arena where, he proudly declared, "I don't need to compete with any other artist. And that is incredibly liberating, because you can just get on with what you want to do. And the moment you do that, the moment you say to yourself you're no longer competing, record sales start to go up. In 1983, I moved to Twickenham with an idea of semiretirement in mind. Instead, the reverse has been true, and I found myself working harder than ever."

Not all of his activities have won the full-blooded approval of his audience. They did, however, scratch itches that he himself needed to relieve. In 1986, he raised many a wry smirk when he agreed to appear at a charity concert being staged in London by Marillion, and even joined the headliners on stage for a version of "I Know What I Like (In Your Wardrobe)." And that same year, he scrapped an already-complete new album cut with Queen's Brian May and vocalist Bonnie Tyler (subsequently issued as *Feedback*) and undertook GTR instead, "just to prove to myself that it was possible to play the game according to the existing rules and make a hit ['When the Heart Rules the Mind'] that way. Once I'd done that, I realized I was perfectly capable of being a team player, I was perfectly capable of understanding it, and it no longer held any interest for me. So I now just make records that appeal to me, and I don't really mind if they sell or not."

In fact, he continued, sometimes a piece of work prospered from obscurity. "It's important to allow yourself to fail, to do things you know are going to fail in the rock arena, but which have never been brought forward." He reflected happily on a catalog of crazy paving that stretched behind him, alive

> "I'm glad I didn't get voted to become Mayor of Carmel."

with acoustic albums, orchestral performances, blues, classical recordings, duets for guitar and flute (*Satie*, a duet with brother John on the music of French composer Eric Satie), and so much more.

"None of these pieces are MTV material. But they are Performance Channel material, and, to my audience, that might be the most important stuff. There's no Machiavellian game plan; I don't approach [my career] like a general.... Whatever one is motivated to do, one should do. At the end of the day, it's all about energy and honesty and passion and commitment. I love music, and I cannot really imagine myself doing anything else full-time. I did a year of charity work, and I almost became a film director at one point...I was at the top of a shortlist for one or two things.... But really, I'm glad I didn't get sidelined and get voted to become Mayor of Carmel or something, because it would slow down one's output for a while."

At least part of Hackett's freedom has been confirmed by his own ability to keep one eye firmly on his own musical roots. Although he purposefully distanced himself from his Genesis past throughout the early years of his career, by the mid-to-late '80s, he was ready to begin embracing it once again; beginning in 1987, when conductor David Palmer and the London Symphony Orchestra undertook a string-driven tribute to Genesis, the amusingly titled *We Know What We Like.*

Appearing alongside bassist Mo Foster and Jethro Tull's Ian Anderson (Palmer himself was Tull's arranger across a number of its early albums), Hackett was one of the stars of a soaringly ambitious effort that drew commendation from no less an authority than George Martin: "[Palmer]'s orchestral coloring has brought out a richness in [Genesis'] music that I had not fully appreciated," Martin wrote in the album's liners. "Listening to his scores, I want to go back to the original Genesis tracks, to hear them again."

We Know What We Like spent most of its time investigating Genesis's late '70s output before soaring toward a closing salvo of "Horizons," "Can Utility and the Coast Liners," and, most impressive of all, "Supper's Ready." Deferring to Genesis's own roots, meanwhile, Palmer also recruited the Charterhouse choir for a couple of numbers, but Hackett himself found his own creativity somewhat stifled by the surroundings.

"I was a hired gun on the David Palmer stuff. (Hackett also performed on Palmer's Pink Floyd orchestration.) He approached me with the idea, [and] even when I was able to give him exactly the original guitar part, he would often argue with me that he knew what the part was, and that it should be played thus…. Really, you just join the orchestra, and you're just one of many. At the end of the day, the umpire's decision is final, as they say. So, I did what kept David happy. I don't think it's the best of my playing. I don't think it's me at my best, but I think that's largely because David turned a deaf ear to my many suggestions, which is why I prefer not to do that kind of thing for a living. So, I occasionally guest on other people's things, but I'm lucky I don't have to make a living that way…. Thank God!"

"Horizons," of course, remains an integral component within Hackett's ever-captivating live show, and 1996 saw Hackett convene what many fans agree could have proven an exquisite alternate reality for the band itself, as he linked with Chester Thompson, bassists John Wetton and Alfonso Johnson, former King Crimson vocalist Ian McDonald, keyboardist Julian Colbeck, and Zombies singer Colin Blunstone for a full-fledged *Genesis Revisited* collection of rerecorded Genesis classics.

Hackett and Colbeck were on an acoustic tour of Italy when the idea first hit. Hackett explained, "I was at my hotel, and a friend phoned me and said, would I mind signing these albums for a chap who'd come all the way from Sicily? So I went down and signed all these Hackett albums, and then this chap reached round his girlfriend and sheepishly asked if I'd sign all the Genesis albums, too. And it made me think that maybe my fans felt that I'd rather the whole (Genesis) thing hadn't happened.

"I suddenly realized that maybe it was time to go back and claim my birthright, so to speak. I spoke to Julian about it on the flight back and he said, 'Why not do it live?' But in the back of my mind, I thought that a studio album would be nice. And I could get to apply the production and other techniques that I had acquired over the years." From the moment of conception, as Hackett began lining up the guest musicians, it became obvious that a full *Genesis Revisited* project could—in logistical terms—never make it out on a conventional tour.

Colbeck remained an avid cheerleader for some kind of concert documentary, however, finally prompting Hackett to arrange a pair of shows, staged at Tokyo's Koseinenkin Hall over Dec. 16 and 17, 1996. By now, however, Hackett's ambitions had far outstripped simply revisiting Genesis. "One of our fans observed that 'great music is timeless and not affected by changes of style, haircuts, or even revolutions.' We wondered what it would be like if occasional members of bands like Frank Zappa's, Genesis, King Crimson, Asia, and Weather Report all got together for one night?

"I'd been talking to John Wetton about putting a band together, and we also talked about getting involved with Ian MacDonald. So I mentioned the chance of doing this Japanese thing and did they fancy doing it?" Each one of the invited players, he explained, "has literally stunned me by his brilliance and versatility over the years, [and] I always wanted musicians who felt at home, no matter how far from their original routes they strayed."

A live set fell into place with ease. "We tried to cover the more salubrious moments of the chaps' history," Hackett explained—Ian McDonald reprising his King Crimson days with "I Talk to the Wind" and "The Court of the Crimson King"; John Wetton serving up an acoustic version of Asia's "Heat of the Moment," which—as Hackett put it—spoke "so much more eloquently than the blockbuster original"; a handful of solo Hackett favorites, and finally, the promised *Genesis Revisited* favorites.

Filmed for a dramatically satisfying home video release, the concerts proved as successful as anybody could have hoped, but still they could not prepare audiences for the main attraction. From the outset, Hackett was adamant that *Genesis Revisited* was never going to be a mere hotch-potch of rerecordings; the bulk of its contents did indeed revisit pastures past…"Fountain of Salmacis," "Los Endos," "Dance on a Volcano," "For Absent Friends," "Your Own Special Way," "Firth of Fifth," and "Watcher of the Skies" were all on board.

But one "new" song, the vast instrumental, "Valley of the Kings," arose to suggest some of the passages that Hackett had seen discarded by the committee back in the day; another, "Déjà Vu," finally brought to light one of the silent legends of Genesis lore, a number Peter Gabriel first wrote around the time of *Selling England by the Pound*, but that had lain untouched and, apparently, unmourned ever since. Hackett, however, recalled it with affection, and linking up with Gabriel, "Déjà Vu" was finally completed.

That unexpected treasure aside, there was no further involvement from any other Genesis alumni. Tony Banks, apparently, expressed interest in appearing on the new version of "Los Endos" before backing out; but, hand on heart, Hackett found no reason to mourn these particular absent friends. Indeed, he professed himself singularly impressed by the manner in which songs hitherto associated only with the vocalists who debuted them—Gabriel and Collins, of course— emerged in the hands of another frontman. "All the Genesis and other songs worked very well. With all respect to Pete and Phil, I think John sounded so perfect singing 'Watcher of the Skies.' That's just my point of view, but Genesis has become so many things since I left. A successful pop group, and I don't think I'm denigrating any of them by saying that, but what was lost along the way was a tremendous amount of detail and atmosphere."

By restoring both attributes, Hackett in many ways restored the very concept of Genesis to an audience that, still awaiting Banks and Hackett's response to Collins's departure, was growing ever more uncertain over what the future held.

In 1975, searching for a new singer, Genesis had failed in every direction and turned inward out of desperation. No such luxury was possible this time. Neither

Banks nor Rutherford professed himself to be any kind of vocalist, and though at least one magazine suggested that they should simply lure Peter Gabriel back to the fold (and another insisted they had tried), it was clear they would need to look elsewhere.

The smart money was always on a blast from the past. From ELP's nomenclaturally forced decision to replace Carl Palmer with Cozy Powell to the veritable merry-go-round of venerable veterans that fired the likes of Asia, Foreigner, and Yes and onto *Genesis Revisited*, there was an unwritten law in recent rock circles that decreed that the oldies must stick together.

Peter Hammill's name floated across one wishful-thinking scenario…String Driven Thing's Chris Adams and Kim Beacon, Rare Bird's Steve Gould…and that was just the Charisma contingent. John Wetton and Colin Blunstone had both proven they could handle Genesis's catalog with aplomb while none less than Ritchie Havens was also mooted as a distinct possibility—and what a union that might have proven. In fact, there was something reassuring for older fans as they sat back and shot the shit with like-minded speculators. Who could come up with the most obscure suggestion of all? Or the daftest…the Peter Gabriel rumor was never going to fly. But how about Marillion's Fish?

What about him? On June 6, 1997, an apparent eternity of uncertainty finally came to an end as Banks and Rutherford proudly unveiled…Ray Wilson?

CHAPTER NINETEEN

NEVERMORE TO GO WANDERING

Ray Wilson was decidedly *not* a veteran. Born on Sept. 8, 1968, he was only six months older than Genesis's first album, which meant he was still in short trousers when Peter Gabriel quit the band and left school around the same time as *Genesis* left the chart. Yet he had certainly squeezed some experience into his short career. Having already cut an album with his first serious band, Guaranteed Pure (familiar to some from its contribution to Fish's *Outpatients 93* project), in 1993 he became the fourth and final member to join former Hue and Cry bassist James Finnegan's new outfit, Stiltskin, just in time to see the group's U.K. profile explode sky high when it recorded a song for a Levi's commercial.

"Inside" had nothing to do with either denims or the ad itself…Quaker girls watching in astonishment as an apparently naked man cavorts in a quiet lake (he's actually breaking in his new jeans). But the hard rocker certainly struck a chord with viewers, who swamped the ad agency's switchboards with requests for the song and reacted with cheated incredulity when it was revealed that it had yet to be released. "Inside" finally hit British record stores at the beginning of May 1994, and was No. 1 just seven days later.

And that was the end of Stiltskin. Serious rock fans disparaged them, writing the group off as a wholly manufactured and manipulated phenomenon; teenyboppers wanted to know only about the song they'd heard on the telly, and everybody else simply yawned and moved onto whatever the Next Big Thing may be—the new single by the Manchester United soccer team, which replaced "Inside" at the top after just one week, was the latest by Wet Wet Wet, which then surmounted the chart for the next four months.

Stiltskin did enjoy one further hit single, as the semisoundalike "Footsteps" staggered to No. 34; an album, *The Mind's Eye*, came and went inside a month. By the time the group released its final single, March 1995's so-cruelly titled "Rest in Peace," Stiltskin were already forgotten; and when Wilson was announced as the new voice of Genesis, even his own fans were staggered. Genesis's army of supporters, on the other hand, was outraged.

Tony Banks was not making excuses when he admitted that the Genesis faithful were never going to be truly satisfied, whoever filled the void. "I think we always felt that we didn't want it to come out like a supergroup or something," he explained, taking a well-aimed potshot at the bands who had taken precisely that route and the fans who hoped Genesis would follow suit. "We wanted…the group to carry on having the kind of character it has."

And that was the end of Stiltskin.

The pitfalls of recruiting a superstar vocalist, after all, should have been plain to all—"If you can imagine any singer you care to name, if you said, 'Steve Winwood with Genesis…'" would it still be Genesis? Or would it be Steve Winwood, who just happened to have a couple of members of Genesis behind him? The group had already been through that kind of experience during the last tours with Collins, where promoters blithely publicized concerts as featuring "Phil Collins *and* Genesis." The last thing the surviving pair needed was a repeat, or even an exaggeration, of that.

Ray Wilson's name first entered the frame in spring 1996. Wilson recalled, "I was in my little studio writing songs; it was ten in the morning, I was making coffee, and Tony Smith was on the phone, 'Would you like to come and audition to replace Phil Collins?' I didn't even know Phil Collins had left!"

In the studio, however, he quickly found himself gelling with Banks and Rutherford, adding his writing talents to theirs as soon as the door to the rehearsal room closed while Israeli-born Nir Zidkyahu and, on three tracks, Spock's Beard's own singing drummer Nick D'Virgilio, took their shot at replacing Collins's percussive contributions.

It would be another 18 months, however, before the trio was ready to allow the world in on the secrets it had created, when Virgin finally unveiled the single, "Congo," a dramatic, tribal chant fired by Zidkyahu's rattling drumming and a remarkably assured vocal from Wilson—but why did so many reviewers and listeners feel compelled to describe his performance as "remarkable" in the first place? As Banks patiently commented before the album's release, it wasn't as if Wilson was an absolute *ingénue*; Stiltskin was massive in its day, no matter how fleeting that day eventually proved, "He'd had enough experience; he'd done it in front of a big audience." And now he was doing it again.

True, "Congo" felt a long way from the days of Collins, but that in itself was no surprise. The Collins days felt a long way from the Gabriel era and, if comparisons needed to be drawn between Wilson and either of his predecessors, a dispassionate ear may well insist that he (and, therefore, the band's entire approach) was closer to the Gabriel ideal than the Collins ideal. Like Gabriel, Wilson had an expressive voice with just a hint of melodramatic husk to its most emotive moments—the sense that he was actually living the words he sang, rather than reading back what was written in front of him. If one wants to be painfully honest (and he has admitted as much), Phil Collins *never* made the group's earliest repertoire his own, meaning Wilson could scarcely fare any worse; in fact, the strength of *Calling All Stations* (as the new album was titled) suggested he may well do a lot better. The big question was, would he be given the opportunity to even try?

From the outset, skepticism was draped over Wilson's involvement in the band. Steve Hackett, watching from afar, admitted, "I think that Ray Wilson has a good voice." But he questioned "whether or not [Genesis] was the right forum for him...it sounds to me like most of the songs have been written by Tony and Mike...." He conceded, "I may be wrong. Maybe he was more involved with the creative process [than it sounds]." But still Hackett was convinced that Wilson was "capable of a lot more than he was allowed to be."

Wilson apparently had few doubts. "We started to get back to what Genesis was," he explained. "Allow the band to breathe again. But the end result was, it wasn't going to be as commercial," and that, more than any of the other challenges that faced Genesis this time around, was where the real difficulties lay.

Once, the last time it had been starting out with a new lead singer, bands such as

Genesis existed within its personal corner of the mainstream, competing only with others of their ilk—King Crimson, Uriah Heep, ELP, whoever. That was no longer the case. Genesis's status had shifted, but so had the industry itself. By the late '90s, there was little room for anyone to simply flourish within a world of its own making. Either groups mixed it with everybody else, or…there's always room for one more on the unemployment line.

The diehard fans didn't make such distinctions, of course; to them, Genesis was always going to be worth more, and saying more, than fellow hit-makers Kylie Minogue, Mariah Carey, and the Firm. But, to the media whose manipulation of the general public's musical awareness grows more pernicious every year, what was a new Genesis record but another piece of product to line up alongside all the other giants of 1997…the Spice Girls (whose latest single was called "Mama"), Gary Barlow and Oasis in the United Kingdom, LeAnn Rimes, George Strait, Puff Daddy in America.

> "We started to get back to what Genesis was. Allow the band to breathe again."

British audiences were at least willing to give the group a chance. While "Congo" breached the Top 30, the album *Calling All Stations* entered the chart at No. 2, with only the seemingly immovable Oasis keeping it from climbing any higher. American audiences, however, were less impressed with Genesis's latest incarnation, the album's eventual peak of No. 54 representing the lowest placing *any* new Genesis album had mustered since *Selling England by the Pound*, 14 years previous.

Neither were matters to improve—rather, they rapidly went from bad to worse. A scheduled tour of the same stateside stadia and arenas that the band had grown accustomed to visiting was organized for November 1997 and then swiftly revised as it became apparent that ticket sales in no way vindicated such largesse. Instead, the group was lined up to hit the theater circuit for the first time in a decade, but that, too, foundered. Where Genesis had once intended playing close to three dozen concerts across the last months of 1997, it instead was scrabbling to find any. A pair of launch gigs in August, at Berlin's BT Tower and the Kennedy Space Center in Florida, were simply industry invitation-only events; French and Danish radio alone offered the group the opportunity to showcase its new material in a live setting.

Matters picked up somewhat in the new year, as the band's European tour went ahead as scheduled and wound up astonishing audiences with a show that utterly dismissed any lingering fears over Wilson's suitability. Whether he was voicing the vintage cuts that justified the tour's so-tempting title of *Genesis Through the Ages* ("Firth of Fifth," "Dancing with the Moonlit Knight," "The Carpet Crawlers," "Follow You, Follow Me") or bringing exuberant strength to the new album's already turbulent "The Dividing Line" and "Alien Afternoon," Wilson was in his element, stepping so readily into his predecessors' shoes that there seemed little doubt that this latest incarnation of Genesis was more than capable of reclaiming the throne from which it had apparently slipped.

Neither did the rest of the setup disappoint. With Chester Thompson choosing not to resume his role in the band, Nir Zidkyahu reprised his studio role as the live drummer, and did so with flair aplenty.

Daryl Stuermer, too, had departed, initially because Genesis's proposed American tour coincided with Phil Collins' jazz dates, an outing to which he was already committed but also, he admitted, because his heart simply wasn't in it any more.

"A lot of things have changed inside Genesis. To close the chapter [of] Genesis was very hard for me. It always was a pleasurable thing. But also, I would miss Chester. I've heard *Calling all Stations* only once, and it differs a lot from the Genesis I know. Like the old days. I miss Phil's energy on the album. Now it's a different band. For me, the new album is not as strong as *Duke*, *Abacab*, or *Genesis*. I like the title track, [but] the album sounds a bit like Tony's best solo album. I think *Calling All Stations* is a good album. But it all sounds so different."

His absence, too, was readily negated, as Banks and Rutherford called in the Corrs's Anthony Drennan, a guitarist of such confidence and style that solos that had once been carved in stone (Hackett-era masterpieces such as "Firth of Fifth") were calmly recast in his own image—a shock for ears that expected the usual note-for-note recitals that Stuermer politely echoed but another indication that this new Genesis had no intention of simply sitting back on its laurels. By the time Genesis finally came off the road at the end of May 1998, all the indications were that recent doubts and fears had already been shunted out of view. Appearing at the massive Rock Am Ring festival in Nuremberg, Germany, both Bob Dylan and the reconvened Robert Plant and Jimmy Page could only hope to warm up the crowd for Genesis.

But it was not to be. As usual, Genesis retreated from view in the wake of the tour, neither confirming nor denying the rumors that now circulated concerning its future. But the total collapse of its American profile had seriously dented the group's confidence, and though Europe's loyalty surely insisted that a future of some sort existed for this most dynamic of configurations, Banks and Rutherford had had enough.

Shattered by what they continued to perceive as a lack of interest, they broke up the band. After almost exactly 30 years and more seismic lineup changes than any group should be able to withstand—imagine the Rolling Stones if Mick Jagger, Keith Richard, and Charlie Watts had all quit over time—Genesis had finally reached its own revelation. "Had they carried on, the next record would have been better," Tony Smith speculated. "It's a shame they weren't given a good enough shot."

> "It's a shame they weren't given a good enough shot."

Tony Banks, too, was swift to reject suggestions that the entire *Calling All Stations* era was a serious miscalculation. "I don't think it was wrong; it was just something we tried. It was a lot of fun to do. In terms of the album, it stands up with any Genesis material. I've got no problem with it. We really just felt that we would never really get a really fair response from the media. Rather than watching the whole thing go downhill, we really thought it was better to knock it on the head. But I had a great time. I really enjoyed the tour and to play with new musicians like Nir and Anthony Drennen. It was a wonderful thing for me, but I felt it was probably wasn't going much further. The feeling was that going down the hill on the other side was a bit unnecessary after being 30 years in the business."

But if the band was dead, of course it would not lie down. How could it, when half a dozen separate careers had all taken wing from its existence in the first place? And why should it when, though there would be no further "new" new releases, there was plenty of older material just busting to get out?

Just weeks after the band came off the road for the last time, but with the news of its demise still pending, Virgin Records finally ended all the uncertainty that surrounded the eternally gestating Genesis boxed sets and prepared *Genesis Archive 1967–75* for released in late June. And, from the outset, it was clear that this was no ordinary package.

Archive included five numbers (including an epic "Supper's Ready") recorded at the London Rainbow during the *Selling England by the Pound* tour in 1973, plus two entire discs worth of the *Lamb Lies Down on Broadway*, recorded at the Los Angeles Shrine in January 1975—the same show that provided the live "Waiting Room" B-side to the "The Carpet Crawlers" single that same year but that had otherwise lain unmolested since then.

And therein lay yet another treat. On the night itself, the tapes ran out as the band prepared to launch into the main set's closing number, "It." As they readied the recording for release, the five players—Gabriel, Hackett, Collins, Banks, and Rutherford reunited for the first time since Milton Keynes 1982—were well aware that a substitute could have been drawn from another show. How much more exciting, though, to actually restage the performance itself? An entire new recording of "It" was made and appended all but seamlessly to the end of the concert.

> "There were a few things [that] were just too awful."

That was not the only "new" recording. Gabriel rerecorded some of his live vocals—most notably those that were so obscured within his muffling Slipperman costume; Hackett reworked a couple of solos from "Dancing with the Moonlit Knight" and another *Lamb* extract, "Fly on a Windshield." Banks replayed a keyboard intro and then explained, "We just want to get rid of any glaring mistakes. If you have a chance to do that, you do."

The five musicians would also convene to record a new studio version of yet another *Lamb* favorite, "The Carpet Crawlers"—or, at least, that was the intention. Ultimately, however, each player recorded his contribution separately ("I did my guitar parts at home," Hackett acknowledged), to be layered together at a later date. Neither would the recording make it onto the box set; rather, it was itself archived for another three years before finally emerging on 1999's single disc *Turn It On Again—The Hits* compilation, as "The Carpet Crawlers 1999." "In fact," Hackett smiled, "it was more like 1996 or 1997."

Elsewhere, the *Archive* box set delved into the group's darkest past, surrendering one entire disc to Anthony Phillips's days with Genesis and a selection that ranged from the tentative pickings of "Patricia" through to the early-1970 BBC session that preceded the recording of *Trespass*. There may have been more such treasures, too, had Tony Banks not put his foot down. Banks admitted he had rejected several possible inclusions because "there were a few things [that] were just too awful, even though some of the things that ended up on it were pretty awful to my mind." Nevertheless, not only were the four discs comprised exclusively of previously unreleased (or, at least, painfully rare) material, including demos dating back to before the group's inception, they also brought a spectacular end to the years that fans had spent mourning the virtual unavailability of any Gabriel-era live material.

There were further blasts from the past on May 11, 1998, as Virgin Records arranged for the five "classic-era" band members to meet the press at Heathrow Airport and then supplemented one lineup with another, as Anthony Phillips and John Silver came along to discuss their own contributions to the box. Neither was Ray Wilson to be left out of the festivities—as VH-1 Europe prepared a *Genesis Day* TV special, he was recruited as the event's narrator. And, at the end of the day, Tony Banks delighted the entire gathering when, standing as if to offer a toast, he instead announced, "We managed to sack the lot of you."

The success of *Genesis Archive*—it reached No. 35 in the United Kingdom, no mean feat for a four-CD box set—made a second volume inevitable; it finally arrived in 2000, to cover the Phil Collins years, and it was, perhaps, indicative of the group's awareness of its rise from cult collectible to mainstream mass-purchase that, whereas *Vol. One* was riddled with rarities, *Vol. Two* took a considerably less dramatic approach.

Of the 34 tracks spread across the three discs, it was true, a little more than one-third comprised in-concert versions of songs that had never appeared on past Genesis live albums while the remainder concentrated on the group's nonalbum repertoire, from those funny little B-side excursions that reliably backed almost all the hits, through highlights of the *Spot The Pigeon* and *Paperlate* EPs, and onto the 12-inch extended remixes that the '80s made *de rigueur*. But a true successor to the original *Archive* box may have found room for the auditions that preceded Collins's elevation to the front line, may have offered some kind of insight into the artistic browbeating that attended Genesis's transformation from flowery epic to grandiose pop, and certainly should have served up more studio outtake material than simply a lengthy "work in progress" mix of "Mama."

None of this bothered the diehard fans, who were simply thrilled to get their hands on three CDs worth of previously unanthologized music, or casual purchasers, for whom the '80s-era Genesis was already a fuzzily nostalgic reminder of the cocktail parties they used to attend and the absurd haircuts they used to sport. But for anybody who regarded Genesis as a band that was worth so much more than that and one that deserves a tribute as spectacular as it could be, *Archive 2* was simply a lost opportunity, and the definitive Genesis box remains securely locked up.

"We want the B-sides, but we also want the classics," the American magazine *Goldmine* complained. "We want the hits, but we also want the experiments. And we want someone to actually put them all in sensible chronological order, and not the butt-over-backwards mélange which we're saddled with here. Genesis had a meaningful history. This is just a bunch of random dates. Or, as they themselves once put it, 'a trick of the tail?' No, a trick of the light."

Although there was (and, at the time of writing, remains) no similar excavations in the immediate pipeline, Collins confessed that he was not averse to further such exercises. "I'm reading a book on Joe Zawinul, being a big Weather Report fan, and there is a tape they mentioned in their book about the legendary performance at Montreux, which is very, very rare. Well, I've got a copy of it from Claude Nobs at Montreux. So, I'm sitting there thinking how much reverence there is about this, and I have it and it's good. But it's in black and white, and it's not DVD quality, but, to fans, it doesn't have to be DVD quality. DVD also means they will always have it, the tape's not going to break, it's not going to lose something, it's not going to get stuck in the machine. So it doesn't have to be DVD quality in terms of high-definition; it's a question of having 'the thing'. So there's lots of gigs that we would take for granted because we don't think they're particularly interesting but from the fans' point of view...."

Other archives yawned open. The year 1998 also brought a *Greatest Hits* collection from Phil Collins that literally bristled with more chart-toppers than any one drummer could ever have dreamed of accumulating—in fact, with more than two

Phil Collins in 1997, achieving more chart-toppers than any drummer ever dreamed of accumulating.

dozen American Top 40 smashes to his name, many people's favorite hits couldn't actually fit onto the disc!

The single-disc Genesis hits package, *Turn It On Again* welcomed 1999 into view while Steve Hackett commenced a massive overhaul of his own back catalog, realigning the majority of his past albums on his Camino label and arranging a series of DVD releases as well. Even Anthony Phillips got into the act, ranging through his closets to compile his *Archive Collection Vol. One*, an absolutely fascinating trawl that reached as far back as his song-writing sessions with Mike Rutherford, at Send Barns in 1969. "I remember," smiled long-time Genesis collector Peter White,

> "You can really get stuck as the curator of a museum of your own making."

"when the only thing you had to worry about was finding copies of the old Charisma 45s, and the occasional obscure European compilation album. Now, every time you leave the house, there's another album you need to pick up to keep the collection complete."

The band members share his bewilderment although, from their point of view, the problem with excavating the past is that one is necessarily compromising the future. Steve Hackett explained, "There's always plans to release all sorts of bootlegs and films…there's a lot of dross, but there's a lot of good stuff as well. But it's all a bit of an archaeological dig really; this is history, and if you're not careful, you can really get stuck as the curator of a museum of your own making."

There was, of course, little danger of that. Mike and the Mechanics re-emerged in 1999 with its second self-titled opus, and Phil Collins, too, had certainly had enough of resting on his laurels. No sooner had the *Greatest Hits* album, and a hit cover of Cyndi Lauper's "True Colors," been absorbed than he was preparing his next masterstroke, scoring the forthcoming Disney animation of *Tarzan*.

Disney's shift into soundtracking movies with "contemporary" music was a subtle one, but was finally catapulted to prominence by Elton John's multi-award-winning score for *The Lion King*. As John's successor, Collins certainly had a hard act to follow, but *Tarzan* drew from both his musical expertise and from his understanding of what a Disney soundtrack should sound like—as many memorable songs as *The Jungle Book*, as many catchy tunes as *Lady and the Tramp*.

Into this basic framework, however, he slammed some surprising forward-thinking elements—overlook the ghastly *NSYNC duet "Trashin' the Camp," and he emerged with at least a handful of numbers (notably the worldbeat of the main theme "Two Worlds") that rate with any of his strongest recent compositions. (Confirming Collins's shift into hardcore family entertainment, a second Disney soundtrack, *Brother Bear*, would follow six years later.)

Peter Gabriel was set to return to the fray, after he was approached, in 1997, to deliver a multimedia performance as part of Britain's end-of-the-century celebrations, to be staged at London's Millennium Dome. He responded with *OVO*, a vast sprawl rooted around the interrelated problems of race relations, family concerns, and environmental issues, played out through a succession of songs, characters, dances, and images.

Conceived by Gabriel and creative director Mark Fisher, together with Micha Bergese (artistic director), Keith Khan (costume and 3D props), author Bob Baker, and Patrick Woodroffe (lighting designer), and described by Fisher as "a live aerial and acrobatic performance on an epic scale," *OVO*'s musical passages ranged from mild ambience through Irish jigs and onto fresh interpretations of Gabriel's own music.

An eclectic and sometimes bewildering smorgasbord, the soundtrack was only somewhat successfully translated onto CD the following year, despite guest appearances from Neneh Cherry, the Cocteau Twins' Elizabeth Fraser, Afro-Celt Sound System, Richie Havens, the Black Dyke Mills Band, and more. *OVO*'s value as an art installation, however, was seldom questioned, and Gabriel's faith in the project was to remain strong. In 2003, he announced plans to rerecord the album in his own voice, rather than those of the myriad guests.

Invigorated by the sheer magnitude of *OVO*, Gabriel now launched into perhaps his most creative period in a decade and a half, as he echoed the synchronicity of *Birdy* and *So* back in 1985/86, by preceding the scheduled release of his next studio album with a new movie soundtrack.

Long Walk Home was the soundtrack to director Phillip Noyce's *Rabbit Proof Fence*, a harsh but beautifully filmed examination of the Australian authorities' now-disgraced practice of removing half-caste children from their aboriginal homes and resettling them in white cities, as part of an undisguised attempt at racial cleansing—it was believed, as one especially horrific sequence of the film makes clear, that sufficient selective interbreeding could ultimately remove all trace of aboriginal color from the blood line.

Recorded with Nusrat Fatel Ali Khan and Shankar returning from past excursions, the Adzido Pan African Dance Ensemble, and producer Stephen Hague, *Long Walk Home* emerged a fabulously atmospheric piece of music. Deeply authentic to its subject matter, within the movie, it blends so seamlessly into the on-screen action as to become almost visual in itself; in isolation, it merges with the night to create a truly transforming soundscape.

Gabriel's third full soundtrack was followed, just months later, by his seventh full solo album, *Up*. Opening with the frighteningly sonically unbalanced "Darkness," intentionally balanced to alternately strain your ears and shatter them, *Up* was on the schedule for four years by the time it was released—no sooner had Gabriel announced the title than both REM and Shania Twain released albums with precisely the same title.

But, whereas those sets could point to contents that readily conveyed the emotional meaning of their titles, Gabriel's definition of *Up* was, contrarily, down among his most uncompromising visions yet, an album that could be compared only to the very bleakest moments of its predecessors yet sounded nothing like either of them. Gabriel may not have appreciated one critic's opinion that, were one to excise the intervening 20 years, *Up* could well have been the follow-up to the fourth *Peter Gabriel* album, but there was certainly a degree of wistful truth to the suggestion.

With its maker now confirmed as some kind of *Grandpere par Enigmatic Excellence* for all who would merge modern technology with traditional arts, for all who would ride a bicycle around the stage while singing "Solsbury Hill," for all who would dare do many or any of the things that Gabriel now regarded as routine performance staples, the stage was set for his continued brushing aside of the industry norm.

Having rushed the *Growing Up: Live* concert DVD into production, and followed through with the career-spanning *Hit* 2CD collection, Gabriel then linked with the online service *themusic.com* to record and release no less than 19 "official bootleg" live albums, one from each night of his summer 2003 tour, and a choice of two box sets compiling the entire tour into one. He then repeated the gesture on an even grander scale in 2004.

Gabriel, in 2003, cuts yet another live album.

The idea itself was not, for once, a Gabriel innovation. A similarly sprawling program was pioneered by Pearl Jam and had already been further popularized by the
Who (among others). Phil Collins, too, had dabbled in "official bootleg" territory,
with 1998's *Live from the Board: Official Bootleg* mini-album teaser for the Big
Band's *A Hot Night in Paris* live album. But still the series positioned Gabriel on a
technological cutting edge that those artists had never countenanced, as he combined with Brian Eno to announce the formation, in February 2004, of MUDDA—
the Magnificent Union of Digitally Downloading Artists.

Gabriel at the keyboard, 2003.

MUDDA grew out of an earlier digital setup, the OD2 downloading service that Gabriel helped establish in 2002 as a reaction to the industrywide mortification ignited by such Internet concerns as the original Napster, which permitted users to freely share and download music with whomever tapped into the service.

Since that time, OD2 had grown to become Europe's leading digital distributor, both among the independent labels that were its initial catchment area and, more recently, the major labels. Now MUDDA intended enlarging upon this premise, to "take advantage of [the new] situation and help transform the music business in such a way that artists are on level terms with record companies, receive fair payments, and have new opportunities to be their own retailer when they choose."

Gabriel declared, "We are now witnessing the most fundamental transformation of the selling of music since records were invented. The economic restraints of the traditional business model have, for all these years, dictated what music can be made and when and how it can be sold. [But], if artists are willing to act together, there are extraordinary opportunities both creatively and commercially." Indeed, at the time of writing, Gabriel is well poised to take advantage of precisely those opportunities—the *Hit* compilation completed his contractual obligation to Geffen, and he has just one more album due to Virgin in Europe.

> "The most fundamental transformation of the selling of music since records were invented."

With now-characteristic serendipity, *Up* was joined on the shelves by new albums by both Steve Hackett (*To Watch the Storms*) and Phil Collins—breaking the six-year silence that was dented only by *Tarzan* and the live jazz album, *Testify* (co-produced with *Tarzan* collaborator Rob Cavallo). Collins's latest delivered a surely, but not necessarily autobiographical, sequence of songs that traced a few years in the life of a middle-aged man, in the throes of marital separation—not the most inviting of descriptions, to be sure, but one that allowed him to indulge in some remarkably tender and certainly heartfelt observations.

Like *Dance into the Light*, it was not a massive seller. By year's end, *Testify* had shifted just 140,000 copies in the United States, another far cry from the multimillion turnover of his '80s and '90s output. But Collins was neither especially perturbed nor, if the truth be told, too disappointed. He told the Reuters news agency, "I'm not in that marketplace anymore, and I'm quite pleased not to be, to be quite honest. I'm 51. I'm not gonna do the things that are required of me to be on MTV, if they were even thinking about having me on it, because I'm too old."

Besides, freedom from the commercial marketplace allowed him to explore the musical territories that he may, had *Face Value* not so dramatically rerouted his life 20 years before, already have been able to pursue. Proudly, he described the Disney *Brother Bear* soundtrack as his own purposefully world music–themed album and, as he prepared for what he tagged his *First Farewell Tour*, during summer 2004, it was with the determination that henceforth, a new Phil Collins record would be very, very different to anything his audience and reputation expected.

German TV offers up a rare glimpse of Collins
the left-handed guitarist.

Collins during the 2004 First Farewell Tour.

There were fresh fields ahead, too, for Mike Rutherford and Tony Banks. Stunned by the death, on July 15, 2000, of Mike and the Mechanics vocalist Paul Young, Rutherford, and Paul Carrack finally reconvened the following year to work on new material, both for a possible Mike and the Mechanics return and otherwise. July 2001 brought the news that Rutherford was also writing with Blur guitarist Alex James, late 2003 saw him penning material for Irish singer Ronan Keating, and while Rutherford spoke enthusiastically of being "almost finished" with the album in fall 2001, he also acknowledged he was under no pressure to actually do so. *Rewired* was finally issued in July 2004.

Tony Banks, too, was preparing his return to the new release racks, as he took over the Air Lyndhurst studios in Hampstead with the 66-piece London Philharmonic Orchestra and conductor Mike Dixon, to begin work on *Seven*, his long-awaited (and even longer-gestating) classical album—it was finally released in March 2004.

Interviewed by the *genesis-music.com* website, Banks detailed, "This particular project [began] after [the] *Calling All Stations* tour ended. I was just writing lots of stuff as usual, and I came up with this piece, which I did on the string synth, and I thought it would be really nice to see how it sounded with a real orchestra, as opposed to doing it artificially as I normally do it. And from there, it was a decision to do a whole album that way, and I wrote the rest of the pieces to go with that. So I used [one] piece from 20 years ago and another about the time of *Strictly Inc.*, which we didn't use at the time, but the bulk of the album was written in the last four or five years. The most recent piece was probably written about a year and a half ago when I decided I needed a slightly uptempo piece."

Writing and recording were laborious processes, particularly once the orchestra came into play, and Banks admitted it was not always a comfortable experience. "I'm always a bit of a panicker when I get in the studio, and I like to do things fast. I know with the group we worked slower, but on my own I tended to work fast. I'm not as good as some people in waiting for something to happen. Peter Gabriel would take ten years before he was happy with something. With me, I get it as quick as I can, while it is still fresh. So you can panic a bit when things aren't going right."

The end result, however, vindicated the painstaking approach, as *Seven* emerged one more in that thin trail of albums that, though they could never have been created *by* Genesis, were certainly styled in the classic vein that the original group's most devout admirers have dreamed of for so many years now.

Indeed, no matter what the various musicians get up to, that is one issue that will never go away.

One Genesis reunion or another has occupied the group's supporters for almost 30 years now, ever since Peter Gabriel departed. And, unlike Genesis, it won't quit. The slightest clue can send the fan club into paroxysms of anticipatory delight; the most off-hand comment can splash headlines over the internet.

That was a lesson Phil Collins learned after he was drawn to discuss the possibility in late 2002. "I would definitely see us doing something together again," he mused and, while he did point out that it would not necessarily go under the familiar old name, still he continued, "as someone who's known for doing anything, you know, doing everything, to me it's just, 'Hey, I'll do that; that's not going to ruin my life. This is just going to be a bit of fun.' So, I would say 'yes.' In either lineup, but for a limited run only. And for a good reason."

Mojo magazine continued with the revelation that Collins had already "indicated to Peter Gabriel and Mike Rutherford that he's happy to take part in a Genesis reunion, but they have to make the arrangements. 'If they set a rehearsal date, I'll show up.'"

In fact, the closest any former members of the group had come to a "public" reunion was when Collins appeared as best man at Peter Gabriel's second marriage, to long-time girlfriend Meah Flynn, in Sardinia in June 2002. But still Tony Banks was drawn to shrug, "People always ask us this question. Phil was obviously saying that there is no reason why we shouldn't. Who knows? Maybe we might do something, but there is certainly nothing planned. It may well be that we'll never do it, [but] we've seen each other quite a lot recently for various reasons. So it's never impossible. To be honest, you can say that we done it once and it's maybe something not to revisit."

Steve Hackett merely laughs when the subject is broached. "We've been hearing that rumor ever since we broke up," he told *Goldmine* magazine in 2003. Anthony Phillips, too, dismissed any such suggestions, not only from his personal standpoint but also that of other past members. "I think it's very, very unlikely that any of that would ever happen. Once you leave Genesis, it doesn't seem to work that people get back together and work as a full-time thing. Mike Rutherford was my original partner for song writing so it's not inconceivable that we could end up working together again. We have done a couple of small television things, so that's not impossible. But I think anything beyond that is in the realms of fantasy."

The final word on such subjects, however, returns to Tony Banks, the one man who, as Tony Smith once insisted, *is* Genesis, and without whom none of the past three decades-plus of adventuring could have happened. "We have no plans, I'm afraid. We certainly have no plans for a tour. We have no plans to do anything."

And then he laughed out loud.

ACKNOWLEDGMENTS

To Peter Guy White and Andrew Gilbert, fellow Genesis aficionados in the days when they were still a secret; thanks for sharing the beginnings. And to Amy Hanson, for helping it reach an end. For encouragement and enthusiasm, gratitude goes out to Jo-Ann Greene, Greg Loescher (*Goldmine* magazine), Chris Hewitt at Ozit Records, my agent Sherrill Chidiac, and everyone at Backbeat Books.

To the musicians and associates who took the time to speak with me over the years, in and out of the interview room—special thanks to Chris Adams, Tony Banks, Mo Foster, Peter Hammill, Jonathan King, Mike Rutherford, and Johnny Warman. I'd especially like to acknowledge the late Tony Stratton Smith, interviewed during the mid-'80s for a proposed book on independent record labels. The book never happened, but Strat's enthusiasm and encouragement more than compensated for that disappointment.

Other abandoned works-in-progress that I pillaged for this project include a 1981 conversation with Phil Collins, undertaken for a fanzine the week before it folded; a 1982 interview with Peter Gabriel, which was shelved when the commissioning editor decided he wanted to write it himself; and the brilliantly titled "Divided Kingdom of Jonathan King," a 50-page article on King's entire career that foundered when it proved impossible to cut down to the required ten pages.

Elsewhere, the backstage report from Peter Gabriel's first solo London show was written for my own 'zine in 1977, and much of the Steve Hackett interview material stems from a summer 2003 interview carried out for *Goldmine* magazine.

Finally, thanks to everybody else who helped bring the beast to life—Anchorite Man, Bateerz and family, Blind Pew, Mrs. B. East, Ella and Sprocket, Gaye and Tim, Gef the Talking Mongoose, the Gremlins who live in the furnace, K-Mart and Snarleyyowl, Geoff Monmouth, Nutkin, the Possum who eats all the pumpkin seeds, Sonny, a lot of Thompsons, and Neville Viking.

FURTHER READING/BIBLIOGRAPHY

Although both are now considerably out-of-date, the most valuable Genesis biographies in my own research library were *Genesis: The Evolution of a Rock Band* by Armando Gallo (Sidgwick and Jackson, 1978—updated 1980 as *I Know What I Like*), a horse's mouth–style documentary of the band's first decade or so; and *Opening the Musical Box: A Genesis Chronicle* by Alan Hewitt (Firefly, 2000); as editor of the band's *The Waiting Room* fanzine, Hewitt has compiled a dense but fact-packed compendium of both band and solo activities, detailing the world of Genesis from disc-/video-/gig-ographical angles. No serious appraisal of the band's career can afford to pass over either of these books.

Other worthy additions to the bookshelf include the following:

Genesis: A Live Guide 1969–1975 (SAF Publishing, 2004)

Genesis: The Illustrated Discography by Geoff Parkin (Omnibus Press, 1981—updated 1984)

The Book of Genesis by Hugh Fielder (Sidgwick and Jackson, 1984)

Genesis by Janis Schacht (Proteus, 1984)

The Phil Collins Story by Johnny Waller (Zomba, 1985)

Peter Gabriel by Armando Gallo (Omnibus, 1986)

Peter Gabriel: An Authorised Biography by Spencer Bright (Sidgwick and Jackson, 1988)

Genesis: A Biography by Dave Bowler and Bryan Dray (Sidgwick and Jackson, 1992)

The Complete Guide to the Music of Genesis by Chris Welch (Omnibus Press, 1995)

Phil Collins: The Definitive Biography by Ray Coleman (Simon & Schuster, 1997)

Peter Gabriel: In His Own Words by Chris Welch (Omnibus, 1997)

Numerous other volumes detail different aspects of Genesis's career. Those referred to most frequently while writing this book include *Rock Family Trees* by Pete Frame (Omnibus Press, various editions); *The Great Rock…*and *Psychedelic Discography* by Martin Strong (Canongate Books, various editions); The *Guinness Book of British Hit Singles…Albums* (Guinness World Records, various editions); *Top Pop Singles…Albums* by Joel Whitburn (Record Research, various editions); *In Session Tonight* by Ken Garner (BBC Consumer Publishing, 1992); and *The Top 20 Book* by Tony Jasper (Blandford Books, various editions).

Magazines and periodicals referenced include the following: *Circus, Creem, Disc, Live! Music Review, Goldmine, Melody Maker, Metal Hammer, Mojo, New Musical Express, Record Collector, Rolling Stone, Sounds, The Waiting Room,* and *ZigZag.*

Websites include the following:

http://www.genesis-music.com/, which is home to the redoubtable Genesis Archive project.

http://www.genesisaz.cwc.net/, which is Martin Dean's heavily detailed A–Z of Genesis.

http://genesis.www-hosting.net/index.html, which is the largest of all Genesis websites, the curio-packed Genesis Museum.

http://www.twronline.net, which is the online home of *The Waiting Room* fanzine

http://www.skwc.com/essent/genesis.html, which is Scott McMahan's all-encompassing discography of band, solo, and related releases, 1967–96.

DISCOGRAPHY

GENESIS
U.K. DISCOGRAPHY

SINGLES

02/68 The Silent Sun/That's Me (Decca F12735)

05/68 A Winter's Tale/The One-Eyed Hound (Decca F12775)

06/69 Where the Sweet Turns to Sour/In Hiding (Decca F12949)

10/70 Looking for Someone/Visions of Angels (Charisma CS 1—withdrawn)

06/71 The Knife, Parts 1 and 2 (Charisma CB 152)

05/72 Happy the Man/Seven Stones (Charisma CB 181)

10/73 Twilight Alehouse (flexidisc free with *Zig Zag* magazine)

03/74 I Know What I Like (In Your Wardrobe)/Twilight Alehouse (Charisma CB 224)

11/74 Counting Out Time/Riding the Scree (Charisma CD 238)

04/75 The Carpet Crawlers/The Evil Jam (The Waiting Room) (live) (Charisma CB 251)

03/76 A Trick of the Tail/Ripples (Charisma CB 277)

02/77 Your Own Special Way/It's Yourself (Charisma CB 300)

05/77 *Spot the Pigeon* EP: Match of the Day/Inside and Out/Pigeons (Charisma GEN 001)

03/78 Follow You, Follow Me/Ballad of Big (Charisma CB 309)

06/78 Many Too Many/The Day the Light Went Out in Vancouver (Charisma CB 315)

03/80 Turn It On Again/Behind the Lines (Charisma CB 356)

05/80 Duchess/Open Door (Charisma CB 363)

09/80 Misunderstanding/Evidence of Autumn (Charisma CB 369)

10/81 Keep It Dark/Naminanu (Charisma CB 391)

10/81 Keep It Dark/Naminanu/Abacab (long version) (Charisma CB 39112)

02/82 Man on the Corner/Submarine (Charisma CB 393)

05/82 *3x3* EP: Paperlate/You Might Recall/Me and Virgil (Charisma GEN 1)

08/83 Mama/It's Gonna Get Better (Virgin MAMA 1)

08/83 Mama (extended)/It's Gonna Get Better (extended) (Virgin MAMA 112)

11/83 That's All/Taking It All Too Hard (Virgin TATA 1)

11/83 That's All/Taking It All Too Hard/Firth of Fifth (live) (Virgin TATAY 1)

02/84 Illegal Alien/Turn It On Again (live) (Virgin AL 1)

02/84 Illegal Alien (extended)/Turn It On Again (live) (Virgin AL 112)

05/86 Invisible Touch/The Last Domino (Virgin GENS 1)

05/86 Invisible Touch (extended)/The Last Domino (Virgin GENS 112)

08/86 In Too Deep/Do the Neurotic (Virgin GENS 2)

08/86 In Too Deep (extended)/Do the Neurotic (extended) (Virgin GENS 212)

11/86 Land of Confusion/Feeding the Fire (Virgin GENS 3)

11/86 Land of Confusion/Feeding the Fire/Do the Neurotic (Virgin GENS 312)

11/86 Land of Confusion/Land of Confusion (extended remix)/Feeding the Fire (Virgin SNEG 312)

03/87 Tonight, Tonight, Tonight/In the Glow of the Night (Virgin GENS 4)

03/87 Tonight, Tonight, Tonight/Tonight, Tonight, Tonight (extended)/In the Glow of the Night/Paperlate (Virgin GENS 412)

03/87 Tonight, Tonight, Tonight/Tonight, Tonight, Tonight (John Potoker remix)/In the Glow of the Night/Invisible Touch (extended) (Virgin DRAW 412)

06/87 Throwing It All Away/I'd Rather Be You (Virgin GENS 5)

06/87 Throwing It All Away (live)/I'd Rather Be You/Invisible Touch (live) (Virgin GENS 512)

—/89 Domino, Part 1 (live)/Part 2 (free with *Invisible Touch* live video)

10/91 No Son of Mine/Living Forever (Virgin GENS 6)

10/91 No Son of Mine/Living Forever/Invisible Touch (live) (Virgin GENDG 6)

01/92 I Can't Dance/On the Shoreline (Virgin GENS 7)

01/92 I Can't Dance/On the Shoreline/In Too Deep (live)/That's All (live) (Virgin GENDG 7)

01/92 I Can't Dance/I Can't Dance (sex remix)/On the Shoreline (Virgin GENSD 7)

04/92 Hold on My Heart/Way of the World (Virgin GENS 8)

04/92 Hold on My Heart/Way of the World/Your Own Special Way (live) (Virgin GENDG 8)

04/92 Hold on My Heart/Way of the World/Home by the Sea (live)/Second Home by the Sea (live) (Virgin GENSD 8)

07/92 Jesus He Knows Me/Hearts on Fire (Virgin GENS 9)

07/92 Jesus He Knows Me/Hearts on Fire/I Can't Dance (the other mix) (Virgin GENDG 9)

07/92 Jesus He Knows Me/Hearts on Fire/Land of Confusion (rehearsal) (Virgin GENDX 9)

11/92 Invisible Touch (live)/Abacab (live) (Virgin GENS 9)

11/92 Invisible Touch (live)/Abacab (live)/The Brazilian (live) (Virgin GENDG 9)

02/93 Tell Me Why/Dreaming While You Sleep (Virgin GENS 11)

02/93 Tell Me Why/Dreaming While You Sleep (live)/Turn It On Again (live) (Virgin GENSD 11)

02/93 Tell Me Why/Dreaming While You Sleep (live)/Tonight, Tonight, Tonight (live) (Virgin GENDX 11)

09/97 Congo (edit)/Papa He Said/Banjo Man (Virgin GENSD 12)

09/97 Congo (edit)/Second Home by the Sea (Virgin GENDX 12)

12/97 Shipwrecked/Phret/7–8 (Virgin GENSD14)

12/97 Shipwrecked/No Son of Mine/Lover's Leap (live)/Turn It On Again (live) (Virgin GENDX 14)

03/98 Not About Us/Anything Now/Sign Your Life Away/Run Out of Time (Virgin GENSD 15)

03/98 Not About Us/Dancing with the Moonlit Knight (live)/Follow You, Follow Me (live)/Not about Us (live) (Virgin GENSD 15)

ALBUMS

03/69 *From Genesis To Revelation* (Decca LK 4990—mono mix)

03/69 *From Genesis To Revelation* (Decca SKL 4990—stereo mix)

10/70 *Trespass* (Charisma CAS 1020)

11/71 *Nursery Cryme* (Charisma CAS 1052)

10/72 *Foxtrot* (Charisma CAS 1058)

07/73 *Genesis Live* (Charisma CLASS 1)

10/73 *Selling England by the Pound* (Charisma CAS 1074)

11/74 *The Lamb Lies Down on Broadway* (Charisma CGS 101)

02/76 *A Trick of the Tail* (Charisma CDS 4001)

01/77 *Wind and Wuthering* (Charisma CDS 4005)

10/77 *Seconds Out* (Charisma GE 2001)

04/78 *And Then There Were Three* (Charisma CDS 4010)

03/80 *Duke* (Charisma CBR 101)

08/81 *Abacab* (Charisma CBR 102)

06/82 *Three Sides Live* (Charisma GE 2002)

10/83 *Genesis* (Virgin GENLP 1)

06/86 *Invisible Touch* (Virgin GENLP 2)

11/91 *We Can't Dance* (Virgin GENCD 3)

11/92 *Genesis Live: The Way We Walk Vol. 1 (The Shorts)* (Virgin GENCD 4)

01/93 *Genesis Live: The Way We Walk Vol. 2 (The Longs)* (Virgin GENCD 5)

09/97 *Calling All Stations* (Virgin GENCD 6)

U.S. DISCOGRAPHY

SINGLES

02/68 The Silent Sun/That's Me (Parrot 3018)

02/73 Watcher of the Skies (remix)/same (Buddah/Charisma 103 promo)

02/73 Watcher of the Skies/Willow Farm (Buddah/Charisma 103)

03/74 I Know What I Like (In Your Wardrobe)/Twilight Alehouse (Charisma 26002)

12/74 Counting Out Time/The Lamb Lies Down on Broadway (Atco 7013)

03/76 Ripples/Entangled (Atco 7050)

02/77 Your Own Special Way/...In That Quiet Earth (Atco 7076)

03/78 Follow You, Follow Me/Inside and Out (Atlantic 3474)

07/78 Scene from a Night's Dream/Go West Young Man (Deep in the Motherlode) (Atlantic 3511)

05/80 Misunderstanding/Behind the Lines (Atlantic 3662)

09/80 Turn It On Again/Evidence of Autumn (Atlantic 3751)

10/81 No Reply at All/Heaven Love My Life (Atlantic 3858)

01/82 Abacab/Whodunnit? (Atlantic 3891)

03/82 Man on the Corner/Submarine (Atlantic 4025)

05/82 Paperlate/You Might Recall (Atlantic 4053)

08/83 Mama/It's Gonna Get Better (Atco 89770)

11/83 That's All/Second Home by the Sea (Atco 89724)

06/84 Taking It All Too Hard/Silver Rainbow (Atco 89656)

08/86 Throwing It All Away/Do the Neurotic (Atco 89372)

04/87 In Too Deep/I'd Rather Be You (Atco 89316)

10/91 No Son of Mine/Living Forever (Atco 87571)

01/92 I Can't Dance/On the Shoreline (Atco 87532)

04/92 Hold on My Heart/Way of the World (Atco 87481)

07/92 Jesus He Knows Me/Hearts on Fire (Atco 87454)

11/92 Never a Time/ (Atco 87411)

—/93 Domino (live)/The Lamb Lies Down on Broadway/interview (Atlantic PRCD 4997—promo)

ALBUMS

—/69 *From Genesis To Revelation* (London PS 643—stereo mix)

10/70 *Trespass* (Impulse 9295)

11/71 *Nursery Cryme* (Buddah/Charisma)

10/72 *Foxtrot* (Buddah/Charisma)

10/73 *Selling England by the Pound* (Charisma 6060)

05/74 *Genesis: Live* (Buddah/Charisma)

11/74 *The Lamb Lies Down on Broadway* (Atco 401)

02/76 *A Trick of the Tail* (Atco 129)

01/77 *Wind and Wuthering* (Atco 144)

10/77 *Seconds Out* (Atco 9002)

04/78 *And Then There Were Three* (Atlantic 19173)

03/80 *Duke* (Atlantic 16014)

08/81 *Abacab* (Atlantic 19313)

06/82 *Three Sides Live* (Atlantic 2000)

CD remasters feature *four* sides live. Others include five studio tracks.

10/83 *Genesis* (Atco 80116)

06/86 *Invisible Touch* (Atco 81641)

11/91 *We Can't Dance* (Atco 82344)

11/92 *Genesis Live: The Way We Walk, Vol. 1: The Shorts* (Atco 82452)

01/93 *Genesis Live: The Way We Walk, Vol. 2: The Longs* (Atco)

09/97 *Calling All Stations* (Atlantic 83037-2)

COMPILATIONS FEATURING UNAVAILABLE MATERIAL

06/97 *Archive 67–75* (Atlantic 82858)

11/99 *Turn It On Again: The Hits* (Atlantic 83244)

—/00 *Archive 2 76–92* (Atlantic 83410)

MISCELLANEOUS

—/87 *We Know What We Like: The Music of Genesis: The London Symphony Orchestra Conducted by David Palmer* (RCA Red Seal 56242)

—/92 *The Royal Philharmonic Orchestra Play Genesis Hits and Ballads* (Edel EDT 5204 US)

—/96 Steve Hackett: *Watcher of the Skies: Genesis Revisited* (Guardian 21943 US)

—/01 Guddal And Matte: *Genesis for Two Grand Pianos* (Camino CAMCD 28)

TONY BANKS DISCOGRAPHY

SINGLES (U.K. UNLESS NOTED)
—/79 For a While/Undertow (Charisma CB 344)

—/79 For a While (remix)/A Curious Feeling (Charisma CB 365)

—/82 The Wicked Lady/Prelude to the Wicked Lady (Atlantic 9825 US)

—/83 This Is Love/Charm (Charisma BANKS 1)

—/83 And the Wheels Keep Turning/Moving Under (Charisma BANKS 2)

—/85 *Soundtracks* EP: You Call This Victory/Lion of Symmetry/Redwing (Charisma CB 415)

—/86 Short Cut to Somewhere/Smilin' Jack Casey (Charisma CB 426)

—/86 Short Cut to Somewhere/Smilin' Jack Casey/K2 (Charisma CB 42612)

—/89 Throwback/Thursday the Twelfth (Virgin VS 1200)

—/89 Throwback/Thursday the Twelfth/This Is Love (Virgin VST 1200)

—/89 I'll Be Waiting/Diamonds Aren't So Hard (Virgin VS 1208)

—/89 I'll Be Waiting/Diamonds Aren't So Hard/And the Wheels Keep Turning (Virgin VST 1208)

—/91 I Wanna Change the Score/Hero for an Hour (Virgin VS 1347)

—/91 I Wanna Change the Score/Hero for an Hour/Big Man (Virgin VST 1347)

—/91 I Wanna Change the Score/Hero for an Hour/Big Man/The Waters of Lethe (Virgin VSCDT 1347)

—/91 The Gift/Back to Back (Virgin VS 1362)

—/91 The Gift/Back to Back/A House Needs a Roof (Virgin VST 1362)

—/91 The Gift/Back to Back/A House Needs a Roof/Redwing (Virgin VSCDT 1362)

—/92 Still It Takes My Heart by Surprise/The Final Curtain (Virgin VS 1406)

ALBUMS
10/79 *A Curious Feeling* (Charisma CAS 1148 UK/CA 1 2207 US)

06/83 *The Fugitive* (Charisma TBLP 1 UK/Atlantic 80073 US)

—/83 *The Wicked Lady* (Atlantic 78-0073)

03/86 *Soundtracks* (Charisma CAS 1173 UK/Atlantic 81680 US)

08/89 *Bankstatement* (Virgin V2600 UK/Atlantic 82007 US)

04/91 *Still* (Virgin V2658 UK/Giant 24441 US)

09/95 *Strictly Inc.* (Virgin 2790)

COMPILATIONS
03/86 Soundtracks (Charisma CAS 1173 UK/Atlantic 81680 US)

—/98 Strictly Banks (SBCD 1)

PHIL COLLINS DISCOGRAPHY

SINGLES (U.K. UNLESS NOTED)

01/81 In the Air Tonight/The Roof Is Leaking (Virgin VSK 102)

03/81 I Missed Again/I'm Not Moving (Virgin VS 402)

05/81 If Leaving Me Is Easy/Drawing Board (Virgin VS 423)

10/82 Thru These Walls/Do You Know, Do You Care? (Virgin VS 524)

11/82 You Can't Hurry Love/I Cannot Believe It's True (Virgin VS 531)

11/82 You Can't Hurry Love/Do You Know, Do You Care? (Atlantic 89933 US)

02/83 I Don't Care Anymore/The West Side (Atlantic 89877)

03/83 Don't Let Him Steal Your Heart Away/Thunder and Lightning (Virgin VS 572)

03/83 Don't Let Him Steal Your Heart Away/Thunder and Lightning/And So to F (Virgin VS 57212)

05/83 Why Can't It Wait till Morning/Like China (Virgin VS 603)

02/84 Against All Odds/Making a Big Mistake (by Mike Rutherford) (Virgin VS 674)

11/84 Easy Lover (with Philip Bailey)/Woman (Philip Bailey) (Columbia 04679 US)

01/85 Sussudio/The Man with the Horn (Virgin VS 736)

01/85 Sussudio/(extended)/The Man with the Horn (Virgin VS 73612)

01/85 Sussudio/I Like the Way (Atlantic 89560 US)

03/85 Easy Lover (with Philip Bailey)/Woman (Philip Bailey) (CBS 4915)

04/85 One More Night/I Like the Way (Virgin VS 755)

04/85 One More Night/(extended)/I Like the Way (Virgin VS 75512)

04/85 One More Night/The Man with the Horn (Atlantic 89588 US)

07/85 Take Me Home/We Said Hello, Goodbye (Virgin 777)

07/85 Take Me Home/(extended)/We Said Hello, Goodbye (Virgin 77712)

07/85 Don't Lose My Number/We Said Hello, Goodbye (Atlantic 89536 US)

07/85 Don't Lose My Number (extended)/Don't Lose My Number/We Said Hello, Goodbye
      (Atlantic 86863 US)

08/85 Take Me Home/Only You Know and I Know (Atlantic 89472 US)

10/85 Separate Lives/Only You Know and I Know (Virgin VS 818)

06/88 In the Air Tonight ('88 Remix)/I Missed Again (Virgin VS 102)

06/88 In the Air Tonight ('88 Remix)/(remix extended)/I Missed Again (Virgin VST 02)

08/88 A Groovy Kind of Love/Big Noise (Virgin VS 1117)

11/88 Two Hearts/The Robbery (by Anne Dudley) (Virgin VS 1141)

11/89 Another Day in Paradise/Heat on the Street (Virgin VS 1234)

11/89 Another Day in Paradise/Heat on the Street/Saturday Night and Sunday Morning (Virgin VST 1234)

01/90 I Wish It Would Rain Down/Homeless (Virgin VS 1240)

01/90 I Wish It Would Rain Down/Homeless/You've Been in Love (Virgin VST1240)

04/90 Something Happened on the Way to Heaven/Do You Remember?/I Wish It Would Rain
      Down (Virgin VS 1251)

04/90 Something Happened on the Way to Heaven (remix)/(demo)/I Wish It Would Rain Down
      (Virgin VST 1251)

07/90 That's Just the Way It Is/Broadway Chorus (Virgin VS 1277)

07/90 That's Just the Way It Is/Broadway Chorus/In the Air Tonight (extended remix) (Virgin VST 1277)

09/90 Hang In Long Enough/Around the World in 80 Presets (Virgin VS 1300)

09/90 Hang In Long Enough/(12-inch mix)/(dub mix) (Virgin VST 1300)

09/90 Hang In Long Enough/(12-inch mix)/Around the World in 80 Presets (Virgin VSCDT 1300)

09/90 Hang In Long Enough/(club mix)/(pop mix)/(dub mix) (Atlantic 8611 US)

11/90 Do You Remember? (live)/Against All Odds (live) (Virgin VS 1305)

11/90 Do You Remember? (live)/Against All Odds (live)/Doesn't Anybody Stay Together Anymore? (live)(Virgin VST 1305)

11/90 Do You Remember? (live)/The Roof Is Leaking (live)/Doesn't Anybody Stay Together Anymore? (live) (Virgin VSCDX 1305)

05/93 Hero (with David Crosby)/Coverage (by David Crosby) (Atlantic 87360 US)

10/93 Both Sides of the Story/Always (live) (Virgin VS 1500)

10/93 Both Sides of the Story/Always (live)/Both Sides of the Demo (Virgin VSCDT 1500)

10/93 Both Sides of the Story/Always (live)/Both Sides of the Demo/Rad Dudeski (Virgin VSCDG 1500)

01/94 Everyday/(demo)/Don't Call Me Ashley/Doesn't Anybody Stay Together Anymore? (live) (Virgin VSCDG 1505)

01/94 Everyday/(demo)/Don't Call Me Ashley/Hang In Long Enough (live)/Hand in Hand (live) (Atlantic 85715)

04/94 We Wait and We Wonder/Take Me with You/Stevie's Blues (Virgin CDG 1510)

10/96 Dance into the Light/It's Over/Take Me Down (Face Value EW 066)

10/96 Dance into the Light/Take Me Down/It's Over (Face Value 87043)

12/96 It's in Your Eyes/Easy Lover (live '95)/Separate Lives (live '95)/It's in Your Eyes/Always (big band)/I Don't Wanna Know (Face Value EW 076)

07/97 Wear My Hat/(mixes) (Face Value EW 113)

11/98 True Colors/Don't Lose My Number/In the Air Tonight/Take Me Home/I Missed Again (Virgin VSCDT 1715)

11/99 You'll Be in My Heart/? (Walt Disney 0100735)

09/01 In the Air Tonight (L'il Kim with Phil Collins)/? (WEA 331)

09/02 Can't Stop Loving You/? (Face Value EW 254)

02/03 Come with Me/? (Face Value)

03/03 The Least You Can Do/Wake Up Call (Face Value 260)

05/03 The Least You Can Do/Wake Up Call/Hey Now Sunshine (Face Value)

10/03 Look Through My Eyes/(instrumental)/(Bulgarian Woman's Choir) (from Disney's *Brother Bear*) (Disney 001)

ALBUMS

01/81 Face Value (Virgin V2185 UK/Atlantic SD 16029 US)

11/82 Hello, I Must Be Going (Virgin V2252 UK/Atlantic 80035 US)

02/85 No Jacket Required (Virgin V2345 UK/Atlantic 81240 US)

11/89 ...But Seriously (Virgin V2620/Atlantic 82050 US)

11/90 Serious Hits...Live! (Virgin PCLP 1 UK/Atlantic 82157 US)

11/93 Both Sides (Virgin 82550 US)

10/96 Dance Into The Light (Atlantic 82949 US)

06/98 Live From the Board (WEA 4781 US)

06/99 A Hot Night in Paris (Atlantic 83198 US)

11/99 Tarzan (Disney 867645 US)

11/02 Testify (Atlantic 83565 US)

10/03 Brother Bear (Disney 860127 US)

COMPILATIONS

02/84 *Against All Odds* (Virgin V2313 UK/Atlantic 89700 US)

    includes "Take a Look at Me Now" plus tracks by Peter Gabriel and Mike Rutherford

—/87 12" ERS (Virgin CDEP 4 UK/Atlantic 81847 US)

11/89 Buster (Virgin V2544 UK/Atlantic 81905 US)

    includes "A Groovy Kind of Love"/"Two Hearts"/"Big Noise"

—/91 Two Rooms: Celebrating The Songs of Elton John and Bernie Taupin (Mercury 83917)

    includes "Burn Down the Mission"

10/98 ...Hits

MISCELLANEOUS

—/90 *Hits of Phil Collins Performed by the Royal Philharmonic Orchestra* (Nouveau 10132 US)

FLAMING YOUTH DISCOGRAPHY

U.K. SINGLES

—/69 Guide Me Orion/From Now On (Fontana TF 1057)

—/70 Every Man, Woman and Child/Drifting (Fontana 6001 002)

—/70 From Now On/Space Child (Fontana 6001 003)

ALBUMS

—/69 *Ark 2* (Fontana STL 5533 UK/Uni 73075 US)

BRAND X DISCOGRAPHY (Releases with Phil Collins only)

U.K. SINGLES

—/79 Soho/Dance of the Illegal Aliens (Charisma CB 340)

—/79 Soho/Dance of the Illegal Aliens/Noddy Goes to Sweden/Poolroom Blues (Charisma CB 34012)

ALBUMS

07/76 *Unorthodox Behaviour* (Charisma CAS 1117 UK)

04/77 *Moroccan Roll* (Charisma CAS 1126 UK/Passport UB 9822 US)

11/77 *Livestock* (Charisma CLASS 5 UK/Passport PB 9824 US)

05/79 *Product* (Charisma CAS 1147 UK/Passport PB 9840 US)

—/80 *Do They Hurt?* (Charisma CAS 1151 UK/Passport PB 9845 US)

—/82 *Is There Anything About?* (CBS 85967/Passport PB 6016 US)

COMPILATIONS

—/86 *Xtrax* (US Passport 6054)

—/92 *The Plot Thins: A History of Brand X, 1976–1980* (UK Virgin CDVM 9005)

05/98 *The Missing Period* (Outer Music 1004)

10/99 *The X-Files: A 20 Year Retrospective* (Outer Music 1011)

06/03 *Trilogy* (Collins on live 1979 disc) (Buckyball 11)

10/03 *Macrocosm: Introducing…Brand X* (UK Virgin 90978)

PETER GABRIEL DISCOGRAPHY

SINGLES (U.K. UNLESS NOTED)

02/77 Solsbury Hill/Moribund the Burgermeister (Charisma CB 301)

06/77 Modern Love/Slowburn (Charisma CB 302)

05/78 D.I.Y./Perspective (Charisma CB 311)

12/78 Solsbury Hill (live) (Sound for Indystry SFI 381—flexidisc)

09/79 D.I.Y./Mother of Violence/Me and My Teddy Bear (Charisma CB 319)

02/80 Games without Frontiers/Start/I Don't Remember (Charisma CB 354)

05/80 No Self Control/Lead a Normal Life (Charisma CB 360)

08/80 Biko/Shosholoza/Jetz Kommt Die Flut (Charisma CB 370)

09/82 Shock the Monkey/Soft Dog (Charisma SHOCK 1)

12/82 I Have the Touch/Across the River (Charisma CB 405)

07/83 I Don't Remember (live)/Solsbury Hill (live) (Charisma GAB 1)

07/83 I Don't Remember (live)/Solsbury Hill (live)/Kiss of Life (Charisma GAB 12)

06/84 Walk Through Fire/The Race (by Larry Carlton) (Virgin VS 689)

06/84 Walk Through Fire/The Race/I Have the Touch (Virgin VS 68912)

12/84 Out Out/Gizmo (Geffen 4953 US)

04/86 Sledgehammer/Don't Break This Rhythm (Virgin PGS 1)

04/86 Sledgehammer (extended mix)/Don't Break This Rhythm (extended mix)/I Have the Touch
   (85 remix) (Virgin PGS 1-12)

04/86 Sledgehammer (extended mix)/Don't Break This Rhythm (extended mix)/I Have the Touch
   (85 remix)/Biko (extended remix) (Virgin PGS 2-13)

10/86 Don't Give Up/In Your Eyes (special mix) (Virgin PGS 2)

10/86 Don't Give Up/In Your Eyes (special mix)/This Is the Picture (Virgin PGS 2-12)

02/87 Big Time/Curtains (Virgin PGS 3)

03/87 Big Time/(extended)/Curtains (Virgin PGS 3-12)

03/87 Big Time/(extended)/Curtains/No Self Control/Across the River/ (Virgin GAIL 3-12)

06/87 Red Rain/Ga Ga (I Go Swimming) (Virgin PGS 4)

06/87 Red Rain/Ga Ga (I Go Swimming)/Walk Through Fire (Virgin PGS 412)

08/87 In Your Eyes/(special mix)/Biko (live) (Geffen 05350 US)

11/87 Biko/No More Apartheid (Virgin PGS 612)

11/87 Biko (live)/No More Apartheid/I Have the Touch (remix) (Virgin CDPGS 612)

06/89 Shaking the Tree/Old Tucson (Virgin VS 1167)

06/89 Shaking the Tree/Old Tucson/Sweeping the Leaves (Virgin VST 1167)

12/90 Solsbury Hill/Shaking the Tree (Virgin VS 1322)

09/92 Digging in the Dirt/Quiet Steam (Virgin PGS 7)

09/92 Digging in the Dirt/(instrumental)/Quiet Steam (Virgin PGSC 7)

01/93 Steam/Games without Frontiers (remix) (Virgin PGSC 8)

01/93 Steam/(remix)/(remix dub)/Games Without Frontiers (remix) (Virgin PGSCD 8)

01/93 Steam/(remix)/Games Without Frontiers (remix)/(live) (Virgin PGSCDSX 8)

03/93 Blood of Eden/Mercy Street (remix)/Blood of Eden (special mix) (Virgin PGS 9)

03/93 Blood of Eden/Mercy Street (remix)/Sledgehammer (Virgin PGSDX 9)

07/93 Come Talk to Me/A Different Drum (Geffen 19263)

09/93 Kiss That Frog/(remix) (Virgin PGSC 10)

09/93 Kiss That Frog/(remix)/Digging in the Dirt (remix) (Virgin PGSDG 10)

09/93 Kiss That Frog/(remix)/Across the River/Shaking the Tree (remix) (Virgin PGSDX 10)

06/94 Lovetown/Love to Be Loved/A Different Drum (Epic 660480)

08/94 *Secret World Live* EP: Red Rain/Come Talk to Me/San Jacinto/Mercy Street (Virgin PGSCDF 11)

06/00 Story of Ovo (Rasco's Rap Version)/? (Real World)

09/02 The Barry Williams Show (radio edit)/(album version)/My Head Is Like That (remix by Royskopp)/Cloudless radio edit) (Virgin PGT 14)

12/02 More Than This (Polyphonic Spree mix)/(Elbow Mix) /My Head Sounds Like That (Royksopp Remix) (Virgin PGST 14)

12/02 More Than This (radio edit) /(Polyphonic Spree mix)/(elbow mix) (Virgin PGSCD 14)

12/02 More Than This/Sky Blue (Martyn Bennett remix) /The Barry Williams Show (Dolby Digital 5.1) (Virgin PGSDVD14)

08/03 Growing Up (Tom Lord Alge radio edit)/(album version)/(Trent Reznor remix) (Virgin PGCD 15)

08/03 Growing Up video/(full album version, Stereo/5.1 and DTS mixes by Tchad Blake)/(stabilizer remix) (Virgin PGSDVD 15)

—/03 Burn You Up, Burn You Down (radio edit)/Darkness (Engelspost remix) (Virgin PGSCD 16)

ALBUMS

02/77 *Peter Gabriel* (Charisma CDS 4006 UK/Atco 36147 US)

06/78 *Peter Gabriel* (Charisma CDS 4013 UK/Atco 19181 US)

05/80 *Peter Gabriel* (Charisma CDS 4019 UK/Mercury SRM 1 3848 US)

07/80 *Ein Deutsches Album* (Charisma 6302 035 Germany)

09/82 *Peter Gabriel* (US title: *Security*)(Charisma PG 4 UK/Geffen 2011 US)

09/82 *Deutsches Album* (Charisma 6302 221 Germany)

06/83 *Plays Live* (PGDL 1 UK/Geffen GHS 4012 US)

03/85 *Birdy* (Virgin CAS 1167 UK/Geffen 24070 US)

05/86 *So* (Virgin PG 5 UK/Geffen 24088 US)

10/89 *Passion* (Real World RWLP 1/Geffen 24206 US)

09/92 *Us* (Real World PGLP 7 UK/Geffen 44732 US)

—/93 *Snowflake* (narration only) (Kizna TOCT 6917-8 Japan)

08/94 *Secret World Live* (Real World PGDCD 8 UK/Geffen 24722 US)

05/00 *Ovo: The Millennium Show* (Real World 849540 UK)

03/02 *Long Walk Home: Music from* Rabbit-Proof Fence (Real World 12238 UK)

09/02 *Up* (Geffen 493536 US)

08/03 *The Peter Gabriel Encore Collectors Box 2003 Tour* (ESD-PG03-CB)

08/03 *The Peter Gabriel Deluxe Road Case 2003 Tour* (ESD-PG03-RC)

08/03 *06/07/03 Mountain View, CA; Shoreline Amphitheatre* (ES-PG03-0607)

08/03 *06/08/03 Irvine, CA;Verizon* (ES-PG03-0608)

08/03 *06/11/03 Dallas, TX; Smirnoff Center* (ES-PG03-0611)

08/03 *06/12/03 Houston, TX; Woodlands Pavilion* (ES-PG03-0612)

08-/03 *06/14/03 West Palm Beach, FL; Sound Advice Amphitheatre* (ES-PG03-0614)

08/03 *06/16/03 Atlanta, GA; Chastain Park Amphitheatre* (ES-PG03-0616)

08/03 *06/18/03 Mansfield, MA; Tweeter Center* (ES-PG03-0618)

08/03 *06/20/03 Holmdel, NJ; P.N.C Bank Arts Center* (ES-PG03-0620)

08/03 *06/21/03 Camden, NJ; Tweeter Center at the Waterfront* (ES-PG03-0600621)

08/03 *06/22/03 Bristow, VA; Nissan Pavilion* (ES-PG03-0622)

08/03 *06/24/03 Wantagh, NY; Tommy Hilfiger at Jones Beach* (ES-PG03-0624)

08/03 *06/26/03 Milwaukee, WI; Marcus Amphitheatre* (ES-PG03-0626)

08/03 *06/28/03 Tinley Park, IL; Tweeter Center* (ES-PG03-0628)

08/03 *06/29/03 Clarkston, MI; DTE Energy Music Theatre* (ES-PG03-0629)

08/03 *07/01/03 Columbus, OH; Germain Amphitheatre* (ES-PG03-0701)

08/03 *07/02/03 Noblesville, IN; Verizon Wireless Music Center* (ES-PG03-0702)

08/03 *07/04/03 Toronto, ON; Molson Amphitheatre* (ES-PG03-0704)

08/03 *07/05/03 London, ON; John Labatt Centre* (ES-PG03-0705)

08/03 *07/06/03 Montreal, QC; Bell Centre* (ES-PG03-0706)

COMPILATIONS

06/76 *All This and World War Two* (Riva RVLP 2 UK)
   various artists collection includes "Strawberry Fields Forever"

01/81 *The Bristol Recorder* 2 (Bristol Recorder BR 002 UK)
   magazine/LP collection includes "Humdrum"/"Not One of Us"/"Ain't That Peculiar" (all live)

07/82 *Music and Rhythm* (WEA K68045 UK)
   various artists collection includes "Across the River"

06/84 *Raindrops Pattering On Banana Leaves* (WOMAD 001 UK)
   various artists collection includes "Lead a Normal Life" (live)

10/84 *Gremlins: Original Soundtrack* (Geffen 24044 US)
   soundtrack includes "Out Out"

11/85 *Sun City: Artists Against Apartheid* (EMI Manhattan MTL 1001 US)
   various artists collection includes "No More Apartheid"

09/87 *The Secret Policeman's Third Ball* (Virgin V2458 UK/90643 US)
   various artists collection includes "Biko" (live)

—/89 *Shaking the Tree: Twelve Golden Greats* (Virgin PGTVL 6 UK)

—/89 *Shaking the Tree: Sixteen Golden Greats* (Geffen 24326 US)

09/92 *Us Before Us* (Geffen—PROMO US)

11/92 *Revisited* (Atlantic 824229)

—/93 *Philadelphia* (Sony 474998 US)
   soundtrack includes "Lovetown"

—/94 *The Glory of Gershwin* (Mercury 522 727 US)
   various artists collection includes "Summertime"

10/94 *Woodstock 94* (A&M 540 322 US)
   various artists collection includes "Biko" (live)

—/94 *Natural Born Killers* (Nothing 6544 92 460 US)
   soundtrack includes "Taboo"

—/95 *Tower of Song: The Songs of Leonard Cohen*
   various artists collection includes "Suzanne"

—/95 *Virtuosity* (Radioactive RAD 11295 US)
   soundtrack includes "Party Man"

—/98 *City of Angels* (Warner Bros 46867 US)
   soundtrack includes "I Grieve"

—/98 *Babe, Pig in the City* (Geffen 25310 US)
   soundtrack includes "That'll Do"

—/02 *The Wild Thornberries* (Jive 48503 US)
   soundtrack includes "Animal Nation"

10/02 *Gangs of New York*
   soundtrack includes "Signal to Noise" (new version)

10/03 *Hit* (Geffen 000148602)

10/03 *Hit* **(includes German language cuts)** (EMI 595396 Germany)

STEVE HACKETT DISCOGRAPHY

U.K. SINGLES

—/78 How Can I?/Kim (Charisma CB 312)

—/78 Narnia/Please Don't Touch (Charisma CB 318)

—/79 Everyday/Lost Time in Cordoba (Charisma CB 334)

—/79 Clocks/Acoustic Set/Tigermoth (Charisma CB 341)

—/80 The Show/Hercules Unchained (Charisma CB 357)

—/80 Sentimental Institution/The Toast (Charisma CB 368)

—/81 Hope I Don't Wake/Tales of the Riverbank (Charisma CB 385)

—/83 Cell 151/Air Conditioned Nightmare/Time Lapse in Milton Keynes/Clocks/Horizons/
   Kim/Please Don't Touch (live)

—/84 A Doll That's Made in Japan (Lamborghini 12LMG 16)

ALBUMS

09/75 *Voyage of the Acolyte* (Charisma CAS 1111 UK)

05/78 *Please Don't Touch!* (Charisma CDS 4012 UK/Chrysalis PV 41176 US)

05/79 *Spectral Mornings* (Charisma CDS 4017/Chrysalis CHR 123)

06/80 *Defector* (Charisma CDS 4018 UK)

08/81 *Cured* (Charisma CDS 4021 UK)

04/83 *Highly Strung* (Charisma HACK 1 UK)

11/83 *Bay of Kings* (Lamborghini LMG 3000 UK)

09/84 *Till We Have Faces* (Lamborghini 25987 UK)

—/88 *Momentum* (Start STL 15 UK)

—/92 *Time Lapse* (Caroline 1839 US)

05/93 *Guitar Noir* (Kudos PERMCD 13 UK/Viceroy VIC 8008 US)

01/95 *Blues with a Feeling* (Herald UK)

08/95 *There Are Many Sides to the Night* (Kudos CD2)

—/96 *Watcher of the Skies: Genesis Revisited* (Guardian 21943 US)

04/97 *A Midsummer Night's Dream* (Angel 56348 US)

—/98 *The Tokyo Tapes* (Snapper 5567 US)

05/99 *Darktown* (Camino CAMCD 19)

—/03 *To Watch the Storms* (Camino CAMCD 31)

COMPILATIONS AND ARCHIVE RELEASES

10/92 *The Unauthorised Biography* (Virgin CDVM 9014 UK)

06/01 *Live Archive 70s/80s/90s* (Camino CAMCD 23)

—/02 *Feedback '86* (Camino CAMCD 21)

—/03 *Somewhere in South America* (Camino CAMCD 29)

—/03 *Hungarian Horizons* (Camino CAMCD 30)

—/03 *Live Archive: Nearfest* (Camino CAMCD 32)

—/04 *Live Archive 03* (Camino CAMCD 33)

GTR DISCOGRAPHY

U.K. SINGLES

—/85 When the Heart Rules the Mind/Reach Out (Never Say No) (Arista GTR 1)

—/85 When the Heart Rules the Mind/Reach Out (Never Say No)/Sketches in the Sun/Hackett to
Bits (Arista GTR 121)

U.S. SINGLES

—/85 When the Heart Rules the Mind/Reach Out (Never Say No) (Arista 9470)

—/85 The Hunter/Sketches in the Sun (Arista 9512)

ALBUMS

—/85 *GTR* (Arista AL8 8400 US)

—/97 *GTR Live* (BFH CD 010)

ROCK AGAINST REPATRIATION DISCOGRAPHY

U.K. SINGLES
—/89 Sailing/(instrumental) (IRS 40)

MISCELLANEOUS
—/87 *We Know What We Like: The Music of Genesis* (RCA 6242 US)
London Symphony Orchestra with STEVE HACKETT

JOHN AND STEVE HACKETT DISCOGRAPHY

ALBUMS
05/00 *Sketches Of Satie* (Camino CAMCD 20)

CAMINO RECORDS LISTING:

CAMCD 08 Steve Hackett: *Bay of Kings*
CAMCD 09 Steve Hackett: *Till We Have Faces*
CAMCD 10 Steve Hackett: *Momentum*
CAMCD 11 Steve Hackett: *Time Lapse*
CAMCD 12 Steve Hackett: *Guitar Noir*
CAMCD 13 Steve Hackett: *Blues With Feeling*
CAMCD 14 Steve Hackett: *There Are Many Sides to the Night*
CAMCD 15 Steve Hackett: *Tokyo Tapes*
CAMCD 16 Chester Thompson: *Joyful Noise*
CAMCD 17 Steve Hackett: *Darktown*
CAMCD 18 Ian McDonald: *Driver's Eyes*
CAMCD 20 Steve and John Hackett: *Sketches of Satie*
CAMCD 21 Steve Hackett: *Feedback 86*
CAMCD 22 Steve Hackett: *A Midsummer Night's Dream*
CAMCD 23 Steve Hackett: *Live Archive 70s/80s/90s*
CAMCD 28 Guddal and Matte: *Genesis for Two Grand Pianos*
CAMCD 29 Steve Hackett: *Somewhere in South America*
CAMCD 30 Steve Hackett: *Hungarian Horizons*
CAMCD 31 Steve Hackett: *To Watch the Storms*
CAMCD 32 Steve Hackett: *Live Archive: Nearfest*
CAMCD 33 Steve Hackett: *Live Archive 03*

ANTHONY PHILLIPS DISCOGRAPHY

U.K. SINGLES
—/77 Collections/God If I Saw Her Now (Phillips 6837 406)
06/78 We're All ss We Lie/Squirrel/Sitars and Nebulous (Arista ARIST 192)

03/79 Um and Aargh/Souvenir (Arista ARIST 252)

07/81 Prelude 84/Anthem 84 (RCA 102)

02/84 Sally/Exocet/The Women Were Watching (Street Tunes JJ 102-12)

11/88 Anthem from Tarka/Rising Spring/Excerpts from Tarka (PRT PYD 18)

ALBUMS

—/77 *The Geese and the Ghost* (Passport PP98020 UK)

—/78 *Wise after the Event* (Passport PB 9828 UK)

—/78 *Private Parts and Pieces I* (Passport PVC 7905 UK)

—/79 *SideS* (Passport 9834 UK)

—/80 *Private Parts and Pieces II: Back to the Pavilion* (Passport PVC 7913 UK)

—/81 *1984* (Passport 6006 UK)

—/82 *Private Parts and Pieces III: Antiques* (Passport PVC 8908 UK)

—/83 *Invisible Men* (Passport 6023 UK)

—/84 *Private Parts and Pieces IV: A Catch at the Tables* (Passport PVC 8919 UK)

—/84 *Private Parts and Pieces V: Twelve* (Passport PVC 8926 UK)

—/85 *Harvest of the Heart* (Cherry Red)

—/86 *Private Parts and Pieces VI: Ivory Moon* (Passport PVC 8946 UK)

—/87 *Private Parts and Pieces VII: Slow Waves, Soft Stars* (Audion SYNCD 308 UK)

—/88 *Tarka* (Baillemont 898 France)

—/91 *Slow Dance* (Virgin CDV 2638 UK)

—/92 *Private Parts and Pieces VIII: New England* (Virgin CDVE 912 UK)

—/94 *Sail the World* (RES 102CD UK)

07/95 *Anthology* (Griffin 542)

—/96 *Private Parts and Pieces IX: Dragonfly Dreams* (Resurgent 229)

07/98 *The Live Radio Sessions* (Sony 59010)

11/99 *The Living Room Concert* (Blueprint 218)

12/99 *Private Parts and Pieces X: Soiree* (Blueprint 319)

05/01 *The Sky Road* (Blueprint 329)

—/03 *Soundscapes* (Recall 458)

—/03 *Battle of the Birds* (Blueprint 359)

COMPILATIONS

—/89 *Missing Links Vol. 1: Finger Painting* (Occasional 1)

—/94 *Missing Links Vol. 2: The Sky Road* (Brainworks BWKD 212)

—/94 *Gypsy Suite 1971–77* (VP 189)

—/98 *The Archive Collection Volume One* (Blueprint 279)

—/01 *Missing Links Vol. 3: Time and Tide* (Blueprint 272)

MIKE RUTHERFORD
DISCOGRAPHY

U.K. SINGLES
—/80 Working in Line/Compression (Charisma CB 352)
—/80 Time and Time Again/At the End of the Day (Charisma CB 365)
—/82 Halfway There/A Day to Remember (WEA WS9922)
—/82 Actin Very Strange/Couldn't Get Arrested (WEA RUTH 1)
—/82 Hideaway/Calypso (WEA WS 9923)
—/84 Making a Big Mistake/Against All Odds (Phil Collins) (Virgin VS 674)

ALBUMS
—/80 *Smallcreep's Day* (Charisma CAS 1149 UK/Passport PB 9843 US)
—/82 *Acting Very Strange* (WEA K99249 UK/Atlantic 80015 US)

MIKE AND THE MECHANICS DISCOGRAPHY

SINGLES (U.K. UNLESS NOTED)
—/86 Nobody's Perfect/Nobody Knows (WEA 7789)
—/86 Nobody's Perfect/Nobody Knows /All I Need Is a Miracle (WEA 7789T)
—/88 Seeing Is Believing/Don't (Atlantic US)
—/91 Stop Baby/Get Up (Virgin VS ?)
—/91 Stop Baby/Get Up/Before (Virgin VSCDG ?)
—/91 Stop Baby/I Think I Got the Message/My Crime of Passion (Virgin VSCDT ?)
02/85 Silent Running/I Get the Feeling (WEA 8908)
02/85 Silent Running/I Get the Feeling/Too Far Gone (WEA 8908T)
05/85 All I Need Is a Miracle/You Are the One (WEA 8765)
05/85 All I Need Is a Miracle/You Are the One/A Call to Arms (WEA 8765T)
11/85 Silent Running/Par Avion (Atlantic 89488 US)
06/86 Taken In/A Call to Arms (Atlantic 89404 US)
01/88 The Living Years/Too Many Friends (WEA 7717)
01/88 The Living Years/Too Many Friends/I Get the Feeling (WEA 7717T)
04/89 Seeing Is Believing/Don't (Atlantic 88921 US)
04/91 Word of Mouth/Let's Pretend It Didn't Happen (Atlantic 87714 US)
06/91 A Time and Place/Yesterday Today and Tomorrow (Virgin VS ?)
06/91 A Time and Place/Yesterday Today and Tomorrow/Word of Mouth (remix) (Virgin VS ?)
02/92 Everybody Gets a Second Chance/The Way You Look at Me (Virgin VS 1396)
02/92 Everybody Gets a Second Chance/The Way You Look at Me/At the End of the Day (Virgin VSCDT 1396)
02/95 Over My Shoulder/(live)/Something to Believe In/Word of Mouth/Always the Last to Know (Virgin VSCDT 1526)

06/95 Beggar on a Beach of Gold (acoustic)/Help Me/Nobody Told Me/Boys at the Front/Little Boy
 (Virgin VSCDT 1535)

09/95 Another Cup of Coffee/? (Virgin VSCDT 1554)

02/96 All I Need Is a Miracle (remix)/? (Virgin VSCDT 1576)

06/96 Silent Running/Plain and Simple/Stop Baby (Virgin VSCDT 1585)

06/99 Now That You've Gone/Word of Mouth (live)/Beggar on a Beach of Gold (live)/Silent
 Running (live)/I Believe When I Fall in Love (Virgin VSCDT 1732)

08/99 Whenever I Stop/(unplugged)/Now That You've Gone (live) (Virgin VSCDT 1743)

08/99 Whenever I Stop/Ordinary Girl (unplugged)/My Little Island (live) (Virgin VSCDX 1743)

ALBUMS

—/85 *Mike and the Mechanics* (WEA 252496 UK/Atlantic 81287 US)

—/88 *Living Years* (WEA 256004 UK/Atlantic 81923 US)

—/91 *Word of Mouth* (Virgin TCV 2662 UK/Atlantic 82233 US)

02/95 *Beggar on a Beach Of Gold* (Virgin 2772 UK/Atlantic 82738 US)

O3/96 *Hits* (Virgin 41448 UK)

05/99 *Mike and the Mechanics* (Virgin 2885)

DARYL STUERMER DISCOGRAPHY

ALBUMS

—/88 *Steppin' Out* (GRP 9573 US)

—/98 *Live And Learn* (Urban Island 1960)

—/00 *Another Side Of Genesis* (Urban Island 1961)

CHESTER THOMPSON DISCOGRAPHY

ALBUMS

—/92 *A Joyful Noise* (Bluemoon US)

RAY WILSON DISCOGRAPHY

GUARANTEED PURE U.K. ALBUM

—/93 *Guaranteed Pure*

STILTSKIN U.K. SINGLES

05/94 Inside/America (Whitewater LEV 1)

09/94 Footsteps/Sunshine and Butterflies (Whitewater WWRD 2)

03/95 *Rest in Peace* EP: Rest in Peace/The Poltroon/Inside (acoustic) (Whitewater WWRD 3)

STILTKIN U.K. ALBUM

10/94 *The Mind's Eye* (Whitewater WWL1)

CUT U.K. SINGLES

—/99 Another Day/I Hear You Calling/Adolescent Breakdown (monitor mix) (Virgin)

—/99 Millionairhead/Reason for Running/Dark (Virgin)

—/99 Sarah/Young Ones (Live)/Reason for Running/Dark (Virgin)

CUT U.K. ALBUM

—/99 *Millionairhead* (Virgin 538)

SOLO U.K. ALBUM

—/01 *Unplugged* (Inside Out 6516)

—/03 *Change* (Inside Out 65550)

GENESIS AT CHARISMA

A full catalog of Charisma single and LP releases 1969–85. Genesis and related releases noted in bold.

SINGLES

Note: CB 100–115 and subsequent gaps 117–190 released by B&C label.

CB 116 Topo D. Bill: Witchi-Tai-To/Jam

CB 120 Rare Bird: Sympathy/Devil's High Concern

CB 122 Van der Graaf Generator: Refugees/Boat of Millions of Years

CB 126 Audience: Belladonna Moonshine/The Big Spell

CB 130 Trevor Billmuss: Whoops Amour/Sunday Afternoon in Belgrade

CB 132 The Nice: Country Pie/One of Those People

CB 137 Lindisfarne: Clear White Light (part 2)/Knackers Yard Blues

CB 138 Rare Bird: What You Want to Know/Hammerhead

CB 141 Audience: Indian Summer/It Brings a Tear/Priestess

CB 152 Genesis: The Knife (Part 1)/The Knife (Part 2)

CB 153 Lindisfarne: Lady Eleanor/Nothing but the Marvelous Is Beautiful

CB 156 Audience: You're Not Smiling/Eye to Eye

CB 158 Trevor Billmuss: English Pastures/Fishing Songs

CB 170 Bell and Arc: She Belongs to Me/Dawn

CB 173 Lindisfarne: Meet Me on the Corner/Scotch Mist/No Time to Lose

CB 175 Van der Graaf Generator: Theme One/W

CB 179 Rare Bird: *Sympathy* EP: Sympathy/Devil's High Concern/What You Want to Know/Hammerhead

CB 181 Genesis: Happy the Man/Seven Stones

CB 185 Audience: Stand by the Door/Thunder and Lightning

CB 191 Lindisfarne: All Fall Down/We Can Swing Together

CB 192 Monty Python's Flying Circus: Spam Song/The Concert

CB 193 Capability Brown: Wake Up Little Sister/Windfall

CB 194 Jo'burg Hawk: Orang Outang/Dark Side of the Moon

CB 195 Audience: Raviole/Hard Cruel World

CB 196 String Driven Thing: Eddie/Hooked on the Road

CB 197 The Group: Bovver Boys/Piraeus Football Club/An Open Letter to George Best

CB 198 Brother Universe: Christmas Carols/We Three Kings

CB 199 Lindisfarne: Court in the Act/Don't Ask Me

CB 200 Monty Python with Neil Innes: Eric the Half a Bee/We Love the Yangtze

CB 201 Graham Bell: Too Many People/Before You're a Man

CB 202 Jo'burg Hawk: Orang Outang/Dark Side of the Moon

CB 203 String Driven Thing: Circus/My Real Herox

CB 204 Howard Werth with Audience: You're Not Smiling/Raviole

CB 205 Clifford T. Ward: Gaye/Home Thoughts from Abroad

CB 206 Jack the Lad: One More Dance/Draught Genius

CB 207 Capability Brown: Midnight Cruiser/Silent Sounds

CB 208 Alan Hull: Numbers/Drinking Song/One Off Pat

CB 209 Graham Bell: 60 Minute Man/The Whole Town Wants You Hung

CB 210 String Driven Thing: Are You a Rock and Roller/Night Club

CB 211 Alan Hull: Justanothersadsong/Waiting

CB 212 Clifford T. Ward: Wherewithal/Thinking of Something to Do

CB 213 The Creation: Making Time/Painter Man

CB 214 Music from Free Creek: Lay Lady Lay/Earl's Shuffle

CB 215 String Driven Thing: It's a Game/Are You a Rock and Roller

CB 216 Darian Spirit: Magic Morning Sun/For All the Years

CB 217 Capability Brown: Liar/Keep Death Off the Road

CB 218 Jack the Lad: Why Can't I Be Satisfied/Make Me Happy

CB 219 Kenny Rowe: Jesus/Water Song

CB 220 Doggerel Bank: Tiny Seed of Love/Down on the Farm

CB 221 Clifford T. Ward: Scullery/To An Air Hostess

CB 222 Darian Spirit: Magic Morning Sun/Hennessy Gun

CB 223 String Driven Thing: I'll Sing One for You/To See You

CB 224 Genesis: I Know What I Like (In Your Wardrobe)/Twilight Alehouse

CB 225 Howard Werth: Lucinda/Jonah

CB 226 National Youth Jazz Orchestra: Gatecrasher/Where's Yesterday

CB 227 Sir John Betjeman: A Shropshire Lad/The Cockney Amorist

CB 228 Lindisfarne: Taking Care of Business/North Country Boy

CB 229 The Friends of St. Francis: The Man Who Turned On the World/How Is the World Today?

CB 230 Bo Hansson: The Black Riders Flight to the Ford/Wandering Song

CB 231 Unicorn: Ooh Mother/Bogtrotter

CB 232 Lindisfarne: Fog on the Tyne/Mandolin King

CB 233 Clifford T. Ward: Jayne/Maybe I'm Right

CB 234 Gary Shearston: I Get a Kick Out of You/Witnessing

CB 235 Darian Spirit: Rock Your Soul/For All the Years

CB 236 G. T. Moore and the Reggae Guitars: I'm Still Waiting/Judgement Day

CB 237 Greep: Gemini/Tradition

CB 238 Genesis: Counting Out Time/Riding the Scree

CB 239 String Driven Thing: Mrs. O'Reilly/Keep On Moving

CB 240 Bert Jansch: In the Bleak Midwinter/One for Jo

CB 241 Gary Shearston: Without a Song/Aborigine

CB 242 Jack the Lad: Home Sweet Home/Big Ocean Liner

CB 244 Chris and Pauline Adams: If Only the Good Die Young/The City at Night

CB 245 Peter Hammill: Birthday Special/Shingle Song

CB 246 PierreCour: Letter to a Teenage Bride/Love Letter

CB 247 String Driven Thing: Overdrive/Timpani for the Devil

CB 248 Clifford T. Ward: Jig Saw Girl/Cellophane

CB 249 Gary Shearston: Dingo/Back of Beyond

CB 250 Graham Bell: You Need a 60 Minute Man/That's the Way It Is

CB 251 Genesis: The Carpet Crawlers/The Waiting Room (Evil Jam)

CB 252 Doggerel Bank: Mr. Skillicorn Dances/Shopping Around

CB 253 Jack the Lad: Gentleman Soldier/Oakey Strike Evictionsy

CB 254 Sir John Betjeman: Licorice Fields of Pontefract/In the Public Gardens

CB 255 Unicorn: I'll Believe in You/Take It Easy

CB 256 Howard Werth and the Moonbeams: Midnight Flyer/Sammy Lee Lane

CB 259 Dennis Neal: Cara Mia/Circus Riders

CB 262 Rare Bird: Sympathy/Beautiful Scarlet

CB 263 G. T. Moore and the Reggae Guitars: Reggae Reggae/?

CB 264 Jack the Lad: Rocking Chair/My Friend the Drink

CB 265 The Montanas: Love Machine/Oh But I Love You

CB 266 Lindisfarne: Lady Eleanor/Fog on the Tyne

CB 267 Bert Jansch: Dance Lady Dance/Build Another Band

CB 268 Monty Python: Lumberjack Song/Spam Song

CB 269 Howard Werth and the Moonbeams: Dear Joan/Roulette

CB 270 Charlie Drake: You Never Know/I'm Big Enough for Me (producer Peter Gabriel)

CB 271 Adams: The Crunch/Hand the Rock On

CB 272 Chris White: Spanish Wine/She's Only Dancing

CB 273 Paul and Avis: Every Time You Touch My Hand/?

CB 274 Snaps: Don't You Worry/Hard Lovin'

CB 275 Tommy Goss: Never Gonna Need Your Love/?

CB 276 String Driven Thing: But I Do/Stand Back in Amazement

CB 277 Genesis: A Trick of the Tail/Ripples

CB 278 Sludge: Out of Nowhere/Living on Borrowed Time

CB 279 Elmer Goodbody Jr.: Do Ya/?

CB 280 Clifford T. Ward: Home Thought from Abroad/Where Would That Leave Me

CB 281 Robert MacLeod: Sing Bird Sing/Between the Poppy and the Snow

CB 282 Chris White: Natural Rhythm/Another Little Miracle

CB 283 Eddy Phillips: Limbo Jimbo/Change My Ways

CB 284 Bob Rowe's OMO: Space Hustle/Rio Convey

CB 285 Paul and Avis: Keep Movin'/?

CB 286 String Driven Thing: Cruel to Fool/Josephine

CB 287 Heads Together: Disco Truckin' Mama/Do What You Wanna Do

CB 288 Dennis Neal: Nothing Good Comes Easy/?

CB 289 Hawkwind: Kerb Crawler/Honky DorkyJun-76

CB 290 Robert MacLeod: When Love Goes/Blue Sky

CB 291 R. D. Livingstone: Roots Man/Mo' Roots

CB 292 R. D. Livingstone: Let's Tango/Midnight Inn

CB 293 Alan Parsons Project: (The System of) Doctor Tarr and Professor Fether/A Dream within a Dream

CB 294 Chris White: Don't Look Down/?

CB 296 Paul Ryan: The Day That Anastasia Romanoff Died/?

CB 297 Van der Graaf Generator: Wondering/Meurglies III, the Songwriters Guild, Part 1

CB 298 Alan Parsons Project: To One in Paradise/The Cask of Amontillado

CB 299 Hawkwind: Back on the Streets/Dream of Isis

CB 300 Genesis: Your Own Special Way/It's Yourself

CB 301 Peter Gabriel: Solsbury Hill/Moribund the Burgermeister

CB 302 Peter Gabriel: Modern Love/Slowburn

CB 303 Chris White: Don't Worry Baby/Child of the Sun

CB 304 Patrick Moraz: Tentacles/Kabala

CB 305 Hawkwind: Quark, Strangeness and Charm/The Forge of Vulcan

CB 306 Intergalactic Touring Band: Love Station/Space Commando

CB 307 Intergalactic Touring Band: Starship Jingle/?

CB 308 Isaac Guillory: Love's Revival/Ship in the Window

CB 309 Genesis: Follow You, Follow Me/Ballad of Big

CB 310 Levinsky Sinclair: Disaster Movies/?

CB 311 Peter Gabriel: D.I.Y./Perspective

CB 312 Steve Hackett: How Can I?/Kim

CB 314 Pacific Eardrum: Sitting On a Daisy/?

CB 315 Genesis: Many Too Many/Vancouver/The Day the Lights Went Out

CB 316 Levinsky Sinclair: Love on the Line/Riding on a Winner

CB 317 Pacific Eardrum: Love on a Merry-Go-Round/?

CB 318 Steve Hackett: Narnia/Please Don't Touch

CB 319 Peter Gabriel: D.I.Y. (remix)/Mother of Violence/Teddy Bear

CB 320 Razar: Idle Rich/1978

CB 321 Steve Joseph: Holding Back the Tears/?

CB 322 Blue Max: Dream Machine/UK

CB 323 Hawklords: Psi Power (remix)/Death Trap

CB 324 Ferrets: Don't Fall in Love/Lies

CB 325 Dazzlers: Phonies/Kick Out

CB 326 Darling: Looking Kinda Rock and Rolled/Dead End Kids

CB 329 Dame Edna Everage: Every Mother Wants a Boy Like Elton/S&M Lady

CB 332 Hawklords: 25 Years (remix)/Only the Dead Dreams of the Cold War Kid

CB 333 Link Wray: It's All Over Now Baby Blue/Just That Kind

CB 334 Steve Hackett: Everyday/Tiger Moth

CB 335 Darling: Do Ya Wanna/Stuck on You

CB 336 Dame Edna Everage: Disco Matilda/Disco Matilda (instrumental)

CB 337 Bill Lovelady: Reggae for It Now/Reggae for Strings

CB 338 Dazzlers: Feeling Free/No One Ever Knows

CB 339 Rikki Nadir/Peter Hammill: The Polaroid/The Old School Tie

CB 340 Brand X: Soho/Dance of the Illegal Aliens

CB 341 Steve Hackett: Clocks—The Angel of Mons/Acoustic Set

CB 342 Darling: Voice on the Radio/Save Me

CB 344 Tony Banks: For a While/From the Undertow

CB 345 The Word: The Naz/Cast Your Bread

CB 346 Vivabeat: Man from China/On Patrol

CB 347 Bill Lovelady: One More Reggae for the Road/On the Road

CB 349 Trimmer and Jenkins: I Love Parties/Thank You Lord

CB 351 Berlin: Over 21/Waiting for the Future

CB 352 Phoenix: Just Another Day/?

CB 353 Mike Rutherford: Working in Line/Compression

CB 354 Peter Gabriel: Games without Frontiers/Start/I Don't Remember

CB 355 Vivabeat: Man from China (US remix)/On Patrol

CB 356 Genesis: Turn It On Again/Behind the Lines (part 2)

CB 357 Steve Hackett: The Show/Hercules Unchained

CB 358 Lee Stirling: Earthquake, Landslide, Hurricane/?

CB 360 Peter Gabriel: No Self Control/Lead a Normal Life

CB 363 Genesis: Duchess/Open Door

CB 364 Mike Rutherford: Time and Time Again/At the End of the Day

CB 365 Tony Banks: For a While (remix)/A Curious Feeling

CB 368 Steve Hackett: Sentimental Institution/The Toast

CB 369 Genesis: Misunderstanding/Evidence of Autumn

CB 370 Peter Gabriel: Biko/Shosholoza/Jetzt Kommt die Flut

CB 372 The Juniors: Do You Love Me?/Babylon

CB 373 Vivian Stanshall: Terry Keeps His Clips On/King Cripple

CB 374 Monty Python: I Like Chinese/I Bet You They Won't Play This Song on the Radio

CB 377 Jim Rafferty: The Bogeyman/Salt Lake City

CB 378 Naughty Culture: Once upon a Time/Doing OK (Anchors Away)

CB 380 Cimmarons: Ready for Love/So Real

CB 381 Naughty Culture: Someday Sunday/T.B.A.

CB 382 Vivian Stanshall: Calypso to Collapso/Smoke Signals at Night

CB 383 Afraid of Mice: I'm on Fire/Down in the Dark

CB 384 Rick Wakeman Band: Julia/Sorry

CB 385 Steve Hackett: Hope I Don't Wake/Tales of the Riverbank

CB 386 Harvest Moon: Tales of Wonder/Take a Dream

CB 388 Genesis: Abacab/Another Record

CB 389 Afraid of Mice: Intercontinental/What Shall We Do

CB 390 Steve Hackett: Picture Postcard/Second Chance

CB 391 Genesis: Keep It Dark/Naminanu

CB 392 Rick Wakeman Band: Robot Man/1984 Overture (part 1)

CB 393 Genesis: Man on the Corner/Submarine

CB 394 She Sherriff: I Forgot More Than You'll Ever Know about Him/This House Is for Let

CB 395 Afraid of Mice: Popstar/What I Want

CB 397 Afraid of Mice: Transparents/That's Not True

CB 398 Afraid of Mice: At the Club/I Will Wait (live)

CB 399 24 Hours: Siberian Sid/Witch Doctor

CB 401 24 Hours: Shipwrecked (I'm Not Coming Back)/Rescued

CB 403 Little Tom: It's Not Unusual/You Never Told Me

CB 404 John Sinclair: The Naz/Straight from the Heart

CB 405 Peter Gabriel: I Have the Touch/Across the River

CB 407 Kinetics: Keeping Up with the Joneses/Ghost a You

CB 409 Lindisfarne/Clifford T. Ward: Clear White Light/Wherewithal

CB 410 Rick Wakeman: Theme from G'Ole!/No Possibla

CB 411 Hank Wangford Band: Ghost Herd (Riders in the Sky)/Pain in My Wrist

CB 412 Alexis Korner: Beirut/Mean Fool

CB 414 Peter Hammill: Just Good Friends/Just Good Friends

CB 415 Tony Banks: You Call This Victory/Redwing/Lion of Symmetry

CB 416 Mercy Ray: She'll Be Home Later Tonight/She's Happy

CB 420 Julian Lennon: Stick Around/Always Think Twice

CB 421 Keep It Dark: Dreamer/Outsider

CB 422 Keep It Dark: Don't Surrender/Far from Home

CB 423 Julian Lennon: This Is My Day/Everday

CB 424 Twelfth Night: Shame/Blue Powder Monkey

CB 425 Twelfth Night: Take a Look/Blondon Fair

CB 426 Tony Banks and Fish: Short Cut to Somewhere/Smilin' Jack Casey

CS 1 Genesis: Looking for Someone/Visions of Angels (withdrawn)

GEN 001 *Spot The Pigeon* EP: Match of the Day/Inside and Out/Pigeons

GEN 1 *3x3* EP: Paperlate/You Might Recall/Me and Virgil

ALBUMS

(This omits budget reissues CHC and CS series, reggae/experimental imprint PREX, and vintage
   radio imprint DCS.)

CAS 1005 Rare Bird—*Rare Bird*

CAS 1007 Van der Graaf Generator—*The Least We Can Do*

CAS 1008 Joseph Eger—*Classical Heads*

CAS 1009 Gordon Turner—*A System of Meditation*

CAS 1011 Rare Bird—*As Your Mind Flies By*

CAS 1012 Audience—*Friend's Friend's Friend*

CAS 1014 The Nice—*The 5 Bridges Suite*

CAS 1017 Trevor Billmus—*Family Apology*

CAS 1018 Jackson Heights—*King Progress*

CAS 1020 Genesis—*Trespass*

CAS 1021 Brian Davidson's Every Which Way—*Every Which Way*

CAS 1025 Lindisfarne—*Nicely Out of Tune*

CAS 1027 Van der Graaf Generator—*H to He Who Am the Lonely One*

CAS 1030 The Nice—*Elegy*

CAS 1032 Audience—*House on the Hill*

CAS 1036 Birth Control—*Birth Control*

CAS 1037 Peter Hammill—*Fool's Mate*

CAS 1039 Atacama—*Atacama*

CAS 1040 Leigh Stephens—*And a Cast of Thousands*

CAS 1049 Monty Python—*Another Record*

CAS 1050 Lindisfarne—*Fog on the Tyne*

CAS 1051 Van der Graaf Generator—*Pawn Hearts*

CAS 1052 Genesis—*Nursery Cryme*

CAS 1053 Bell and Arc—*Bell and Arc*

CAS 1054 Audience—*Lunch*

CAS 1055 Spreadeagle—*The Piece of Paper*

CAS 1056 Capability Brown—*From Scratch*

CAS 1057 Lindisfarne—*Dingly Dell*

CAS 1058 Genesis—*Foxtrot*

CAS 1059 Bo Hansson—*Lord of the Rings*

CAS 1060 Atacama—*The Sun Burns Up Above*

CAS 1061 Graham Bell—*Graham Bell*

CAS 1062 String Driven Thing—*String Driven Thing*

CAS 1063 Monty Python—*Previous Record*

CAS 1064 Jo'Burg Hawk—*Jo'Burg Hawk*

CAS 1065 Darien Spirit—*Elegy to Marilyn*

CAS 1066 Clifford T Ward—*Home Thoughts*

CAS 1067 Peter Hammill—*Chameleon in the Shadow of Night*

CAS 1068 Capability Brown—*Voice*

CAS 1069 Alan Hull—*Pipedream*

CAS 1070 String Driven Thing—*The Machine That Cried*

CAS 1071 Hot Thumbs O'Riley—*Hot Thumbs O'Riley*

CAS 1073 Bo Hansson—*The Magician's Hat*

CAS 1074 Genesis—*Selling England by The Pound*

CAS 1076 Lindisfarne—*Roll On Ruby*

CAS 1077 Clifford T Ward—*Mantle Pieces*

CAS 1078 Various—*The Parlour Song Book*

CAS 1079 Doggerel Bank—*Silver Faces*

CAS 1080 Monty Python—*Matching Ti and Handkerchief*

CAS 1082 National Youth Jazz Orchestra—*NYJO*

CAS 1083 Peter Hammill—*The Silent Corner and the Empty Stage*

CAS 1084 Robert John Godfrey—*Fall of Hyperion*

CAS 1085 Jack the Lad—*Jack the Lad*

CAS 1086 Sir John Betjeman—*Betjeman's Banana Blush*

CAS 1087 Refugee—*Refugee*

CAS 1088 Bernard Haitink—*The Life Story of Mahler*

CAS 1089 Peter Hammill—*In Camera*

CAS 1090 Bert Jansch—*LA Turnaround*

CAS 1091 Gary Shearston—*Dingo*

CAS 1092 Unicorn—*Blue Pine Trees*

CAS 1094 Jack The Lad—*The Old Straight Track*

CAS 1095 GT Moore and the Reggae Guitars—*GT Moore and the Reggae Guitars*

CAS 1096 Sir John Betjeman—*Late Flowering Love*

CAS 1097 String Driven Thing—*Please Mind Your Head*

CAS 1098 Clifford T. Ward—*Escalator*

CAS 1099 Peter Hammill—*Nadir's Big Chance*

CAS 1101 Various—*Beyond an Empty Dream*

CAS 1102 Doggerel Bank—*Mr. Skillicorn Dances*

CAS 1103 Monty Python—*And the Holy Grail*

CAS 1104 Howard Werth and the Moonbeams—*King Brilliant*

CAS 1105 G.T. Moore and the Reggae Guitars—*Reggae Blue*

CAS 1106 Gary Shearston—*The Greatest Stone on Earth…*

CAS 1107 Bert Jansch—*Santa Barbara Honeymoon*

CAS 1108 Lindisfarne—*Finest Hour*

CAS 1109 Van der Graaf Generator—*Godbluff*

CAS 1110 Jack the Lad—*Rough Diamonds*

CAS 1111 Steve Hackett—*Voyage of the Acolyte*

CAS 1112 String Driven Thing—*Keep Yer 'and On It*

CAS 1113 Bo Hansson—*Attic Thoughts*

CAS 1114 Robert MacLeod—*Between the Poppy and the Snow*

CAS 1116 Van der Graaf Generator—*Still Life*

CAS 1117 Brand X—*Unorthodox Behaviour*

CAS 1118 Chris White—*Mouth Music*

CAS 1119 RD Livingstone—*Home from Home*

CAS 1120 Van der Graaf Generator—*World Record*

CAS 1121 Paul Ryan—*Scorpio Rising*

CAS 1122 AFT—*Automatic Fine Tuning*

CAS 1123 Dame Edna Everage—*Housewife Superstar*

CAS 1124 Adrian Wagner—*Instincts*

CAS 1125 Peter Hammill—*Over*

CAS 1126 Brand X—*Moroccan Roll*

CAS 1127 Bert Jansch—*A Rare Conundrum*

CAS 1128 Joseph Eger—*20th Century Classics: Shostakovich*

CAS 1129 Joseph Eger—*20th Century Classics: Stravinsky*

CAS 1130 Sir John Betjeman—*Sir John Betjeman's Britain*

CAS 1131 Van der Graaf—*The Quiet Zone/The Pleasure Dome*

CAS 1132 Bo Hansson—*Music Inspired by Watership Down*

CAS 1133 Pacific Eardrum—*Pacific Eardrum*

CAS 1134 Monty Python—*Instant Record Collection*

CAS 1135 Adrian Wagner—*The Last Inca*

CAS 1136 Pacific Eardrum—*Beyond Panic*

CAS 1137 Peter Hammill—*The Future Now*

CAS 1138 Brand X—*Masques*

CAS 1139 Viv Stanshall—*Sir Henry at Rawlinson End*

CAS 1140 Dame Edna Everage—*The Sound of Edna*

CAS 1141 RD Laing—*Life Before Death*

CAS 1142 Blue Max—*Blue Max*

CAS 1144 Darling—*Put It Down to Experience*

CAS 1145 The Dazzlers—*Feeling Free* (ureleased)

CAS 1146 Peter Hammill—*PH7*

CAS 1147 Brand X—*Product*

CAS 1148 Tony Banks—*A Curious Feeling*

CAS 1149 Mike Rutherford—*Smallcreep's Day*

CAS 1150 Phoenix—*In Full View*

CAS 1151 Brand X—*Do They Hurt?*

CAS 1152 Monty Python—*Contractual Obligation Album*

CAS 1153 Vic Stanshall—*Teddy Boys Don't Knit*

CAS 1154 Sir John Betjeman—*Varsity Rag*

CAS 1155 Afraid of Mice—*Afraid of Mice*

CAS 1157 John Arlott—*Talks Cricket*

CAS 1158 Michael Nyman—*The Draughtman's Daughter*

CAS 1159 Various—*Songs for a Modern Church* (reissue of *Beyond an Empty Dream*)

CAS 1160 Peter O'Sullevan—*Talks Turf*

CAS 1161 Opposition—*Intimacy*

CAS 1162 Rick Wakeman—*G'ole*

CAS 1163 Rick Wakman—*Cost of Living*

CAS 1164 Unity—*Heat Your Body Up*

CAS 1167 Peter Gabriel—*Birdy*

CAS 1168 Mercy Ray—*Swoop Swoop Rock Rock*

CAS 1169 World's Famous Supreme Team—*Rappin'*

CAS 1173 Tony Banks—*Soundtracks*

CAS 1174 Twelfth Night—*Twelfth Night*

CBR 101 Genesis—*Duke*

CBR 102 Genesis—*Abacab*

CDS 4001 Genesis—*A Trick of the Tail*

CDS 4002 Patrick Moraz—*The Story of I*

CDS 4003 Alan Parsons Project—*Tales of Mystery and Imagination*

CDS 4004 Hawkwind—*Astounding Sounds Amazing Music*

CDS 4005 Genesis—*Wind and Wuthering*

CDS 4006 Peter Gabriel—*Peter Gabriel*

CDS 4007 Patrick Moraz—*Out in the Sun*

CDS 4008 Hawkwind—*Quark, Strangeness and Charm*

CDS 4009 Intergalactic Touring Band—*Intergalactic Touring Band*

CDS 4010 Genesis—*And Then There Were Three*

CDS 4011 Nik Turner's Sphynx—*Xitintoday*

CDS 4012 Steve Hackett—*Please Don't Touch*

CDS 4013 Peter Gabriel—*Peter Gabriel*

CDS 4014 Hawklords—*25 Years On*

CDS 4015 Patrick Moraz—*Patrick Moraz*

CDS 4016 Hawkwind—*PXR5*

CDS 4017 Steve Hackett—*Spectral Mornings*

CDS 4018 Steve Hackett—*Defector*

CDS 4019 Peter Gabriel—*Peter Gabriel*

CDS 4020 Keith Dewhurst and the Albion Band—*Lark Rise to Candleford*

CDS 4021 Steve Hackett—*Cured*

CDS 4022 Rick Wakeman—*1984*

CGS 101 Genesis—*The Lamb Lies Down on Broadway*

BG 1 Various—*Repeat Performance*

BG 2 Hawkwind—*Repeat Performance*

BG 3 Van der Graaf Generator—*Repeat Performance*

BG 5 Lindisfarne—*The Singles Album*

CADS 101 Various—*Music from Free Creek*

CLAM 1 Malcolm Maclaren—*Would You Like More Scratching?*

CLASS 1 Genesis—*Live*

CLASS 2 Lindisfarne—*Live*

CLASS 3 Various—*One More Chance*
   (Various artists collection includes "Happy the Man" remix)

CLASS 4 Monty Python—*Live At Drury Lane*

CLASS 5 Brand X—*Livestock*

CLASS 6 Bert Jansch—*Avoet*

CLASS 7 The Dazzlers—*Feeling Free*

CLASS 8 Various—*Heat from the Street*

CLASS 10 Trimmer and Jenkins—*Live from London…*

CLASS 11 The Desperadoes—*The Desperadoes*

CLASS 12 Rick Wakeman—*The Burning*

CVLD 101 Van der Graaf—*Vital*

GE 2001 Genesis—*Seconds Out*

GE 2002 Genesis—*Three Sides Live*

GENLP 1 Genesis—*Genesis*

HACK 1 Steve Hackett—*Highly Strung*

JLLP 1 Julian Lennon—*Valotte*

MMDL 2 Malcolm MacLaren—*Fans*

MMLP 1 Malcolm MacLaren—*Duck Rock*

OPLP 1 Opposition—*Promise*

PG 4 Peter Gabriel—*Peter Gabriel*

RSC 1 Rock Steady Crew—*Ready for a Battle*

TBLP 1 Tony Banks—*The Fugitive*

TSS 1 Various—*The Charisma Disturbance*

PHOTO CREDITS

INDEX